Corporate Image Management

For my family —
Violet,
Ryan and Patrick

Corporate Image **Management**

A Marketing Discipline
for the 21st Century

Steven Howard

Butterworth-Heinemann
Linacre House, Jordan Hill, Oxford OX2 8DP
225 Wildwood Avenue, Woburn, MA 01801-2041
A division of Reed Educational and Professional Publishing Ltd

☫ A member of the Reed Elsevier plc group

OXFORD   AUCKLAND   BOSTON
JOHANNESBURG   MELBOURNE   NEW DELHI

First published 1998
Reprinted 1999

© Steven Howard 1998

All rights reserved. No part of this publication may be reproduced in
any material form (including photocopying or storing in any medium by
electronic means and whether or not transiently or incidentally to some
other use of this publication) without the written permission of the
copyright holder except in accordance with the provisions of the Copyright,
Designs and Patents Act 1988 or under the terms of a licence issued by the
Copyright Licensing Agency Ltd, 90 Tottenham Court Road, London,
England W1P 9HE. Applications for the copyright holder's written
permission to reproduce any part of this publication should be addressed
to the publishers

British Library Cataloguing in Publication Data
A catalogue record for this book is available from the British Library

ISBN 0 7506 4594 6

Cover design by Samm & Matt Design
Typeset by Diana Piper
Printed and bound in Great Britain by
Biddles Ltd, Guildford and King's Lynn

Contents

		Preface	vii
		Acknowledgements	ix
Chapter	1	Introduction	1
	2	Corporate Image Management in a Rapidly Changing World	7
	3	Corporate Image Management as a Catalyst for Change	13
	4	The Value of a Good Corporate Image	28
	5	Making the Corporate Image Management Program Succeed	40
	6	Corporate Image Management and its Impact on the Marketing Process	51
	7	Corporate Image Management as a Marketing Discipline	65
	8	Corporate Image as a Strategic Weapon	79
	9	Managing and Marketing the Corporate Image	103
	10	The Image Management Development Process	124
	11	The Corporate Identity System	140
	12	Implementing a New Corporate Image System	153
	13	The Importance of the Corporate Image on your Communications and Audiences	164
	14	Making the Corporate Image Management Program Succeed (Worth Repeating)	178
	15	Can You Manage Change?	187
	16	The Value of Outside Resources	201
		Epilogue	216
		Glossary	218
		Index	221

Preface

I have been involved on both sides of the corporate image development equation—as a client and as a consultant. Moreover, I have spent the entire 20-plus years of my adult life as an eternal student of marketing.

An area that has enthralled and challenged me throughout my career is the fundamental marketing question: 'Why (and how) do people decide to purchase services and products?' And, most importantly, is there one over-riding motive that can be leveraged by the astute marketeer?

The harder I looked at this topic, the greater became the perceived corporate image as a major, and often *the main*, determining factor in a wide range of observed purchasing decisions. These observations, in over two dozen markets around the world, led me to explore this linkage further.

At first, I was convinced that the corporate image was merely one of several factors that played a key role in most purchasing decisions. Then I started to analyse the slow development of the concept of relationship marketing—a subject which no one, in my opinion, had adequately defined and described.

The juncture of these two thoughts caused the proverbial light bulb to 'click on'. The keys to the thinking about both of these subjects—corporate image and relationship marketing—lay not in analysing how they had been used as successful marketing tools in the past, but rather how they could be moulded into the most dynamic marketing tools of the future.

I knew this was going to be a tough topic to cover when the regional publisher of this book kept sending me e-mail messages reminding me to 'be sure to obtain approval for all the corporate logos and images you want to use'. Apparently my initial outline and copy brief did not explain adequately how I was going to approach the subject of corporate image management from the perspective of a marketing management discipline.

So, dear reader, you will purposely find no corporate logos inside this book. There are plenty of books on corporate image and corporate identity practices written from a design perspective—several by some of the top designers who have approached this topic. Instead, here you will find

Preface

a holistic approach which treats corporate image as a management and marketing issue—an issue that we feel will become the key determining factor in a larger portion of purchase decisions (by both individuals and organisations) well into the 21st Century.

Thus, the topics we will cover in this book include:
- the impact of change on corporate image management,
- corporate image management as a catalyst for change,
- how the value of a good corporate image impacts the organisation's perceived worth, its hiring practices, and its future marketplace success,
- ways of making the corporate image management program succeed,
- the impact of the corporate image on the marketing process, and its use as a strategic marketing weapon,
- the five phases of the corporate image development cycle,
- tips on implementing a new corporate identity system,
- a checklist for success,
- a checklist for avoiding failure, and
- how to choose and use outside resources to help you create and manage a corporate image for your organisation.

Throughout the book, we will focus on how to manage and market the corporate image, and why doing so has enormous implications for the development of mutually beneficial relationships with the organisation's key constituents.

Likewise, this is not a book about corporate image advertising. Again, there are several books on this subject, written by some of the top practitioners in the advertising field. While I devote a section of the book to a discussion on how to communicate a new corporate image, you will find that the majority of that section concentrates on internal communications. The reason: I feel strongly that the corporate image should be a reflection of the corporate ethos, culture and personality. Thus, it has to be communicated as much through corporate behaviour patterns as by marketing communications messages.

Lastly, we will place a great deal of emphasis throughout the book on defining the differences between managing the corporate image (as a marketing discipline) and managing the corporate identity (as a design discipline). By using corporate image management as a management and marketing tool, you will be better placed to lead your organisation to higher levels of success, no matter what your competitive environment.

Acknowledgements

This book is the culmination of countless hours of discussing, analysing, debating and arguing with William E. Carlson, Jr how to implement corporate image management programs. These discussions enriched us both and created the foundation for this book. Without his support, assistance and input, both before and during the writing of the manuscript, this book would never have seen the light of day.

My deepest appreciation also goes out to the two professionals who greatly assisted me in the writing and editing process: Brendan Atkins, who did a stunning job of editing my often rambling thoughts and elongated sentences into a coherent and tightly written style. The reader is the true beneficiary of his editing skills. And Rosemary Peers, whose tenacity and patience were much needed skills as this writer continuously missed promised delivery deadlines. Her ability to keep the editorial production process moving smoothly towards final completion is simply amazing.

It is also a culmination and a reflection of all that I have learned about the power of the marketing process, mostly from my previous bosses:

- Ed and Angel Allen—who embued me with the spirit and power of being a self-employed entrepreneur,
- Ed Morrett, Ralph Oliva and Frank Walters at Texas Instruments—who taught me the power of effective communications, the necessity of always getting the message right, and the ability to turn tough tasks into opportunities to excel,
- the late David McAuliffe—who constantly challenged me to develop creative solutions to selling and marketing situations, and
- David Smith—who preached the gospel of being customer focused in every facet of business.

To my clients, I would like to express my thanks and gratitude for the ways in which they continuously challenge me to expand my thinking—most specifically James Cassin, Brian Thom, Margaret O'Connor and Nancy Elder at MasterCard International; Tan Soo Nan, Heng Lee Cheng and Mano Sabnani at DBS Bank; and Dr Philip Hines at the Citibank Asia Pacific Banking Institute.

Acknowledgements

I would also like to pay recognition to the many successful business people I have had the pleasure of meeting or working with through the years: Ian Batey, Jeff Beaumont, Ian Buchanan, Jack Cason, Jennie Chua, Phil Gibson, Mohd. Azlan Hashim, Richard Helfer, Owen Landell-Jones, Lee Eng Lock, Lim Chin Beng, H. Eugene Lockhart, Ron Meyer, Victor Ow, Sig Rogich, Tan Chee Chye, Wong Sheung Sze and many others.

Add to these my friends and colleagues who have helped me formulate my thoughts and beliefs: Clemens Bach, Dorian Ball, Jenny Bigio, Philip Bigio, Michael J. Bonner, Patti Botcher, Peter Dehio, Greg and Pam Dohm, Chan Siew Ling, Danny Chow, David Franklin, Haris Manaf, Carl Howard, Andrew Hoodwin, Patricia Hu, Ted Jernigan, Irwin Kelaart, Benedict Leong, Presley Lomax, Andrew Mainprize, Peter Robinson, Emma Silipo, Jurgen Schlotzer, Melvin Tan, Dianne Tetreault, Amrish Thomas, Herman Ubbink, and again many others. Also, a special mention to Clive Merifield, a man who embodies true friendship and whose concept of friendship knows no bounds.

And lastly, four very special people in my life, each of whom has had a significant impact:

- John Roddy—an example of a true professional and a wonderful family man. He has been my role model from the day we first met in 1980.
- Ron Kaufman—a special friend who keeps me motivated, challenged and forward looking. Though we never seem to have enough time to spend with one another, we remain constantly connected.
- Deirdre Ball—who has been my colleague, partner, alter ego, sounding board, motivator and true friend for almost two decades.
- My father, the novelist Clark Howard—who showed me the power of the written word and always encouraged me to broaden my thinking through reading, writing and experience.

Steven Howard
Singapore
February 1998

Author's Note

Throughout this book, 'billion' refers to the US billion (one thousand million).

I love this game!™ is a trademark of the National Basketball Association.

If it touches the customer, it's a marketing issue™ is a trademark of Howard Marketing Services.

MasterCard—The Future of Money™ is a trademark of MasterCard International.

The advertisement quoted on pages 28–29 is under copyright of McGraw-Hill Corporation.

The following product and corporate names used in this book are trade marks or registered trade marks:

Adidas	IBM
American Airlines MasterCard	Jaguar
American Express	KFC
Apple-II	Kleenex
Audi	Kodak
Avis	Lexus
Bacardi	Lincoln-Mercury
BMW	Luvs
Cadillac	Macintosh
Cirrus	Maestro
Coca-Cola	MasterCard
Disneyland	Mercedes-Benz
EuroCard	Microsoft
Fortune 500	Mount Blanc
Frito-Lay	Nescafé
General Motors MasterCard	Nestlé Crunch
Gold MasterCard	Nike
HongkongBank Care for Nature MasterCard	Oldsmobile
	Pampers

Author's Note

Pepsi
Perrier
Pizza Hut
7-Eleven
Shell MasterCard
Swatch
Taco Bell

Tide
Tokyo Disneyland
Visa
Walt Disney World
Windows
Xerox

Chapter One

Introduction

The corporate image is a dynamic and profound affirmation of the nature, culture and structure of an organisation. This applies equally to corporations, businesses, government entities, and non-profit organisations. The corporate image communicates the organisation's mission, the professionalism of its leadership, the calibre of its employees, and its roles within the marketing environment or political landscape.

Every organisation has a corporate image, whether it wants one or not. When properly designed and managed, the corporate image will accurately reflect the organisation's commitment to quality, excellence and relationships with its various constituents: current and potential customers, employees and future staff, competitors, partners, governing bodies, and the general public. As a result, the corporate image is a critical concern for every organisation, one deserving the same attention and commitment by senior management as any other vital issue.

Historically, thinking and writing about the subject of corporate image has come from the area of graphic design, with most attention given to name selection, typography, logo design and usage rules, colour palettes, uniforms, and the appearance of corporate stationery, forms and marketing collateral (brochures etc). This approach no longer suits the global, dynamic, cross-border and cross-cultural world in which a growing number of today's businesses and organisations operate. What is needed, instead, is a practice called corporate image management. This is a holistic

Corporate Image Management

management discipline designed to prepare organisations to compete for resources, partners, customers and market share well into the early years of the 21st Century.

Corporate image management is founded upon modern corporate identity practices with the marketing premise that *everything an organisation does, and does not do, affects the perception of that organisation and its performance, products, and services*. These perceptions affect its ability to recruit the financial resources, people and partnerships it needs to attain its goals and objectives.

This approach evaluates corporate image from a marketing, rather than a graphic design, perspective. The premise has two predominant concerns for companies entering the 21st Century:

- an understanding that the corporate image is a major strategic concern that can have a direct impact on the level of success the organisation achieves through its other marketing and management efforts, and
- an understanding that a coherent corporate image needs to be integrated into the organisation at all levels.

Looked at from a marketing perspective, corporate image management becomes an on-going, synergistic management tool, rather than a one-off 'corporate image exercise' as currently practised by most organisations and almost all corporate identity consultants. Corporate image management, therefore, becomes a comprehensive and all-embracing process that internalises a new skill set for managing relationships between constituents at all levels in the organisation. Its goal is to enable sustainable relationship advantages to be developed with key audiences. Since the process of corporate image management is on-going, these relationship management skills are applied to all current, prospective and future relationships. It applies equally to commercial, non-profit and government organisations.

By incorporating a post-graphic design management process into the practice of corporate image management, today's organisational leaders can develop an integrated approach to communicating the organisation's identity to each of the organisation's constituents. Corporate image management focuses on the very heart and soul of the organisation, even to the extent of evaluating why the organisation exists and determining its key purposes. It represents one of the highest levels of functional control of the organisation.

Perhaps more importantly, its value as a marketing tool is greater because it provides a mechanism for the organisation to:

- differentiate itself from competition,
- create recognised added-value to the products and services marketed or delivered by the organisation, and
- attract and maintain customer relationships in order to prosper in an increasingly competitive and constantly changing global marketplace.

Corporate image management, therefore, also represents the highest level of brand personality and characteristics that can be created and communicated to customers and marketing partners. From both a marketing and management perspective, corporate image management needs to be integrated into the organisation's development at all levels, starting from the top.

The Corporate Image

The corporate image comprises all the visual, verbal and behavioural elements that make up the organisation. In many respects, the corporate image should be a dynamic actualisation of the Chief Executive Officer's vision, integrated with the corporation's mission and strategic plan. It should be thoroughly planned and constantly managed in order to support and sustain the corporation's mission. If managed effectively, it should protect the organisation against competition from new competitors or from current competitors offering new products and services. Unfortunately, this is usually not the case.

The corporate image combines the organisation's self-perceptions with those of its constituents. It is the *raison d'être* of the corporate body and gives direction and meaning to the whole enterprise. Thus management of the corporate image should be a primary concern of the Board of Directors, the CEO and the senior management, working in conjunction. Again, unfortunately, this is usually not the case.

However, in today's world of deteriorating brand power, rising perceptions of parity products, reducing employee loyalty, and increasing competition, the management of the corporate image has taken on renewed

Corporate Image Management

importance in management and marketing processes. A weak or strong corporate image can make a significant difference in terms of a company's sales volume and its stock price. It will also affect the marketability and acceptability of the company's products, services and human resources. A strong corporate image is obviously better than a weak image, but most important of all, from a marketing perspective, is the need to communicate and to deliver through action a clear, concise and consistent image to all target audiences. Having a coherent corporate image can make a significant competitive difference in marketing results, recruitment expenses, staff morale, employee turnover and share P/E (price/earnings) ratios.

The corporate *identity* is the visual representation of the company and should not be confused with the corporate *image*. This visual representation usually takes the form of a corporate signature and a corporate symbol or logo. These distinguish graphically between the corporation and its competitors, and positions the enterprise visually in the global marketplace through a consistent use of typeface, colour palette and logo identifier.

Previously, the company's visual identity system was sufficient to project and protect the image of the organisation. Today, all aspects of the corporate image need to be managed, from the refinement of the mission statement to how well the troops on the front-line understand, communicate and portray this mission. Management of the corporate image integrates the corporate culture with the process of managing change and it requires the best leadership, communication and training skills the organisation can muster.

Corporate image management entails the creation of a corporate language, behaviour patterns, symbology, tradition and dialogue that focus on an appropriate expression of the company. The dialogue matches the expectations and understanding of both customer and employee about what the organisation stands for, where it is heading and what its core strengths, traditions and principles are. It also develops relevance within every single aspect of the company, its products and its services, and results in perceptions that become the key to long term success. In a way, corporate image management is the purest definition of total quality management: if everything is relevant to the company or its customers, then nothing retained is wastage.

A phased process, such as the one described in considerable detail later in this book, will help to develop a corporate image management system that is thoroughly based on the organisation's characteristics, the perceptions of its key internal and external audiences, and the position it occupies in the marketplace. Not until this position is understood can a corporate identity be developed or modified. And it is only through careful monitoring of the implementation phase that the image can be refined and marketed successfully.

Change Management

A successful identity system, combined with a planned image management system, will assist the organisation to manage change and remain flexible in its response to changing market conditions, competition and innovation. Implementing a corporate identity system is also a useful way of changing a company's image by providing a catalyst for the initiation of internal and external reforms vital to successful marketing and the creation of highly efficient and flexible organisational structures.

The result of this new management discipline is an optimal image management system for the organisation. This creates an internal image network sufficiently entwined and developed that it can disseminate information within the entire company with little or no supervision. This not only saves valuable response time when handling customer interactions, it also frees senior management's time to meet and deal with new or unforeseen challenges and opportunities.

It is worthwhile examining in some detail how change management and corporate image management processes can be used successfully. Used properly, these can effect significant cultural change in the most staid of organisations without necessarily losing skills and goodwill. Chapter Three will explain this process further and gives a detailed case study.

Summary

Corporate image management is one of the most potent marketing and management tools available for senior executives to use in ensuring the viable execution of the corporate vision. Not only does the corporate image management process provide senior management with the highest level of functional control of the organisation, it also provides one of the most powerful strategic marketing weapons available in the corporate arsenal. Progressive corporate leaders will use this new discipline to drive

Corporate Image Management

their organisations forward in victory in today's and tomorrow's marketing battlefields.

This book will help you to:

- effect and manage change using a systems approach,
- manage the total corporate image from a marketing perspective,
- provide the organisation with a necessary and effective infrastructure for maintaining an innovative and stimulating work environment, and
- develop and manage a marketing communications strategy that builds a clear, unambiguous and definitive understanding of the organisation's desired corporate image.

It will give you the tools to gain the competitive edge to help ensure that your organisational objectives are both achievable and achieved.

The underlining principle of this book is simply this: *if it touches the customer, it's a marketing issue.* Nothing touches the customer more than how he or she perceives your corporate image. This fundamental perception will be the major factor that determines whether the customer will decide to conduct business with you and, more importantly, enter into a long-term and mutually rewarding relationship with your organisation.

There may be no greater marketing issue than corporate image management in today's increasingly competitive markets. In short, corporate image management will be a key marketing discipline well into the next century. The ultimate battleground for winning and maintaining customer relationships now takes place in the minds, hearts, emotions and perceptions of the customers.

Chapter Two

Corporate Image Management in a Rapidly Changing World

The clichés and admonitions about change are numerous enough to fill a book on their own. Suffice it to say that two facts about change are readily apparent as we end the second millennium:

- change is everywhere, particularly within the business environment, and
- the rate of change is probably faster and broader for a larger portion of the earth's population today than at any other time in history.

The forces reshaping the world economy are more numerous, more interwoven and combine to be more powerful than any other combination of economic and political change since the Industrial Revolution. Change is happening so rapidly that the countless reorganisations, restructures, downsizings, mergers, break-ups and new business start-ups make the business community seem almost out of control. Not only has this created an element of uncertainty (particularly for the workers affected), but consumers and customers are baffled and disturbed as they become unsure about the companies behind the available products and services. In the process, of course, many companies have done their images little good.

What types of change are being faced by managers? The following listing is not meant to be exhaustive, but it indicates that change is prevalent and affects many aspects of the business-customer relationship.

Corporate Image Management

- Global competitors in local markets. Your competitor is no longer just the other firm down the street. It's the new start-up or the established multinational whose home base may be halfway around the world. The emergence of the Internet as a hub for electronic commerce will simply magnify and exacerbate this trend.

- Competitors from other industries entering your turf. Who's the biggest threat to the 7-Elevens and other small convenience stores around the world? The major oil companies, as they add groceries and sundry items to the products stocked and sold at petrol stations. Who's the biggest threat to the major oil companies for the sale of petrol to car owners? Supermarkets, which in some countries are now installing petrol pumps outside their huge hypermarkets.

- New concepts of quality. While many consumers still look for high quality, the definition of what is 'quality' is changing quite fast. Many consumers now seek 'real values', not superficial styling or trendy items. Real value may be defined by function as easily as it might incorporate artistic elegance and craft.

- Lack of consumer trust. The combined effect of product-tampering problems, toxic shock syndrome, the Perrier recall, the failed launch of 'New Coke', mad cow disease, hepatitis-infected fruit given to school children and numerous other safety scares has left consumers in a quandary about who and what to trust. In 1987, an Opinion Research Corporation study showed that 72% of American consumers thought advertising was at least fairly believable. Within two years, that number had dropped to 62%, with over a third of the public finding advertising to be unbelievable.

- Deterioration in the power of branding. Consumer marketeers have done an awful job of protecting the value of their brands. Too many marketeers have begun to rely on price promotions, discounts, etc. Consumers, who once bought name brands they trusted during times of economic slowdowns, turned to generic brands, store brands and promotional items during the 1992–93 recession. When Philip Morris cut the price of Marlboro cigarettes in April 1993, the entire Dow Jones Industrial Average dropped over 100 points. In the four months following 'Marlboro Friday', the top 25 makers of brands lost over US$4.75 billion in market value. To fight off generic products, Proctor & Gamble cut the prices on their products Luvs and Pampers three times in a single year.

To cope with these many changes in the market environment, a plethora of new business management concepts has been created over the past two decades. Managers have tried to diversify by building conglomerates, to decentralise by spinning off unlinked entities and to re-engineer businesses based on core competencies. In terms of marketing, we have witnessed a continual movement from one hot topic to another, including excellence, customer service, customer delight, service quality, niche marketing and now customised marketing.

What is a manager or corporate leader to do? How can they choose from the dichotomies being expounded by the omnipresent management consultants and MBA professors: centralisation or decentralisation? consensus-building or top-down decision making? matrix, hierarchical or flat organisation structures? core competencies or customer requirements?

Fortunately, common sense is starting to prevail in the management literature and the corporate boardrooms. It is based on the understanding that there is no Holy Grail or single way of providing the leadership, organisational structure and management processes required by each and every business situation.

CEOs can use corporate image management, however, as their operating platform to determine, select and implement other leadership, management and marketing tools as the vehicles to drive organisations towards their goals. A successful identity system will assist the organisation to manage change and remain flexible in its response to changing market conditions, competition and innovation. (The use of corporate image management as a catalyst for change will be discussed in the next chapter.) Managing the corporate image process assists senior management to initiate internal and external reforms vital for marketing excellence.

Marketing Excellence

Marketing excellence is firmly linked to a strong corporate image. Further, the appearance of one tends to foreshadow the occurrence or likelihood of the other. This leads to the belief that *companies, brands and services succeed as a direct result of the organisation's corporate image and marketing excellence.*

Corporate Image Management

In business, it is not unusual to become caught up in the heat of the immediate commercial battle while losing sight of the greater goal of winning the war. In fiercely competitive and rapidly changing international and domestic markets, the success stories are about managers who correctly identified consumer, client and customer needs and met these in a creative way. They are also about companies who had the internal strength from knowing who and what they are, and where they are heading, three of the most critical elements for managing the corporate image.

Corporate Culture

The reason for failure in the marketplace is seldom lack of investment. It is usually the result of poor marketing performance and the failure to develop a culture within an organisation that supports creative, strategic and market-driven change. This is the reason why corporate image management needs to go beyond the mere visual aspects of logo, symbol and signature. It needs to reach the deeper concerns of shaping a functioning organisation that can adapt to changing market conditions.

Cultural change in organisations is not impeded by the existence of routine or repetitive 'do-it-as-ordered' jobs, but results from the confinement of some people within their job's perceived limitations. Disenchantment (or internal division) sets in when people are not given the chance to think beyond the limits of their own duties. People need to see and understand the larger corporate picture or direction and contribute from their own experiences to the search for more effective ways of getting the job done. The whole re-engineering movement has been tarnished because the human element was often brutally brushed aside in the rush to develop more streamlined and automated processes.

In 1993, *Fortune* magazine advised its readers, 'Forget old notions of advancement and loyalty. In a more flexible, more chaotic world of work, you are responsible for your career'. Has corporate loyalty flown out the door? It's more likely that it was shoved out, along with the so-called non-essential staff, by the re-engineering doctors. The implications for corporate image and organisational culture are immense. In the past, corporate culture was easier to manage because employees naturally learned how things were done in the organisation as they grew in it over periods of 15, 20, 25 or more years. Having an unwritten code of conduct could suffice when the organisation provided lifetime employment. Today, many companies are wandering adrift without a coherent corporate culture. They lack universal acceptance of corporate goals and objectives because they are staffed by employees equally adrift who consider their current employer merely a temporary stop on the road to their personal and individual goals. Their continued employment has not made them grateful or more loyal, merely more scared and concerned about when the next set of layoffs will be coming.

Organisational arteries harden when job definitions become barriers and when people in the more constrained jobs become viewed as a different and lesser breed. The sum of these constraints, and the resultant loss of corporate loyalty by the remaining staff, represents a tremendous waste of corporate energy that is waiting and wanting to be recognised, focused and utilised. By using the corporate image management process, management can uncover this latent energy and channel it towards the corporation's goals and objectives.

Corporate image management will also help senior executives to deal with another of the critical issues facing management today: corporate ethics. As *The Economist* asked in 1995, 'How can a company ensure that its code of ethics is both followed and enforced?'. The sure-fire way is to develop a corporate culture that not only emphasises ethical behaviour, but also punishes and ostracises those who do not live up to the desired standards. Very rarely can a single employee engage in unethical behaviour without other employees being 'in the know' or at least suspicious. A corporate culture, communicated and spread throughout the organisation, that exhibits zero tolerance for unethical behaviour and that is intricately tied to the corporate image is management's best form of assurance. This works better than having internal policy police and a bundle of quarterly forms submitted, analysed and then stacked in some compliance officer's cupboard.

Disintermediation

With advanced forms of communication, and the greater development and ready use of the Internet for electronic commerce, the middle person or company in many transactions will be eliminated, a process called disintermediation. Companies and organisations will be in a better position to take customer orders, pass them on to suppliers, and have their own labels placed onto the products. While this will eliminate some

Corporate Image Management

warehousing, distribution and inventory costs, it will also tend to identify companies directly with their products.

To take an example, most shoppers do not care whether Proctor & Gamble makes Tide, Downey, Luvs or Pampers. For the most part, consumers are still buying brands without really knowing or understanding the company behind them. But unless P&G wants to establish thousands of different web sites for each of its products, it is going to have to start telling people, 'We are the people behind those brands you use and trust'. In other words, P&G will need to determine its desired corporate image for consumer audiences, not just for the investment community, and work out how to communicate this image effectively.

Once again, the perception of an organisation's corporate image by its many constituents becomes the key to winning the marketing battle.

Chapter Three

Corporate Image Management as a Catalyst for Change

A predominant management theme since the early 1980s has been the introduction of new leadership from outside whenever massive internal change is required. The new leadership puts its plans together, takes the company through an exciting period of positive change, and the bottom line results are applauded by the investment community. Unfortunately, most of these changes are of the swift and immediate kind, such as cost containment and trimming of staff ranks. While financially sound and prudent, the company is no longer what it used to be. And while the new leadership team is committed and shares a common vision, neither the public nor the staff know much about the new values of the new organisation.

As a result, internal disenchantment sets in. The younger and brighter staff, those whom the new leaders had counted on to strengthen the middle management ranks, start to leave. Dissatisfied comments are heard regarding wages, benefits and of not 'being informed of the company's activities'. There may be some staff that management would like to see leave the company, but who stay, recognising the security of their employment. On the other hand, the more desirable staff may leave because they do not have a clear picture of what the future holds for them.

The new leaders are so busy tearing down the old structures that they fail to design and communicate what they are building. The public doesn't

Corporate Image Management

see the company in its new light, so they depart to competitive offerings. The staff doesn't know or understand what is going on, and so the most capable—who are also the most mobile—depart for other opportunities.

Changing the old ways may be necessary for short-term financial survival. At the same time, however, it is critical to create the value systems and corporate culture that will enable and promote long-term growth and survival. Otherwise, it's like putting the corporate patient on a life support system for a short time, only to allow it to die a slower, more agonising death later.

The corporate image management process is significant for senior executives desiring to infuse change within their organisations. The revitalisation of a well-established organisation and its products or services is inherently more complex than a traditional corporate identity graphics program. The creation or modification of a deeply seeded corporate culture—especially where long-term employee loyalty and long-term corporate employment are no longer in vogue—is even more difficult and even less graphically definable.

The solution to both lies within the marketing and management discipline of corporate image management.

Leveraging Corporate Image Management

Is there a better way to effect change within an organisation? Is there a better way to create and inculcate a new corporate image within an organisation?

A change in an organisation's corporate identity, whether a large-scale revamp or an updated modification of an existing look, provides an opportunity for the entire organisation to 'rally around' the new identity. It should be based upon agreed corporate culture and values. By leveraging the corporate image management process, the entire organisation becomes focused on collectively implementing management's desired changes and strategies for future growth, within the framework and structure of a new or revised corporate culture.

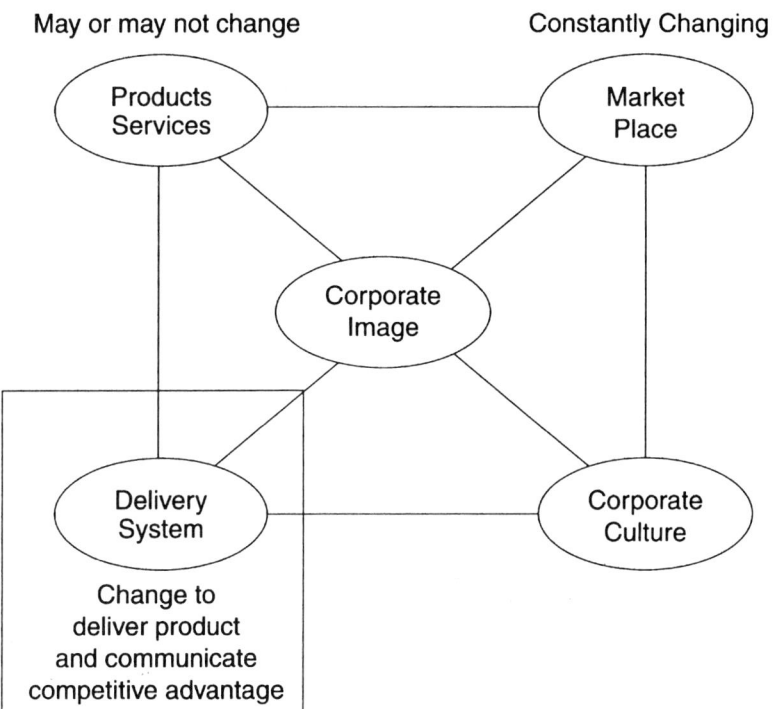

By leveraging the corporate image management process, the entire organisation can become collectively focused on implementing desired changes and strategies for future growth, within the framework of a new or revised corporate culture.

Using the corporate image management process as a catalyst to drive change often results in an opportunity for the entire organisation to rally around the new identity and for all of the organisation's constituents to develop a sense of belonging and engagement with the new identity.

At the same time, the corporate image management process helps individuals and groups to align themselves with the planned changes and to work together in unity to implement the desired change.

Corporate Image Management

An innovative, growing, changing organisation needs a work force at all levels that has not become so stuck in the rhythm of routine jobs that it cannot easily adapt to a new drumbeat. For positive change to be a way of life, rather than an occasional shock, both the crew and the captains have to be engaged in effecting and managing change. And, while still performing the day-to-day tasks that keep the business running, both groups have to ensure that the external identity and internal image of the organisation remain in harmony.

A new corporate identity provides all critical parties—staff as well as management and associated business partners—with a sense of belonging to the new corporate identity system. This system embodies the appearance and feel of the new image and the new identity is supported by the foundation stones of the vision statement, mission statement, corporate quality statement, image marketing objectives, corporate philosophy, corporate values and key points from the organisation's strategic plan.

Active Involvement and Understanding

No staff member, employee or manager, can be expected to act independently or with initiative on behalf of the company without knowing and understanding the corporate vision, mission, philosophy and strategic direction. To ensure the desired results, the corporate image management process includes the involvement of all levels of staff within the planning, analytical, implementation and monitoring stages. This helps to win acceptance and commitment from the very people who will be responsible for implementing the new corporate identity and who will be held accountable for believing in and performing within the new corporate image.

This methodology is particularly useful when companies have diverse business activities that span multiple markets or multiple customer audiences, as witnessed during a project within a financial services company in Malaysia. This company had a relatively new CEO engaged in massive change throughout the organisation. In fact, this change was taking place so rapidly that each of the business units and most of the staff could not keep pace. At a two-day off-site meeting to discuss the corporate and individual business unit vision and mission statements, it quickly became clear that the CEO's top-down vision thinking had not won acceptance or understanding at lower levels.

Corporate Image Management as a Catalyst for Change

To start with, not one of the six business units referred to the corporate vision, mission or goals in their own planning documents. Secondly, none referred to the business plans or products of the other five operating units, even though four of them shared customers or distribution channels with at least one of the other units. This was an organisation heading off in six independent directions, piloted by a CEO who was on a flight path of his own. It was little wonder that the front-line operational and marketing staff below felt clueless about their company. It was also little wonder that an internal research study showed that employees felt more closely identified with their own business units (each of which had its own legal name) than they did with the parent company.

In the end, the corporate image management process for this company did not result in a name change (one was created, but never implemented because the CEO departed before it could be announced). It served however to bring about a refined vision and mission for the company, with a set of key corporate values, revised and linked vision and mission statements for each of the business units, the development of a corporate image strategy plan, and a set of strategic marketing objectives.

Change Process

What happens after the vision is created, the mission set, and the values put into place? How does senior management go about aligning the employees, business partners, shareholders, customers and others with the business strategy? The easy answer is communications. The difficult answer requires a systematic process that augments the involvement of all appropriate parties.

Critical to the success of change management is a project structure built around a steering committee. This team comprises the top manager from each business unit and support department, along with other key individuals, as determined by the nature of the business. Part of the commitment to success requires that the steering committee has the active and constant participation of senior-level managers from each unit. This is not a task force to which junior staff can be assigned to attend the meetings and report back the discussions and action items to the senior managers. That would be a recipe for failure.

The steering committee will guide and direct the project consultants (usually an outside resource). It will also be responsible for evaluating the

Corporate Image Management

feasibility of the ideas and approaches taken throughout the various phases of the project. When possible, representatives of the steering committee should work with the consultants in implementing each phase.

Project teams, comprising lower-level representatives from cross-sections of each business unit (eg Human Resources, Finance, Administration, Manufacturing, Marketing, Operations, Technology), will be formed to collect and interpret both internal and external data. These project teams are critical in providing insights into current issues and concerns buried within the individual business units and work groups. They will also help to identify culturally sensitive issues (those that impact on the current corporate culture or on sociological norms). The four key objectives for forming project teams are to:

- involve all levels and areas of the organisation and gain their inputs,
- establish a two-way communication link and network with all work groups, departments, and business units within the organisation,
- provide an on-going methodology and process for continual feedback and evaluation of the corporate change effort, and
- gain early acceptance and commitment to the idea of change and to the new programs that evolve from this process.

By using cross-divisional and cross-company participation in this process, the units are brought closer together and develop a greater understanding of what each unit contributes to the overall whole. In the process of discussing the company's strategy, the core competencies, strengths, and interests of each unit are identified, discussed, evaluated, understood and accepted by all the other parties. Like pieces in a puzzle, each element is analysed, shaped and put into place. In some instances, these inputs from the project teams result in modifications of the organisational vision or mission. In many cases, this process results in some restructuring of responsibilities, duties or processes, changes that are more readily accepted because they are initiated by the people who will be affected directly.

In almost all cases, this process allows the employees to identify and list what they feel are the core values and attributes of the organisation. Because the project teams invest many hours in identifying, discussing, modifying, shaping and agreeing to these core values, management receives a unified set of values and attributes. These values are not only believed and shared by the rank and file, but also have the commitment, understanding and individual internalisation by the organisation's body public.

Implementation of Change

Now that everyone has a better feeling and idea of the role they and their unit plays in the future direction of the organisation, the related elements of implementation need to be put into place. Part of the communication process is to ensure that everyone understands that all jobs and activities in the organisation are interconnected and that everyone is contributing directly or indirectly to a measurable corporate goal.

Complete and open communication, with accessible information for all, is essential to keep the process moving forward along the desired path. If information is kept to a select few, then the rest of the organisation is like a marooned boat, strategically structured and sound, but waiting for the rising tide to get it moving.

I advocate sharing of the corporate vision, mission, values and objectives with as many parties as possible without jeopardising the competitive and strategic advantages that they provide. Examples are managers, staff, employees, business partners, outsourcing partners, suppliers, union management and leaders, key customers and others. Written documents and manuals that provide supporting rationales and data for the new corporate elements and direction need to be developed and distributed freely within the organisation. These provide the background material needed by those not involved in the deliberations of the project teams and steering committee for ascertaining the logic, justification and meaning behind the new programs and new directions.

Individual business unit implementation programs should be developed with input and guidance from the project teams and, if appropriate, the steering committee. The goal is to ensure uniformity and effectiveness, along with an across-the-board feedback mechanism.

In many instances, formal training and train-the-trainer sessions will be required in order to assemble a group of internal coaches and practitioners that help to develop and shape the desired corporate culture. Top management, through their involvement in the steering committee, should actively follow the work of the change implementors and support these efforts with sufficient financial and human resources to ensure uniform implementation and absolute acceptance.

Corporate Image Management

A Catalyst for Change—Case Study

A good example of the corporate image management process as a catalyst for change occurred when Singapore's Commercial and Industrial Security Corporation (CISCO) engaged an image management company to modernise its logo, and perhaps its name, to improve its commercial activities.

CISCO

CISCO is a statutory board organisation in Singapore with both national security and commercial operations. It is a component of Singapore's Ministry of Home Affairs and its key role is to serve as the country's national auxiliary police force. In addition, CISCO provides a wide range of commercial security services to commercial, industrial and government enterprises in Singapore and an increasing number of South-east Asian markets.

Because of its dual role as both a non-profit, official auxiliary police body and a revenue-generating corporate entity, CISCO has long had a split personality, both internally and externally. In addition, its limited resources have traditionally been split between those pushing to upgrade the auxiliary police force and those wanting to increase revenue and profits from the commercial operations.

In its role as the auxiliary police force, CISCO has no competitors. CISCO was founded for the purpose of providing supplementary security services in Singapore, particularly to government entities and businesses with high risks (ie banks, gold and jewellery shops, manufacturing facilities). CISCO is the only entity outside the other official police forces in Singapore that is allowed to provide armed protection services.

In the commercial world however CISCO has several competitors, particularly in the areas of security consultancy, security management services, computer security, computer recovery, security training and the provision of security storage facilities. Naturally, as a government-linked organisation, CISCO has certain advantages within Singapore in obtaining contracts and business within the commercial and industrial sectors. Unlike its armed protection services, it does not have a monopoly in this area, which means that it must bring a more customer-focused and marketing-aware attitude to this part of the business.

The growth problem

In 1992, the CISCO board determined that future growth would come mostly from its commercial activities. Also, in line with strategic Singapore government thinking, its commercial activities were identified potentially for future privatisation (but the auxiliary police force functions would always remain within the Ministry of Home Affairs). At that time, less than 24% of CISCO's group turnover of approximately S$70 million came from commercial activities.

Environmental factors that affected this decision included the realisation that the auxiliary police functions were highly labour intensive and required a fairly unskilled (but trainable) work force. However, Singapore's ever tightening labour supply, combined with a reducing pool of unskilled labour resources, would have a negative impact on CISCO's ability to grow this portion of its business mix. In addition, new technology was coming on stream that could reduce the need for armed security services and thus would open up CISCO's fairly closed domestic markets to the threat of substitute competition.

This was not a clear-cut decision by the board, which (like the company itself) was divided in thought between giving priority to auxiliary police or to commercial activities. The board comprised a mixture of political appointees with long backgrounds in the public service sector and people with commercial enterprise experience. Significantly, the general manager and CEO of CISCO, Mr Chan Boon Kiong, was not a member of the board. Instead, he reported directly to the chairman of the board.

CISCO's corporate image

One of the major problems facing CISCO in the early 1990s in implementing a growth strategy based on the development of its commercial activities was the weak image of CISCO in the commercial marketplace. CISCO was seen to be less customer friendly, more bureaucratic, less flexible and more expensive than many of its commercial competitors. This perception was based on customer inputs, management observations, and a quantitative field research study conducted amongst customers and prospects. Hence, the board directed senior management to change and improve the corporate image of CISCO while simultaneously developing plans to rapidly grow its commercial operation's revenues and profits.

Corporate Image Management

According to Mr William Carlson, the senior consultant on the project, 'The consultants immediately determined that CISCO suffered from a negative market image, one that was derived solely from its auxiliary police force activities'. Conducting further market and internal research, the consultants concluded that:

- CISCO was perceived exclusively in the market as the provider of armed guards in banks and goldsmith shops,
- the majority of people within CISCO, including middle managers, had little or no idea what functions or services were provided by CISCO outside their own operating areas,
- the commercial activities of CISCO were structured around departments that had grown in a haphazard fashion, resulting in overlaps of services being provided and duplication of internal resources,
- there was no centralised marketing function within the company,
- CISCO was perceived as a very low-tech company,
- staff took little pride in being associated with CISCO,
- the organisation faced numerous difficulties in recruiting technical and marketing staff due to the poor image of the company,
- the organisation had a 'statutory board' mentality throughout the company, even in areas that operated solely in the commercial sector, and
- in the public's mind, only the Public Utilities Board had a lower image than CISCO compared with other government-linked commercial enterprises. CISCO was far down the totem pole from the likes of Singapore Telecoms, Jurong Town Corporation, Keppel, Sembawang, Singapore Airlines and even the Port of Singapore Authority.

According to Mr Carlson, 'Rather than focus on creating a new image, one that was unlikely to be supported by the internal workings of the organisation, we recommended that CISCO senior management consider a major restructuring of the organisation into strategic business units (SBUs), which would allow each SBU to build specific expertise in its product and customer areas and to establish a deeper understanding of underlying customer needs'.

The board was at first reluctant to even consider the structural change recommendations. In addition, although Mr Chan was the first civilian CEO of CISCO, he came to the organisation with 18 years of government administrative service in the Ministry of Labour and the Ministry of Home

Affairs. Despite a long career in the public sector, Mr Chan readily understood and supported the need for quick, massive organisational change.

Fortunately, for both CISCO and the consultants, a new chairman was appointed at this time, one who came from the commercial world. The new chairman, Mr Sim Cheok Lim, was the marketing director of Shell Eastern Petroleum (Private) Ltd and had extensive marketing and management experience in the region. He had been a board member since 1987 and had been one of the stronger advocates for the commercial growth strategy.

Mr Sim also realised that CISCO would have to become a marketing-driven organisation if it were to achieve the long-term goals of the commercial growth strategy. And while many board members and senior managers in CISCO felt that change could not occur quickly within CISCO, Mr Sim was not discouraged. What others thought was impossible, Mr Sim saw not only as achievable, but as mandatory if he was to lead CISCO to commercial glory.

Following up on the previous external research, the consultants conducted extensive internal research on CISCO's image with employees, their friends and family members, and analysed the organisation's internal working procedures, issues and policies. Some of the key findings related to the issue of change were:

- the human resource department was perceived by employees, management and the consultants as generally weak,
- this department was the most resistant to change as it collectively felt that any organisational change would dump massive amounts of new work and procedures on the department,
- there was no central department to lead the proposed change, and
- new operating procedures and company policies would need to be developed to cater for any new organisational changes.

Because of the lack of a central body or department to act as the change leader, CISCO created a series of task forces. These task forces were to investigate each of the key areas related to the proposed changes (eg policies, hiring criteria, internal communications, SBU structure). They were populated by representatives from across the company, including staff from the auxiliary police force departments, the commercial enterprise sections and the support staff areas. Each task force selected its own leader and structure and a senior consultant from the consultancy was assigned to be the lead facilitator of each group.

The new CISCO

The newly created CISCO organisational structure was designed to support its dual role as the national auxiliary police and as a commercially driven company. In doing so, the new structure was divided into statutory board functions, support departments and subsidiaries. Six new SBUs were created to handle both statutory functions and commercial operations.

The internal structure of CISCO now emphasised performance management of specific customer product and service areas, rather than internal processing. With this new structure CISCO is better positioned to gain greater market intelligence and to understand customer needs—the two criteria that had been identified as necessary for the company to continually upgrade its product and service offering.

As more products and services were transferred to the commercial SBUs, eventually only the CISCO Auxiliary Police and CISCO Security Consultancy operations would remain as statutory functions. These two operations were viewed as extremely sensitive and critical to the support of the country's security. The other SBUs were defined by product lines and type of customer and were grouped under three key areas: Security Services, Security Systems and Security Facilities.

In addition, a new Group Marketing function was formed to coordinate security audits and the integration of services to customers whose complex security needs required the products or services of more than one CISCO SBU.

Most importantly, to fully integrate the changes of the new group structure, a set of core values was developed, to be shared and executed by all entities within the organisation. These core values were defined as: professionalism, reliability and integrity.

The development of these core values was critical to the successful implementation of the new organisation's structure. By getting management and staff to collectively determine and write their own core values, rather than dictating these from above, Chairman Sim was rewarded with a set of beliefs that were practised by the organisation he headed, and that he could employ too.

Another valuable spin-off from the methodology employed by Mr Sim is that his fellow board members, not previously known for their quick decisions, immediately approved and agreed to both the core values and the organisational structure designed by Mr Chan and the CISCO task forces. This happened for two reasons:

- the bottom-up approach and cross-company participation on the task forces made it hard for the board to argue with or disagree with the final recommendations, and
- the active participation of the outside consultants in the entire process gave the board a sense of security that the recommendations were rooted in value judgments that had been examined from outside the confines of the organisation.

Through the process of change management, a new set of key performance indicators for all parts of the organisation was created. These aimed to provide meaningful and measurable parameters for guiding continual improvement in CISCO's performance and almost all are strongly customer-oriented (as opposed to the previously used internally focused parameters).

Soon after the creation of the new SBU structure, CISCO embarked on an advertising and marketing communications campaign to explain the new CISCO to the Singapore market. The messages were designed to show that 'the integration of high technology and highly trained personnel makes CISCO a unique security group'. The author's observations at the time were that this campaign had an immediate impact in changing people's impressions, feelings and knowledge about CISCO.

Reacting to change

For an organisation that was so steeped in bureaucratic processes, the CISCO employees readily adopted the new structure and procedures. One obvious reason for this is the participatory nature of the process used throughout the 16-month period when the structural change was being debated, discussed, planned and implemented. Another factor was that all task force members were given special recognition, treated to lunches by senior management or to dinners with the general manager, or rewarded in other ways. In addition, as each new SBU was formed, a lunch or tea

Corporate Image Management

'get together' was held for the staff (sometimes with their customers) so that everyone immediately felt part of the new team.

Two new newsletters—one for employees, the other for customers—were created to explain the new organisation structure, and to inform all employees about new policies, procedures and adjustments as they occurred. This helped to prevent 'whispering campaigns' from disturbing the communications flow. The customer newsletter helped customers understand which SBU to call to handle their specific requests, queries or problems.

Resistance to change was kept to a minimum, as the senior management and board showed appropriate leadership skills and allowed the CISCO staff to 'think for themselves' and participate in the process from day one.

Lessons from the case study
The methodology employed by CISCO's senior management resulted in an organisation that had a clearer focus and that could better identify and meet commercial customer needs. During the process, the role of CISCO was redefined to that of 'loss prevention', which provided a much wider scope than its previous focus on 'security'.

As a result of the new marketing-driven direction of the company, several business units, in particular those providing security training, consultancy and systems services, began to identify overseas business opportunities and to develop a presence for CISCO in neighbouring markets in the region.

In an unfortunate example of impermanent change, the CISCO corporate image advertising campaign turned out to be a one-shot expenditure rather than a long-term investment. The original campaign ran in early 1995 over a period of four months, but little has been seen or heard from CISCO since. Without a continuous investment in an on-going corporate image campaign, the public attitude and perceptions of CISCO are more likely to revert closer to their previous levels than to be maintained at the desired image.

The CISCO experience clearly shows how the corporate image management process can be used by a board or CEO as a catalyst for change. Whereas the original brief to the image consultants was to design a new public image for CISCO, what actually took place was a complete restructuring of the organisation, from top to bottom. With the SBUs aligned with key customer groups and named to facilitate customer understanding of their functions, CISCO became an organisation with a clearly defined purpose and direction, a written set of core values, and an internal structure that could clearly support, rather than undermine, the new corporate image. The irony of this case is that, in the end, very little changed in the visual aspect of the CISCO corporate image (the logo underwent very minor modifications and the expected name change never occurred).

Corporate Image Management as a Catalyst for Change

Chapter Four

The Value of a Good Corporate Image

Walter Landor, often cited as the pioneer of corporate image, remarked 'Only superficial people refuse to judge by appearances'. Although flippant in tone, there is truth in Mr Landor's comments. After all, how else are we to judge an unknown or unfamiliar company, organisation, city, country, or product if not by appearances?

As individuals, we're taught to dress properly, in accordance with our local customs and cultural nuances. Who amongst us hasn't put on his or her best suit, dress, shirt or tie when going to meet someone deemed important, whether it's for a job interview, a date, or a major social gathering? Our appearances are important, especially to those who are not familiar with us. The same holds true for our companies and organisations.

McGraw-Hill understood this concept as far back as the 1950s, when they ran advertisements in the trade press telling companies why they need to advertise in the company's business, professional and technical magazines. The copy platform was quite simple, yet effective:

> 'I don't know who you are.
> I don't know your company.
> I don't know what your company stands for.
> I don't know your company's customers.
> I don't know your company's record.
> I don't know your company's reputation.
> Now—what is it you wanted to sell me?'

The Value of a Good Corporate Image

In today's world, where information travels around the globe at the speed of thousands of electronic bytes per second, your potential customers, suppliers, employees, partners and other important audiences are asking themselves similar questions. Are your employees capable of giving unified and believable responses to these questions?

To understand the value of a good corporate image, compare your initial thoughts when you read the names of these two companies: Johnson & Johnson and Exxon. How about when you think about The Coca-Cola Company and Perrier? Any differences? No doubt there is, especially for the first pairing.

Both Johnson & Johnson and Exxon were not long ago faced with difficult, headline-generating, attention-grabbing problems. For Johnson & Johnson, it was the well documented product tampering scare that hit their market-leading Tylenol product. For Exxon, it was the oil spill from the *Exxon Valdez*. In both cases, the companies were subjected to the highest levels of public scrutiny. Johnson & Johnson came through the test with its corporate reputation not only saved, but actually enhanced thanks to the open, honest way it dealt with the public, its distributors, the media, employees, shareholders and everyone else. Sadly for Exxon, its corporate reputation was tarnished, not so much by the damage from the actual oil spill, but from the way the company's employees and management dealt with the situation. No amount of slick, glossy corporate advertising will rectify the damage done to Exxon's reputation; only time, and the future conduct of the company, will do that.

For the past several decades, ever since the mid-1960s when the 'anti-establishment' mentality began to spread, corporations have rarely been positioned as 'Mr Nice Guys', particularly by the popular media. More often than not, business leaders in films, TV shows, the theatre, and the general, non-business press, are likely to be depicted as dishonest, egoistic, and exploitative thugs. Now, even companies are being portrayed as bad guys; as a result of its handling of the *Valdez* oil spill, Exxon has, in many ways, become a caricature of the 'corporate villain'. As an example, in Kevin Costner's movie *Waterworld*, the huge, decaying ship that sinks at the end of the movie is named *Exxon Valdez*. How much worse could it get for a company? Fortunately for Exxon, *Waterworld* was not a box-office hit produced by the likes of Steven Spielberg; had it been so, it would be appropriate for Exxon (formerly Esso) and its management to seriously discuss another name change.

Corporate Image Management

A good corporate image is a fragile thing and, once damaged, is extremely hard to repair. Compare the situations of Coca-Cola and Perrier. The former made a terrible marketing blunder with the introduction of New Coke. Consumer reaction was so negative that the company had to revert to putting 'old Coke', cleverly renamed Coke Classic, back on the store shelves. And while The Coca-Cola Company may have suffered some short-term damage to its reputation as an astute marketing company, there was no ill effect on its corporate reputation.

Perrier, on the other hand, was not so fortunate. In the early 1980s, Perrier 'owned' the market for fizzy bottled water drinks. Many people around the world would order a 'Perrier and lemon', or some such combination, when dining or when requesting a non-alcoholic drink in bars and pubs. Perrier had established a name that dominated this category, similar to Bacardi's in the rum segment. Then Perrier suffered chemical problems in the production of their product. At first the company blamed natural causes, then said it was a slight manufacturing problem. Eventually Perrier had to admit that the problem was bigger than originally stated. And while the problem was fixed, Perrier's corporate image was not. Today, one rarely hears 'Perrier and lemon' ordered at the lunch table; rather, it has become the generic 'mineral water and lemon'.

Why are consumers, and people in general, so tough on companies when cracks appear in their corporate images? I believe it goes to the desire of people to build intangible relationships with the individuals and entities with which they interact. Consciously, and more often unconsciously, we all want to *relate* to the products, services and companies with which we deal. It's a lot like people's emotional relationships with athletes, music and movie stars and other cultural icons. We get upset when these 'heroes' don't live up to our image of them. We think we understand the Mike Tysons, Michael Jacksons, Maradonas, and Hugh Grants of the world. But actually we don't, and when we find out that these cultural symbols are fallible, we become very unforgiving.

The same holds true with companies and other organisations. If you disappoint us, we not only go away, we're likely to talk negatively about you to others. A marketing saying goes 'If a customer is happy with their experience with a company, they may tell one to four people about it, but if unhappy or disappointed, they are likely to tell as many as 19 people'. Depending upon who's telling the anecdote, the number 19 fluctuates between 12 and 30. No matter what the exact number, the truth is still the same—we are all unforgiving at times when companies and organisations do not live up to *our* images of them. And we're more eager to broadcast to our friends, families, colleagues and business partners the bad experiences we have with organisations than the positive ones. What this says about human nature is probably worthy of a book itself.

Of course, it is not *impossible* to recover from a damaged image. The powerhouse IBM is good example of a company that has had its ups and downs in the marketplace and on the stock market. The share value of Big Blue dropped into the low $70s (from highs around $120 per share) earlier this decade as investors turned away from a company they saw as unimaginative, misdirected and struggling to maintain both market share and customers. The fabled IBM, which liked to claim that 'No one ever got fired for recommending IBM', had been able to use its reputation for dominance and solid after-sales service to push customers to pay more for its products than competitors could charge for theirs. But as technology made computers both cheaper and more reliable, and after-sales service could be handled by third-party providers, the bulky IBM was unable to display the nimbleness required to stay ahead in the rapidly changing computer industry.

It took IBM, and its new CEO Lou Gerstner, a couple of years to get Big Blue's house back in order. Of course, some pundits wrote that IBM was so slow to change because the powerful weapon of its existing reputation was a barrier to internal change. Today, the shares are about to trade again in the low 100s, but only after a two-for-one stock split! IBM has been a key component of the famed 1995–97 bull run on the New York Stock Exchange and investors no longer see it as misdirected and struggling.

Financial Value

Proof of the financial value of a corporate image surfaced a couple of years ago when a Florida real estate developer, Charles Cobb, paid US$1.33 million to purchase the name and trademark logo for Pan Am World Airways. Over US$1 million dollars—for the name and logo of a bankrupt organisation and an airline that inauspiciously is just as likely to be remembered for the tragic aeroplane bombing over Lockerbie, Scotland

Corporate Image Management

in 1988 than for its pioneering and historic role in the aviation industry. At the time of the purchase, the famed Pan Am skyscraper above Central Station on New York's Park Avenue had already been renamed the Met Life building. But according to Cobb, he purchased the rights to the Pan Am identity because 'It's one of the best recognised names in worldwide travel. It's a good vehicle for an international set of properties'.

When you combine the Pan Am story with reports of the huge premiums over book value being paid on Wall Street and other financial capitals to acquire the likes of RJR Nabisco, Parker Pen Holdings Ltd, VeriFone, Turner Broadcasting, Martini & Rossi, Chemical Bank, and other companies, it is obvious that the financial and corporate investment community has reached two conclusions. These are that:

- building a product brand name from scratch is too costly relative to the buying an existing one, and
- the financial value in a good corporate image is worth every bit as much, and sometimes more, than the value found in the hard assets on the balance sheet.

This linkage between a strong corporate image, valuable product brands and the price that buyers are willing to pay for them will only strengthen as consumers move from a desire for product and service excellence to a demand for relationship excellence.

The intangible value of a corporate image even has the accounting profession talking. With investors clamouring for more nonfinancial information reporting from publicly listed companies, accountants are struggling with ways of capturing and reporting a range of nonfinancial criteria. These include the corporation's brand or name equity, the degree of customer loyalty, the overall status of employee relations, and the company's ability to avoid regulatory problems. Of course, some standardisation will need to be developed, for it will do little good to investors if companies use different accounting formulas to measure and report these kinds of criteria. And we all know how long it takes to develop or change standardised accounting rules and policies. But, even if a firm financial value cannot be placed on these issues, astute financial investors have realised that there is great hidden value to be found in the non-balance sheet areas of organisations with good corporate images and powerful brands.

Marketplace Value

The understanding of a valuable corporate image also extends to the marketplace. For instance, in Europe the well-established EuroCard credit card association has begun to recognise the global power of the MasterCard brand franchise. EuroCard, which is already partly owned by MasterCard International, another card payments association, has long insisted on maintaining its own identity throughout Europe. As such, international consumers visiting Europe are more likely to find EuroCard decals in store windows than MasterCard decals. In recent years, however, MasterCard has concentrated on the importance of global acceptance of its three card payment brands: MasterCard, Maestro and Cirrus. As a result, the executives managing EuroCard, realising the importance of leveraging the worldwide global brand image of MasterCard, are now in the process of slowly dissolving the EuroCard name and converting to the more powerful, universally recognised MasterCard brand name. This will take place first in merchant windows and point-of-sale logo displays, and then eventually onto the cards held by European consumers (who currently have a valued relationship with the EuroCard brand name). In the near future, the use of MasterCard cards by overseas visitors to Europe is likely to escalate, as consumers see the familiar interlocking circles of the red and yellow MasterCard logo.

Can the corporate image be a direct linkage with customers? There's little doubt, as we will discuss later. BSN, Europe's third biggest food company, certainly believes in the power and value of the corporate image, and in the benefits of having an easily recognisable, memorable name as a direct linkage with customers. In 1994 the company changed its name from BSN to the Danone Group, the name of one of its best known product lines. At the time of the name change Danone dairy products were second only to Coca-Cola in terms of branded sales across Europe. It was also the market leader for fresh milk products in over 30 countries. It is certainly easier for consumers to begin to understand and develop a relationship with a company called Danone, than with three letters that don't stand for anything. Not surprisingly, other major branded food manufacturers, including H. J. Heinz and Britain's McVities, began allocating a higher portion of their respective advertising budgets to promote the corporate name, rather than individual product names, at about the same time as the Danone name change.

Corporate Image Management

A corporation with a clearly defined identity and, as we'll explore later, a coherent and concise image, is more likely to stand out in the marketplace as a beacon drawing both repeat customers and trial users. Studies from around the globe have shown that, all other things being equal, the stronger a company's image, the more likely the purchasing public will assume that the products produced and the services tendered by that company are better, of higher quality and worth more in actual price.

Studies have also shown that, the more entrenched the corporate image in the minds of the public, the more likely negative elements or negative stories about the company will be edited or filtered out of the observer's consciousness. For instance, if you see a leaking Mont Blanc fountain pen, and you have an entrenched positive image of Mont Blanc, you are more likely to attribute the fault to carelessness by the user of the pen, rather than to a production quality error by Mont Blanc. The mind says, 'Mont Blanc is a good, reliable and reputable company. Their pens thus do not leak. Therefore, the leak must be the fault of the user, not the maker'. Of course, if the fault is later learned to have been the manufacturer's, and there are other negative experiences with Mont Blanc products, services or employees, then Mont Blanc would follow Perrier and others whose products and service delivery failed to live up to expectations and entrenched perceptions.

How prevalent or important is the corporate image to future product development? In a word: extremely. Again, note your own thought processes as you read through the next example. In Europe, a major, well-known manufacturer of consumer branded goods is entering the automotive market with a well-known German producer of cars. What kind of car would you expect this joint venture to develop? A well-built, modern, middle class or luxury automobile that is likely to live up to a high level of quality standards? That's what most of us would think at first.

Now, let's identify the branded consumer products manufacturer who is part of this joint venture partnership. It's Swatch. Now what kind of car do you expect it to be? Hip, colourful, jazzy, spirited, small, cute, etc? Of course, I expect it to come with matching and switchable wheel rims and steering column, so I can change the colours every day of the week if I so desire. And even when you learn that the German automotive partner for Swatch is none other than Mercedes-Benz, your idea of what the car is going to look like, and how it will be positioned in the market, doesn't change much.

It is for this reason that companies also need to be very careful about the types of joint ventures or joint marketing programs they enter. Mercedes-Benz, with a worldwide reputation for quality, luxury and status could do immense damage, over the long haul, to its corporate image if it allows the new Swatch Car to carry the Mercedes name or the famed Mercedes star on the bonnet. Can you image how Mercedes owners would feel if this hip, colourful, low-price little Swatch car parks next to their big, sedate, bulky, luxurious Mercedes sedan in the parking lot at the golf club? If that were allowed to happen, my prediction is that today's Mercedes owners would become Audi, BMW and Jaguar owners the next time they purchased a new car. Fortunately the folks at Mercedes-Benz are too smart to let this happen and the Swatch car will not be marketed under the Mercedes name.

The Value of a Good Corporate Image

In a similar vein, look at the strategic decision Toyota Motor Company took when it decided to launch a high-end luxury car called Lexus. They went to great lengths to dissociate the Lexus name from Toyota, even demanding that dealers in the United States who sold both brands had to establish separate dealerships and service facilities for the Lexus brand. From what I've read, this decision was taken because market research had shown that American car owners did not believe that a high calibre luxury car, one designed to compete with Mercedes, Volvo, BMW, Audi, Cadillac and the Lincoln-Mercury town car, could be built by a Japanese manufacturer. So, rather than try to convince people otherwise, Toyota created the non-Japanese sounding Lexus name and took steps to purposely segment this product from the corporate image of the Toyota name. The marketing success of the Lexus has now shown the American consumer that luxury and superior quality can emanate from Japan.

Still not convinced about the market value of a name? Here's another example from the automotive world. In Freemont, California a joint venture between Toyota and General Motors is called New United Motor Manufacturing Inc. (NUMMI). The plant produces two almost identical cars, the Toyota Corolla and the General Motors Geo Prizm. Being almost identical, they should sell for approximately the same price and depreciate at about the same rate, correct? Perhaps so, but they don't. The Toyota Corolla sold in 1989 for about 10% more than the GM Geo Prizm. It then depreciated more slowly than the Geo Prizm, resulting in a second-hand value almost 18% higher than the American branded model after five years.

Corporate Image Management

Why the differences? One has to assume that the relative strength of the Toyota brand and corporate name over the General Motors name, in the late 1980s, played the first significant role. If car buyers perceived a Toyota to be superior to a GM car in the same model class, they would be willing to pay a higher sticker price. But that wasn't the entire difference, according to a study by the Boston Consulting Group. The BCG study reported that the after-sales service provided by the Toyota dealer network sustained, and even boosted, the perceived edge of the Toyota name. In other words, the corporate image *management* process taken by Toyota to ensure that the service department at its dealer network wouldn't tarnish or deteriorate the Toyota name helped to reinforce the positive attributes of the Toyota identity. These had already given it an edge in the marketplace *vis-a-vis* a direct, almost identical competitor manufactured in the same facility using the same materials and labour. This example shows the direct value of a strong and well-managed corporate image.

Human Resource Value

A strong corporate image is also a valuable human resource tool, for two reasons. First, having a good reputation makes it easier to attract and recruit the talent required to grow your business and to develop deeper customer relationships. Second, a positive corporate image reduces your recruitment costs. This is because talented people are just as likely to seek you out, and those you want to pursue will need less wooing and require less time and energy to bring them on board.

Think about it. How many top performing or graduating computer engineers would choose Apple Computer over IBM, Compaq or Digital? Is a senior executive, with a family to feed and children to educate, going to take the gamble of a mid-career move to Apple when rumours of its purchase alternate with those of its imminent demise? One of the reasons why companies find it so hard to pull out of free-fall is that their capable people usually jump ship first, and it's then damned difficult to recruit the talent needed to bring stability and direction to the organisation.

A respected reputation not only attracts and retains the best talent available, it also enables the organisation to cherry-pick and woo talent away from competitors. Of course, potential employees have the same concerns as customers and prospects: is this the type of organisation that represents the values and beliefs with which they want to be identified?

It's the total reputation and image of the organisation, not just its reputation for wonderful financial results or market-leading products and services, that are evaluated by potential employees.

Turnover problems can also be reduced by managing the corporate image in such a way as to foster a two-way sense of loyalty, teamwork and commitment between the organisation and its employees. Employee satisfaction is a lot like customer satisfaction: it's okay until someone else comes along and offers employee delight or customer delight. And in the future, I would argue, even these higher standards of gratification will be replaced by the measures that truly count: employment relationships and customer relationships.

Asian Perspectives

The success of many businesses in Asia, particularly outside Japan, has been due to the business flair or networking capability of the founding head of family-owned and family-managed businesses. With decision-making concentrated at the top, opportunities are quickly seized and contractual agreements agreed to and sealed with a handshake. As a result, the corporate image of the firm is often equated with the personal image of the individual or family running the business. Reputations are built over time, as are business and commercial relationships. This system has served the rapidly developing and emerging markets in Asia well, up to a point.

As Asian companies age and the markets mature, they are beginning to understand the need for building and managing a corporate reputation. Asian firms with family or highly ethnic names that are well known only in their local markets are finding it extremely difficult to enter western markets with their products, or even to gain funding and financing. While the concepts of global franchises and corporate image building are western, they are now readily being adopted and adapted by an increasing number of Asian firms. For similar reasons, as these firms grow in size and identify overseas markets as critical for achieving their expansion goals, business can no longer be conducted solely on a personal basis using the family name or a network of personal connections. Rather, new corporate identities need to be created in order to develop international business relationships and to capture new prospects in foreign markets.

Corporate Image Management

More importantly, the management of a new identity will need to be based on the sum totality of the organisation, and not created as a one-off design exercise resulting in a new name and a cleverly designed, and rationally justified, logo.

An Unfixable Problem

There's one 'corporate image' suffering from inaccuracy, misinterpretation and naivety that we'll all be hearing about in the next two to three years. Worst of all, it's something that cannot be fixed, partly because there's no single 'hero' or entity to fight its battle. If I were offered this particular item as a corporate image management client, I'm afraid I'd find the challenge too difficult and would personally turn it down as an unfixable problem.

The 'client' I'm talking about is the new millennium, which officially doesn't begin until just after the stroke of midnight, Greenwich Mean Time, on 1 January 2001. Unfortunately for this 'client', a large portion of the world will celebrate its arrival a full year earlier, preferring the populist date of 1 January 2000. Thousands of people have already booked hotel ballrooms, ocean liners, special round-the-world time-zone tracking flights and other venues to celebrate the start of the new millennium on 31 December 1999, a full year before its actual arrival.

To correct this misperception would take a pro-active, highly engaged, and multimillion dollar corporate image management program on behalf of the Year 2001 and its brother The 21st Century. Quite frankly, I don't think any amount of effort or expenditure is going to sway the general population not to party heartily on the last day of 1999. It might be easier to try and act on behalf of the Year 2001 cousin, known as the Third Millennium. That will also start officially on 1 January 2001, although I'm already hearing people call it the Second Millennium.

Summary

The corporate image permeates everything that constitutes the corporate body. It's the platform, or operating system, for how we perceive and evaluate every company, organisation, product, country, place and movement. Its value cannot be underestimated or overlooked, not in a

The Value of a Good Corporate Image

world where access to information is quick, easy and comes at the click of a few buttons.

Consumers, employees, stakeholders, partners, prospects, governments and the general public want to know the answers to the questions of what your organisation is, what it stands for and what its role in the society is. But information content is no longer enough. Your key target audiences want to put this information into context, which is why you can't simply change or enhance your corporate image with a multi-million dollar advertising campaign that runs every couple of years. Your corporate image needs to be thoroughly thought out, planned, nurtured, executed, monitored and, when necessary, modified.

It's your most valuable commodity and deserves to be treated as such.

Chapter Five

Making the Corporate Image Management Program Succeed

Corporate image management is not a design assignment or a graphic solution. It is not creating a new name or new logo for the organisation and it is much more than 'strategic design'. In fact, there is often too much emphasis placed on selecting a name, logo and colours during a corporate identity exercise, rather than on understanding the fundamental core of what the name and symbol are intended to represent or project.

Most importantly, corporate image management is not a one-off task, but rather a continuous process and on-going program. Or at least it should be, if taken from a marketing perspective. As we stated in Chapter One, *if it touches the customer, it's a marketing issue*. The importance of the corporate image is that it not only touches the customer, but it also reaches out and grabs all of the organisation's other key constituents.

If you ask a public relations person what affects the corporate image, their answer is likely to be that it is created and managed through news releases and press articles, by key staff making public appearances and speeches, and through customer and employee testimonials and community relations. Ask an advertising executive, however, and he or she is more likely to say that the corporate image is a reflection of the advertising and promotional activities of the company.

Turn around and ask a design company the same question and the response will cover the importance of a unified nomenclature system and symbol used with conformity and consistency throughout the organisation. Now ask an architect to ponder this subject and you'll be told the importance of having a solid structural appearance (or of owning your headquarters building) and creating a livable and functional working environment.

Making the Corporate Image Management Program Succeed

Naturally, all of these factors will have positive or negative effects on how an organisation is perceived. The interesting thing is that different audiences may develop contrary opinions on whether a particular factor is beneficial or detrimental to the organisation's image. For instance, while competitors or the public may be impressed with a gigantic headquarters, the staff or customers may interpret this to be a huge waste of funds and resources that could otherwise have gone to either higher salaries or lower product prices.

That's the key point to understand. As we'll say many times in this book: *everything an organisation does, and does not do, has a direct impact on its corporate image*. The corporate image comprises all of the above elements, and all other factors that leave an impression on the observer. The corporate identity, which we'll cover in greater detail below, is just one of the many major influences on the corporate image. Unfortunately, it's often the one element that is given too much attention, particularly in the early stages of developing a new corporate image.

How can something that the organisation does *not do* affect its image? Very simply, a financial group that does not provide private banking services within its array of products and services is going to be a different organisation from the conglomerate that does. Similarly, a hotel that does not provide a business centre or health club facilities is in an entirely different category from the hotels that do. This strategy of not providing a certain type of service, or not doing something that others do, is equally adroit at creating a market segmentation as that of continually trying to offer more than the competitor.

Compare the overseas editions of the *Wall Street Journal* with the global newspaper *International Herald-Tribune*. Dow Jones produces both the *Asian Wall Street Journal* and the *European Wall Street Journal*, both full of daily stock tables, financial stories and business reports. The *IHT* on the other hand, has a broader array of international, regional and US news, a comprehensive sports section, crossword puzzle, comic strips, and general interest articles in addition to its more limited business and financial coverage. The *IHT* is also published six days a week, compared to only five for the two Dow Jones papers.

Dow Jones is an organisation that is fully entrenched in the field of business and financial news reporting. When it started the *Asian Wall Street Journal* in the early 1980s, the *IHT* (which is jointly owned by the New York Times and Washington Post companies) had been established for well over five decades. However, the *IHT* had not yet started regional advertising and editorial editions for Asia.

Dow Jones has clearly differentiated its *Asian Wall Street Journal* from the only other major daily newspaper circulated across the region by keeping within the confines of business and financial news reporting. By *not* broadening its editorial product in Asia into the areas of lifestyle, leisure or sports reporting, its corporate image has remained consistently linked to business and financial reporting. Had the company launched a more general interest newspaper across Asia in the 1980s (say an *Asia Today* paper based on the *USA Today* format), the corporate image of Dow Jones would undoubtedly have changed.

What goes into the corporate image? In a word: everything.

Strategic Understanding, not Strategic Design

A successful corporate identity will visually separate and distinguish the organisation from both its competitors and from others operating within the same geographic region. While the design of the corporate identity (meaning the name, nomenclature system, symbol and corporate colour palette) is important, it is not the only strategic issue management faces when considering how to make its corporate image management program successful.

Management must remember that the corporate identity is merely a reflection of the organisation. It is by no means the definition of who or what the organisation is today and what it is striving for in the future. You cannot define your organisation through a symbol, name or colour scheme. Rather, you need a well-defined corporate identity system to express to the organisation's constituencies, and to the world at large, who and what the company is. This will be in terms of the factors that senior management have determined are most critical in ensuring the organisation's future success.

This requires a strategic understanding of where the organisation has been in the past, where it is today, and, most importantly, where it is heading in the future. In effect, it means understanding the true nature and personality of the organisation, and then viewing this personality from the customer's perspective. If the organisation has the persona to attract the right kinds of customers in the future, then it already has a foundation on which to base the expression of its corporate identity. If it does not, then the corporate image management process must begin by identifying these personality gaps and the action steps required to correct the problem, and not by designing a new logo or new typeface for the corporate signature.

To many of us in the marketing arena, the key strategic marketing issue for the 21st Century will be how to develop, build and maintain relationships with customers, employees, suppliers and other key partners. (More on this follows in the next chapter.) The ability to do so is absolutely essential for the mutual benefit of constituents.

There is a perception amongst many consumers and professional buyers that we have entered an era of parity products. As a result, price becomes the sole differentiating factor, with the low-price provider winning the business or the order. However, when the organisation is able to develop a distinct personality, persona or product, then consumers use criteria other than price to make purchase decisions. Witness the continued phenomenal success of Disneyland, which has celebrated its 40th anniversary. No other amusement park *in the world* has been able to create a personality to remove Disneyland as the number one family destination.

The only amusement parks that even come close to matching Disneyland's popularity are its sister parks, Walt Disney World in Florida and Tokyo Disneyland in Japan. Interestingly, even when families have been to either of these parks, they still desire to visit the original Disneyland in Southern California 'one day'. This is the drawing power that a strong

Corporate Image Management

corporate image, which is consistently and properly managed over time, can create and sustain.

Customers will buy on price when they cannot find a difference between competing offers in terms of quality, service, convenience, character or some other value-determining criteria. But, while competitors can quickly mimic, match or surpass your product, quality, service delivery, or distribution methodologies, they cannot imitate a well-defined corporate personality. To make your corporate image program succeed, you must understand and manage the elements comprising your corporate personality and leverage these to differentiate your organisation from your competitors. This is fundamentally more important than concentrating on how to create an impressive, but perhaps superficial, new look for the organisation.

Without a doubt, consumers are now more intelligent and better judges of corporate character than ever before. They can readily distinguish a solid, quality corporate personality from one created artificially and cleverly. They also remember organisations that have let them down by not living up to their expectations (Perrier) as effortlessly as those who have matched or surpassed expectations (Johnson & Johnson). When it comes to choosing preferred relationship partners in the next century, consumers will go with quality and fundamentals, not with flash and false symbolism.

Organisations that do not focus on managing the fundamental characteristics of their corporate personalities risk ending up with identities that are artistically slick but meaningless and empty-hearted to their critical audiences. When strategic design attempts merely to 'create' a point of differentiation for the organisation, rather than reflect real and deep-seated differences, consumers and business partners may be fooled, but only for a short period. Corporate image management practices will not be successful if they merely paint over the fundamental flaws in the organisation.

This point becomes clearer when you recall one of the stories from *Alice in Wonderland*. The Queen of Hearts wants all of her roses to be red, and so the Jacks dutifully go out and paint all of the roses in the garden. This is fine in theory, but the following spring, the roses will bloom again in their original colours. Organisations launching a new name, logo or mission statement without making any modifications within the organisation are like the Queen of Hearts—willing to accept the appearance of short-term solutions without recognising the consequences of failing to formulate real, long-term solutions.

To illustrate further, consider sales professionals who want to improve their sales performance and the rewards that go with doing so. If they simply go out and buy new suits in order to 'create' a better impression, they may indeed see a short-term increase in sales performance. But if they evaluate areas for improving personal selling skills, and invest the same amount of money in sales training courses, books, self-motivation tapes and other educational materials, their long-term results will assuredly be far greater. Instead of a cosmetic change, they will have worked on essential elements that are more likely to ensure a better long-term result.

To make their corporate image management programs succeed, managers need to analyse the strengths and weaknesses of their organisations, and identify both the elements that can be leveraged for future success and the factors that need to be rectified or modified. The process needs to start with a full understanding of the organisation's capabilities, combined with a vision of its direction for the future. This first step will create real differences within the corporate persona for any new or modified name and symbol to represent.

Where to Start

The best way to start this internal analysis is often with the help of an outside resource. Unfortunately, the normal tendency is to call one of the design-based consultants who specialise in corporate identity work. I say 'unfortunately' because few of the design-centred firms have the management resources, experience or expertise to conduct an objective, full-scale internal analysis. Rather, they tend to base the design process on creative intuition.

The alternative, however, is equally frustrating. A management consultancy firm can help you to devise and understand strategic plans and initiatives for fulfilling the competency gaps identified by thorough research. However, they often lack an understanding of design and the subtleties inherent in creating organisational nomenclature systems, symbology and even colour selection.

Corporate Image Management

Thus, the decision of whether to be strategy-led or design-led needs to be based on:

- the organisation's current positioning status relevant to the market and an analysis of its most pressing marketing needs, and
- whether your internal team leader for this process has greater strengths in strategy formation or creative design management.

The outside resource should ideally compensate for any weaknesses found internally, either in terms of research analysis, strategy development or creative management.

Of course, this also means that the decision-making management team will need to be willing to listen to the outside consultant and be willing to accept its recommendations. Too often, a strong internal person or persons will try to drive the external consultants into making internally preconceived recommendations or force a creative design compromise that suits someone's particular internal agenda. The latter may be reluctantly accepted and implemented by the design team, particularly if the company is eager to get the project completed and to deposit the design fees into their bank account.

On what basis should an organisation decide to alter its corporate image or the visual projection of its corporate persona? While this is a matter of corporate judgment, it should be a decision based on evidence that is both qualitative and quantitative, developed through research of all audiences, internal and external. The goal of the research is to provide senior management with a clear understanding (based on facts, not personal opinions) of how the organisation is perceived by its constituents, for what it is known and remembered, and how these perceptions compare with competitors and management's desired image.

A complete change in both name and visual identity is quite rare in the corporate world. However, as corporations and organisations evolve through time, it is often necessary to update and modernise the visual imagery and appearance associated with the entity. For some, it may be important to show a long history and thus making changes to a 60-year old typeface and logo would be wrong. For others though, a look that is six decades old might project an old-fashioned image out of tune with the modern world. Either way, the decision should be rooted in solid research and analysis, and not be made simply because a new CEO has taken charge of the organisation (although this is probably the number one cause worldwide of corporate identity changes).

Small, entrepreneurial firms are often better at conducting this analysis than major conglomerates. Being small and nimble, such firms are more likely to have unified decision-making teams and an agreed set of vision and goals at the start of the process.

For the opposite reason, many mergers fail when attempting to create a new entity from two disparate ones with clashing cultures. Management might think that a new name and symbol will give the staff of the combined new entity something to rally around, but if they haven't taken the time to create a unifying corporate culture for the new entity, then failure is more than likely. After all, if the new symbol doesn't represent anything, what is there to rally around?

How can management expect loyalty to a mere symbol when we live in a world in which businesses do not cultivate loyalty? Or one where our favourite sports team may move to a different city if they get an offer for better facilities? Or when our favourite sports stars will jump to an opposing team for a higher pay cheque? This is why the new symbol has to represent something that is truly meaningful to the staff, rather than a string of high-minded platitudes or catchy slogans.

The problem is compounded if the employees perceive that the main priority of senior management is determining which senior level managers stay and who is going to be the CEO, COO, CFO, etc. When the efficiencies described in a proposed new merger are of cost savings, staff reductions, and elimination of duplicate areas, is it any wonder that both employees and customers start to consider their other options?

In the 1990s, senior management has played the merger game with an eye on Wall Street and other financial centres. In an era of relationship marketing, the merger game will need to be conducted with an understanding of customer needs. The efficiencies will be described as better customer delivery, improved product lines, the marriage of two corporate cultures, or better products developed by combining manufacturing or R&D operations. This approach will also require that corporate image management be practised as a marketing discipline rather than a design function.

Corporate Image Management

Focus Internally First

Once a decision is made to modify or create a new corporate image, it is natural for the senior management team to want to develop an associated corporate identity quickly and begin to communicate this internally and externally as rapidly as possible. This is definitely an area where speed is not a virtue.

Before the organisation can begin to develop and communicate its desired corporate image, it is important to get the entire corporation squarely on the road towards the desired corporate entity. This is a long, arduous journey and there are no bonus points for taking shortcuts. The final destination is more important than the time taken to get there. The chosen destination should not, by the way, be a set of criteria that becomes the basis for the development of a new corporate image advertising campaign: that is a communications goal, not a corporate image management goal.

In a typical corporate identity exercise (the approach I *do not* advocate), the goal is to quickly identify and agree upon a set of criteria that can be communicated externally in order to give the organisation some sort of market advantage, real or otherwise. Here, the focus is more external than internal and often on a specified set of competitors or likely competitors. The key question is usually phrased, 'How do we distinguish ourselves from companies A, B and C?'. Or, 'How can we create a market advantage through positioning our company?'.

This sort of image positioning relies more on style than substance and often attempts to hide any weaknesses or soft areas that contradict the desired positioning. This process may also result in trivial differences being exaggerated to the extreme, sometimes to the point where they are meaningless to the customer anyway. Do I really care if you are 'Asia's first airline' or the first to fly non-stop from point A to point B? Probably not. I'm more likely to care about your current on-time track record, type of aircraft and seat configuration used on my route, and whether your flight schedule is convenient to my schedule. Gone are the days when I'll automatically adjust my travel schedule to meet the timetables of a particular airline, without at least checking for other alternatives and options first. Except for a handful of carriers that have differentiated their product and service offers through distinctive and consistent corporate image management practices, all airlines are pretty much on a parity basis

Making the Corporate Image Management Program Succeed

for this traveller. And I speak as one who has spent the last 18 years averaging almost one flight a week on journeys across Asia, the Pacific, and sometimes beyond.

The better methodology for creating a desired corporate identity is to develop internal patterns of behaviour throughout the organisation that support and substantiate the desired corporate image. Then, spread these methods across the organisation internally in a manner that produces genuine enthusiasm and pride. As the desired behaviours become consistent, it will be noticed and praised by the customers (assuming, of course, that these behaviours are both relevant and important to the customer base).

In the retail bank division of Citibank in Singapore, where I worked in the early 1990s, customer delight became the war cry. It became the focus of almost all internal communications and we even had internal customer service awards given to staff who had provided superior service (or customer delight) to another staff member. Like a bad cold, this focus on satisfying customer needs became contagious and spread like wildfire throughout the division. Years later, I can hardly recall going into a single meeting where the subject of the customer, or a particular customer, wasn't raised. Without so much as a single ad praising the customer service activities of the bank, Citibank gained a stellar reputation in Singapore for providing the best and most personalised customer service of all the retail banks in the market.

This methodology not only permeates the desired behaviour pattern through the organisation, it also teaches staff how to behave when their supervisor is not monitoring their activities. Equally as important, customers are not only pleased and happy to retain their business relationships with the organisation, they will also refer and recruit new customers. More importantly, the public projection of the organisation's corporate image and personality can now be based on a significant point of difference that can be substantiated through action rather than lofty copywriting. If, in the best of all worlds, this point of differentiation becomes a company value (from the customer's perspective), then the organisation has also achieved a value-added component that could allow for a premium pricing differentiation as well.

Organisations that can differentiate themselves based on substantiated personality characteristics and traits are also better positioned to project

Corporate Image Management a corporate identity that integrates numerous design and marketing communications disciplines: advertising, public relations, architecture, product design and service delivery, packaging, and corporate identity practices. If these are fully imbued across the organisation, then the job of incorporating and integrating the characteristic across a multitude of design elements and communications channels is so much easier and practicable. Better still, the organisation builds trust with its key target audiences and constituencies. As the next century approaches, and the world becomes more of a field of heightened global competition, there's nothing better than trust for building a business franchise, or for establishing a relationship with customers, suppliers, employees, partners and all others of importance to the organisation.

Chapter Six

Corporate Image Management and its Impact on the Marketing Process

Corporate image management is not only a critical aspect of the marketing function, it can (and will) have a significant impact on the marketing process. This is so particularly as companies, organisations and customers move into the realm of seeking, building and maintaining relationships. As will be stated many times in this book, the underlining premise for this philosophy is the belief that *if it touches the customer, it's a marketing issue.* Nothing has the potential to *touch the customer* in more ways, to deeper degrees and to a greater and more meaningful extent than the corporate image of the organisation.

Through the years, the marketing process has evolved from one art form to another. More and more companies are now competing on a global basis. This fact, in an era of more knowledgeable customers, will require organisations to raise their marketing prowess if they are to win in the early years of the next century. The winners will be those who integrate the management of their organisation's image into every aspect of their market and product matrixes.

Recent trends in marketing can be broadly classified as:

    1960s   product excellence
    1970s   product positioning and branding excellence
    1980s   service excellence
    1990s   dialogue excellence (two-way communications *with* customers) and distribution excellence

Corporate Image Management

This is an admitted over-simplification of the evolution of marketing excellence because some companies, and even some countries, have been either ahead or behind these trends. For instance, Singapore Airlines began the rise of service excellence within the airline industry in the 1970s, well ahead of most of its competitors. On the other hand, Qantas Airways redefined product excellence in the airline industry in the 1980s when it became the first to offer a Business Class section. After the proliferation of Business Class across every major international airline by the end of the 1980s, SIA took the marketing process a step further by branding its Business Class service as Raffles Class.

For every industry, there is a time when high levels of commercial success are guaranteed simply by manufacturing and distributing an innovative or very good product. However, once a plethora of competitors has fully entered the field, product excellence alone is no longer sufficient to ensure marketing success. Thus comes the need to develop brand names and personalities in order to differentiate one product from another, or to carve out entire new product categories in the collective conscious of a defined market.

Nor have countries been immune to this process. The label 'Made in Japan' in the 1960s and early part of the 1970s connotated low quality, low reliability, imitation and cheap to the large majority of customers. Today, of course, this no longer holds true. Not only are products from Japan often seen as superior in quality and reliability to those from other parts of the world, but numerous product innovations (such as the Sony Walkman) have been created there. Japanese companies have spent much of the last two decades in achieving both product excellence and positioning excellence for their firms and their products.

No matter what the industry, the marketing environment will progress to a stage where product excellence and distinct brand personalities no longer are the key factors in purchase decision-making. At this stage, customers begin to demand excellent service from organisations in addition to high quality product features and associated personalities. This trend surged simultaneously in North America and Asia in the 1980s. The United States economy developed from a manufacturing base to a service economy, while Asian traditions and culture ensured that service was integral to its products.

Once a high level of service excellence is reached within an industry, the market share leader will be the organisation that develops the highest level of dialogue excellence with its customer base. I would agree with the many consumers who find a lack of dialogue excellence in the 1990s, but at least a start has been made. Many organisations have begun to develop two-way communications processes with key customers in order to continuously monitor customer needs. Unfortunately, many of these initiatives have been bastardised by organisations more interested in simply tracking customer purchasing behaviours and by inept attempts to develop so-called 'loyalty marketing' programs. The latter are often poorly disguised attempts to buy loyalty through reward schemes and bonus point systems that have as much to do with loyalty building as coupons and discount cards.

However, for those companies who have understood how to make it easy for customers to communicate with them, the world is literally beating a path to their stores. Or, in the case of Internet-based firms, beating an electronic path to their virtual reality outlets.

Case study—Amazon.com

An excellent example is Amazon.com, the Internet bookstore. Most reviewers rave about the technological aspects of Amazon.com, which enable the company to sell millions of book titles to customers around the world without stocking more than a mere handful in its Seattle warehouse. There is no doubt that this is a truly exceptional case study of a distribution strategy. But from our perspective, it is much more than a story on how to use technology to reach global markets and how to sell globally without investing in expensive distribution channels and financing large inventories.

At Amazon.com they make it easy to be a customer. And they make it easy to communicate with them. Even more, they have built-in, *proactive* communications procedures that give customers the feeling that the company has combined product, marketing and service excellence into an offering that they no longer want to live without.

When you go to the Amazon.com web site (http://www.amazon.com), the attractive home page invites further interaction with clear instructions and pleasing graphics. You can search for desired books by title, author's name and subject matter. Once you select a book and 'place it'

Corporate Image Management

into your 'shopping basket', the site automatically gives you a list of other titles by the same author, or by other authors on the same or similar subject. There is no hard sell involved, simply an understanding of common reading and purchasing habits that says 'Others who have purchased the title you've just selected have also shown an interest in the following'. It's up to the customer to decide whether to look at the review notes for these suggested options, to go on to another author or subject category, or proceed to the 'check-out' line to confirm his or her purchases.

The pro-active communications do not stop there, however. Within a few minutes of placing an order, customers receive an e-mail confirmation of their order, the purchase price, the shipping details, and clear instructions on how to contact Amazon.com should any of the information be found incorrect. Then, when the books are shipped a few days later, the customer receives another unsolicited e-mail with details on the shipment, an approximate delivery date, and further clear instructions on how to contact Amazon.com if anything goes astray during the delivery process.

Throughout the communications process, there is no attempt by Amazon.com to hard-sell, up-sell or cross-sell the customer (other than during the initial buying process). And there are no phoney or gimmicky loyalty points programs, no weekly or monthly electronic 'News from Amazon.com' or constant barrage of discount offers and special savings messages that attempt to entice the buyer back to the Amazon.com web site.

Dialogue marketing does not mean constant and continuous communication. It should mean relevant and appropriate communication. That's what Amazon.com does. It says to its customer 'We offer convenience and a huge range of products. When you purchase from us, you will receive professionalism and accuracy in processing and delivery of your orders. If at any time we do not meet your standards, we are easy to reach'. If the customer is happy with the quality of the Amazon.com service, he or she will communicate by revisiting the Amazon.com web site the next time an interest in purchasing a book arises.

By the way, Amazon.com also captures certain information about the customer at the time of the first purchase and assigns that individual a customer number. If the person uses the customer number on future orders, there is no need to re-enter shipping details or credit card information, unless the customer wishes to change it from the previous purchase. This not only eliminates customer frustration at having to re-key basic information, it also prevents errors from entering the order entry process. For someone like myself, who is often willing to pay a premium for convenience and confidence in the buying process, the Amazon.com methodology is one I'd like to see replicated by numerous other organisations with which I deal.

The corporate image management process is designed to foster dialogue excellence, particularly in companies that have not yet achieved this stage of marketing excellence. A marketing advantage of the corporate image management process is that it forces two-way dialogues with the organisation's entire range of key target audiences.

Relationship Marketing

Relationship marketing will be one of the key success factors in the next couple of decades. We have already begun to move from mass marketing to individualised marketing in many sectors and industries, one of the unique aspects of relationship marketing.

John Nesbitt has called the 1990s 'the age of the individual'. This age has just begun and even new 'mass marketing' media such as the Internet require the application of individualised marketing techniques. Freedom of choice is becoming the way of the world as customers find opportunities to buy products and services from beyond their normal geographic or product scopes. These decisions are going to be based as much on the perceived relationships they have with the organisations as on product characteristics, brand personalities, price and delivery convenience.

The credit card industry is quickly moving from dialogue excellence to relationship excellence. The Gold MasterCard card, created by MasterCard International in 1981, was the first bank card created especially for a higher income market segment. The product allows customers to tell their banks that they desire a credit card with a higher credit line or one with enhanced services over the bank's standard level card. This relationship marketing has been taken a step further with the introduction of co-branded and affinity credit card programs, such as the General Motors MasterCard, the Shell MasterCard, the American Airlines MasterCard, and the HongkongBank Care for Nature MasterCard programs. By choosing affinity or co-branded

Corporate Image Management

credit card programs, consumers identify and align themselves with programs and organisations they desire to support.

A significant stride into the next sphere of relationship marketing will be taken by the card payments industry when the reloadable chip card becomes an ordinary method of payment for millions of cardholders. By using integrated circuit technology to replace the magnetic stripe found on the back of today's plastic cards, the industry will not only greatly reduce fraudulent and counterfeiting abuses of credit cards, it will also have a system in place in which to delve deeper into relationship marketing. The reloadable feature of a MasterCard chip card, for instance, will enable the bank issuing the card to design reward programs tailored to individual usage and buying behaviours. Banks will also be able to put debit, credit and pre-paid functions onto a single card. This will provide cardholders with a wider range of payment options, deepening the product relationship between the cardholder and the issuing bank and encouraging repeat business by the cardholder.

It is safe to project that a significant proportion of future growth for many businesses and organisations will come from repeat purchases from loyal customers. Loyalty is a direct function of the relationship between the customer and the organisation providing the goods or services. Thus, corporate image management will be a direct means to future growth due to its direct impact on the ability of the organisation to build and maintain a mutually supportive and loyal relationship with a key portion (or all) of its customer base.

Loyalty, however, cannot be bought. It has to be won. It has to be earned. True loyalty will not result from reward schemes and customer loyalty point schemes. These are simply marketing tools which 'buy' repeat business. Yes, they are valid marketing techniques, for we all know that it is less expensive to sell to a current customer than to acquire a new one. But, like coupons and price promotions, these types of programs also raise the cost of doing business and are effective only as long as the reward schemes are kept in place. Drop the schemes and you will suffer a direct hit on your customer base. Thus, they should not be confused with loyalty programs that aim to develop true customer relationships.

To understand the difference, let's define what a customer is. When does a prospect become a customer? Most people say it is at the time of purchase.

I suggest not. Customers who make their first purchase of your product should be thought of as *trial users*. They become customers when they *purchase something from your organisation for the second time*.

What keeps a customer loyal? For the most part it is the consistent level of product quality, brand characteristics and service excellence received each time a purchase is made. Consistent receipt of those three attributes will lead to repeat purchases, which in turn lead to brand, product or corporate loyalty. This loyalty will be the basis for relationship excellence in the coming years, not the type of loyalty based on frequent-flyer mileage points, discount cards and other tactical marketing techniques.

The corporate image of the organisation is an inherent component in all three attributes: product quality, brand characteristics and service delivery. The key to delivering these attributes in such a way as to build and maintain solid customer relationships is through consistent delivery by everyone associated with the organisation. The better your organisation can do this, the deeper and longer lasting will be the relationships with your customers.

Managing Consistent Delivery

Singapore Airlines has long had the reputation for service *par excellence* in the airline industry, and with good cause. However, for those of us destined to fly on this carrier on a regular and frequent basis, the stellar service and corporate image of SIA have recently tarnished and need a bit of polishing. Some of this is because of recent inconsistencies in their product and service delivery, which detracts from their corporate image. Here are two examples.

Firstly, we mentioned above that SIA branded its Business Class service as Raffles Class in order to differentiate it from other airlines. This was a strong marketing excellence move from an airline renowned for its marketing abilities. However, at some point the airline began to differentiate its Business Class delivery on certain routes. Raffles Class passengers on flights between Singapore and Penang, and between Singapore and Kuching, are not entitled to use the special Raffles Class passenger lounge facilities. In addition, wine service is no longer available on the Singapore-Penang route. When this was experienced a couple of years ago, not a single front-line staff member could explain why a full-fare paying

Corporate Image Management

Business Class passenger was not entitled to use the Business Class lounge facilities. A minor point, to be sure. But it was at this time that I began to take greater notice of other service problems on SIA and began flying on Malaysia Airlines between Singapore and Kuching. I also reasoned that I should not have to forego the use of Business Class lounge facilities at Changi Airport just because some executive within SIA felt I should.

Secondly, and in a similar move, SIA has recently stopped its wine and premium champagne service in First Class on the flights between Singapore and Kuala Lumpur, Malaysia. Here again, the front-line staff are unable to explain, other than 'We have stopped serving these items on this sector'. Here again, it is a minor point. Or is it? Wasn't the Singapore Airlines stellar reputation partially built on an advertising platform that spoke of Dom Perignon and crystal glasses for all First Class passengers? After so many years of consistent product and service delivery (Dom Perignon was served on this sector up until at least 1995), what could possibly be the benefits of downgrading its delivery?

As the old story goes, a chain is only as strong as its weakest link. The image of SIA was built on a distinctive product and service delivery. Now parts of that delivery are showing chinks in the armour. The corporate image of any organisation is only as strong as its own weakest attributes. When an organisation like SIA has built its corporate image around a distinctive product and service delivery, then management should understand that the corporate image will suffer when the activities that established the image are discontinued.

Years ago, SIA was able to charge a premium for its Business Class service over other airlines serving the same sectors, yet many business travellers around the region were very loyal to SIA. After all, the service was perceived to be far superior to that provided by other airlines, and the charm of the Singapore Girl on board easily matched that found in the airline's wonderfully produced advertisements and commercials. And the service was delivered consistently across all routes. At the time, loyalty to SIA was built on service and product delivery.

Unfortunately for the airline, other carriers have since closed the product and service delivery gaps with SIA and their on-board cabin crews are equally charming and competent. Did the SIA service standards go down?

Not necessarily and, even if so as shown above, only by small amounts. The problem for SIA is that the other airlines have increased their own capabilities in terms of both product and service.

When SIA was the first airline in Asia to fly the Boeing 747-300, it branded the plane Big Top and was the only Asian airline to fly this new high-tech plane for about 14 months. More recently, SIA was the first Asian carrier to fly the super modern Boeing 747-400, dutifully branded as Mega Top. This time, however, another Asian carrier had its own 747-400s in service within months of SIA. The product gap was closed more quickly than ever before.

Today, 'loyalty' to SIA is partially built on the Passages frequent flyer mileage program, which the airline joined along with Malaysia Airlines, Cathay Pacific and SIA subsidiary Silk Air. Speak to frequent business passengers today and the Passages program is one of the most derided customer loyalty programs in the South-east Asian market. The most common complaint: it takes too many kilometres to earn any decent kind of free ticket award. The second most common complaint: kilometres are earned only when flying Business and First Class, but many organisations now restrict Business Class travel to flights over a certain minimum number of hours. Thus, the frequent business traveller who is hopping around the ASEAN region on SIA, MAS or Cathay Pacific in economy class isn't earning any kilometres—and isn't building any specific loyalty or special relationship with any of these three carriers.

By being extremely innovative in developing excellence in products, product positioning and service, SIA achieved an extremely high and valuable corporate image. As the airline celebrated its 50th anniversary in 1997, its management was faced with many difficult challenges, many of which relate to the management of its future corporate image. Can it overcome competitive forces and management decisions and reach the next marketing plateau, that of relationship marketing, based on true customer loyalty?

For many organisations, not just SIA, it is time to start marketing the relationship. Customers, however, cannot have a relationship with a company, product or brand with which they are not totally familiar. Hence, corporate image management is needed as the driving force to reach the level of relationship marketing.

Corporate Image Management

Marketing Communications

As our organisations move from dealing with people in general to dealing with individuals as unique customers, the role of corporate image management becomes ever more important. In the past, it was thought that merely designing and clearly communicating a consistent corporate identity was enough. Today, we realise that it is the corporate image that must be clearly and consistently communicated, not a graphically pleasing corporate identity.

As with the marketing trends identified above, recent years have also seen a series of new trends in marketing communications. We have seen:

> Monologue Advertising ⟶ Dialogue Advertising
> Passive Consumers ⟶ Involved Participants
> Mass Marketing ⟶ Contact Marketing
> Integrated MarComm Strategies ⟶ Database Driven Strategies

Dialogue excellence links the product, marketing and service excellence stages with the relationship marketing stage. A successful relationship, for both organisations and individuals, can only be formed through excellent dialogue skills. If you cannot communicate clearly, openly and honestly with one another, there is no chance for the development of a meaningful relationship. We understand this instinctively when it comes to forming and maintaining interpersonal relationships. The same holds true for relationships between organisations, and between organisations and people.

There is no doubt that we have entered an era where dialogue excellence is feasible, not only with customers but with all of our key organisational constituents: employees, shareholders, the financial community, the press, local community groups, customers, prospects, and partners. Witness the explosion of the Internet and e-mail as a convenient form of frequent communication.

An example of dialogue excellence is the Avis web site on the Internet. While planning a recent holiday to the United States, I asked my father to make a rental booking with my usual car rental agency. He was unable to book a station wagon for me, so he ordered some other model. Having not lived in the US for many years, I was not familiar with that model, so I went to the agency's web site. There was little information available about this particular model and I left not knowing a whole lot more than when I had logged onto my computer moments earlier.

Since I was already on-line, I decided to look at the Avis web site. Was I ever impressed! It provides colour photos and detailed descriptions of the cars and trucks available for rent, segmented by geographic region. There were two models similar to the one my father said he had confirmed for me. But neither was exactly the same as the one offered by the other agency. Now that I felt armed with enough information, I went ahead and made a booking on the Internet with Avis for my two-week stay the following month. A booking confirmation number was immediately given. Then I sent my father an e-mail asking him to cancel the booking with the other car rental agency.

To me, Avis understands the meaning of dialogue excellence. It means providing customers and other audiences with all of the information they need to know in order to make a relationship-building experience. I had been a loyal, if small, customer of the other firm for years. I rent fewer than five cars per year in the US. And while their product levels had always been consistent, their service level (in terms of providing enough information to make a purchase decision) was no longer sufficient to meet my changing needs. Now my loyalty has moved to Avis...a loyalty relationship based on meeting my customer requirements through dialogue excellence, not on bonus points, loyalty schemes or other marketing ploys.

Whether the Internet is a technological panacea for selling or not, it is undoubtedly a viable marketing and marketing communication tool for those who understand how to design and develop dialogue excellence with key organisational audiences. This dialogue excellence will lead to the development of relationship building for smart, marketing-savvy organisations, as Amazon.com and Avis have already done with this consumer.

The evolution towards dialogue excellence has been an interesting phenomenon to watch. Technological advances as early as the 1960s, particularly in the broadcast media, enabled organisations to begin targeting marketing communications messages at intended audiences based on the language capabilities or the media-consuming patterns of those audiences. These advances also allowed, for the first time, organisations to create and project corporate image positions to large portions of the market at one time. This monologue, or one-way, communication was

Corporate Image Management

aimed at relatively passive consumers who accepted the messages as the cost of watching their favourite television shows or listening to their favourite radio channel.

Today, with the ubiquitous remote control channel changer, consumers are no longer so passive, even while sitting and watching the television. Thus, marketeers and others have moved into dialogue advertising, featuring direct response mechanisms like coupons, reply cards, and 24-hour toll-free telephone call centres. The aim is to solicit immediate and direct feedback from the target audience, often as a prelude for developing a database so that future communications activities can be targeted more specifically.

Eventually, organisations will start to develop databases of customers' wants or preferences, in order to tailor products and services instead of marketing messages; then, the evolution from dialogue excellence to relationship excellence will truly be underway. The path, however, will be fraught with missteps and bungled attempts by organisations trying to jump on this bandwagon without fully understanding the processes and techniques involved.

As I write this book I am sitting in a guest room in a five-star hotel in Jakarta managed by a well-respected Asian hotel chain. I'm here for two weeks and upon check-in was given a lovely note from the head of housekeeping thanking me for my planned long-term stay in this hotel. The note was accompanied by a form that allowed me to choose when and how I wanted my nightly turn-down service (what time, leave drapes opened or closed, number of pillows on bed, etc).

I was duly impressed. This was a hotel that seemed to understand how to conduct dialogue excellence with customers. I completed the form and left it on the bed the next morning (as instructed). In the seven days I've been here, not one of the instructions given or options selected on that form has been followed. The first rule of dialogue excellence has been consistently broken:

> *If you are going to ask your customers what they want and how they want it, you should have processes in place to deliver upon their requests.*

As in the SIA example above, inconsistent performance in one area has led me to notice and become concerned with other service delivery inadequacies (breakfast room opened late one morning, messages not delivered to the room promptly, etc). Sure enough, this has had a negative impact on my overall perception of the image of this hotel. And, sure enough, when I return to Jakarta in two weeks I'll be staying at a different five-star hotel run by the other major Asian-based hotel management company.

Are these examples of service problems, customer service issues or corporate image issues? Are these truly marketing problems? If you are asking yourself either of these questions at this point, then my whole premise has not been delivered to you: *if it touches the customer, it's a marketing issue. Nothing touches the customer more than the corporate image of your organisation.*

Partnership Marketing

What is next after relationship marketing? Very few organisations need to worry about this right now. However, there is every indication that the emerging concept is partnership marketing. This is an application of relationship marketing to marketing partners, rather than with customers.

Again, some companies are ahead of the curve and others are watching from afar. Partnerships are becoming critical to many businesses these days, and take the form of collaboration in such areas as research and development, sourcing of raw materials, back room processing, shared production, and joint marketing activities. An example of what may have been a life-saving partnership arrangement is the August 1997 announcement that Microsoft would take a US$150 million equity stake in Apple Computer. As Apple Computer founder Steve Jobs told the MacWorld convention in Boston in making this historic announcement, 'The concept that for Apple to win Microsoft must lose was no longer valid'.

We have already seen a diverse range of partnerships: Hewlett-Packard, Sony and Philips to produce a new Digital Video Disk technology; MasterCard International, Visa, IBM and others teaming up to establish a Secure Electronic Transaction protocol to enable safe electronic commerce over the Internet; Northwest Airlines and KLM establishing a jointly branded World Class business class service across both airlines.

Corporate Image Management

In each case the partners will have to determine how the particular project will affect their corporate images and the corporate images of the other partners. Equally, companies will want to ensure that their potential partner prospects fit with their own corporate image and corporate culture. Partnerships, like business itself, rely on people, and you don't want to risk having the people at another firm jeopardise your own corporate image.

You don't think that's possible? Consider then whether the ValuJet corporate image was damaged when people employed by another company wrongfully loaded hazardous oxygen containers onto its plane that crashed in a Florida swamp in 1996 (as ValuJet claims as at this writing).

Or how about Pepsi-Cola? It chose three personalities to be its brand spokespeople in the 1980s and 1990s: Michael Jackson, Madonna and Mike Tyson. All three were subsequently dropped because of controversies surrounding their images. Through no fault of their own people, the Pepsi-Cola corporate image could have been damaged by their choice of their marketing partners.

The corporate image is a delicate and sensitive matter needing constant managing and nurturing. The impact of the corporate image will become more pronounced as organisations attempt to move up the marketing hierarchy from excellence in products, services and positioning to excellence in dialogue, relationships and partnering.

Chapter Seven

Corporate Image Management as a Marketing Discipline

Let us state the obvious: your organisation has a corporate image, whether you want it or not.

Your organisation also has a mission and a strategic plan—again whether you want one and whether you like it or not. This mission and plan may not be summarised, verbalised or even structured. But, at a minimum, it is a compilation of the combined efforts of the organisation's business units and people, whether they are pulling together as a coherent whole in the same direction or not.

Almost no one would argue that the organisation's image and strategic planning should be left to chance or fate. Every chief executive worth his salt knows and understands the importance of giving the organisation a precise set of goal statements, action plans and corporate guidelines as a precursor to achieving the defined organisational objectives. So why should it be any different with the corporate image?

It shouldn't. The corporate image needs to be planned, monitored and managed, just like any other strategic activity of the organisation. Unfortunately, in many cases the corporate image is rarely planned and almost never managed.

This may result from the primary thinking in recent years that the corporate image was something to be created by design consultants. It was then to be communicated by the organisation's public relations and advertising

Corporate Image Management

agencies to important target audiences. Employees were expected to fall into line behind the new image and to communicate it to customers at all times. The 'keeper of the image', usually a junior executive in the communications department, had the main function of ensuring that the new, beautifully crafted logo and corporate typeface were used consistently within the guidelines provided by the design consultants. The result is that after several years, the agreed solitary corporate identity crafted by the designers becomes diffused, abused and misused before it deteriorates into a multitude of associated images and identity platforms. Management then begins to wonder why 'customers no longer understand us' and why 'staff turnover is at our highest levels ever'.

This concept of designing a corporate identity to be projected to a selected audience, what can best be described as strategic design, was a valid approach during the age of positioning excellence. Corporate identity as a design function was another way of creating a unique positioning platform for the organisation, one designed to give it a competitive edge in the marketplace. This methodology would still be sensible today, particularly for companies or countries that are still progressing through the early stages of marketing excellence (product excellence, positioning excellence, service excellence).

However, for organisations and markets progressing beyond the early stages of marketing excellence, the design approach to corporate image management is no longer sufficient. The goal today is to manage the organisation's image, or images, as well as possible in order to build, maintain and represent the true core values of the organisation and its people, products, brands, processes and beliefs.

Image management does not equate to a corporate image advertising campaign or a series of internal off-site meetings that attempt to instil a new corporate culture. This is the old way of thinking, where the corporate identity design process is completed when the identity standards and guidelines manual is delivered.

The design approach to corporate identity is characterised by seven features:

- one-way communication from the executive offices to the staff,
- one-way communication from the organisation to its key audiences,

- expression (often graphically) of attributes that the organisation or brand wishes to broadcast,
- a focus on managing the creative process,
- the aim of reflecting and positioning change,
- a one-time event produced within an arbitrary time frame, and
- a reflective process, but not value-adding.

Under the design approach, the objective is the creation of a tangible element or elements, such as a new name, logo, symbol, typeface and colour palette. The tangible element or elements will often become the focus of a one-way, informational advertising, public relations or other marketing communications campaign. The ability of the organisation to communicate the new identity is an integral part of the design process and the decision-making process. Both the development of the design elements and the marketing communications are one-off events for the organisation, with the hope that the effect of both will last for the foreseeable future (or at least as long as the tenure of the current CEO).

The design approach to corporate identity development has successfully applied the techniques of branding at the organisational name and identity level. This technique has successfully helped thousands of companies create their own marketing advantages by differentiating themselves from competitors. These advantages, however, are both temporary and short lived. They are temporary because markets move from emphasising positioning excellence to service and dialogue excellence, and short lived because management rarely invests the same level of marketing and communications dollars to the promotion of the corporate identity as is required by the product brands. What is the first thing cut by management during times of financial problems? Advertising budgets. And what portion of the advertising budget is demolished first? Corporate advertising.

It is the attitude that the corporate image is 'nice to have, a luxury, not a necessity' that prevents organisations from attaining dialogue excellence and relationship excellence with its key audiences. When the corporate image is nothing more than a projected identity, little harm comes to an organisation that does not feed, nurture and promote it. But where it was created to be the point of differentiation in the market place, lack of support for the corporate image allows gaps for aggressive competitors, who may then steal market share, customers and employees.

Corporate Image Management

Managing the Corporate Image

Is the design approach still suited to today's marketing environments? In a word: no. The marketing environment is moving up the marketing excellence ladder to the rungs of dialogue excellence and relationship excellence. In an age of marketing relationships, organisations must manage their images more closely.

'Management' is the most important word in the phrase corporate image management. In the design approach, the words 'image' or 'identity' would be more important because its final objective is the creation of the image or the identity. With the corporate image management approach, there is no final destiny or end objective. The process of continuous management is both the methodology and the destination.

Corporate image management takes the concept of the design approach several steps further, because it:

- focuses on the process,
- aims to enable and to incorporate change throughout the organisation,
- monitors internal and external environments and the continual development of the organisation and its image,
- is expressed both graphically and organisationally (sometimes even resulting in the reorganisation of the corporate structure),
- is a continuing process (ie it's an investment, not a one-off expense),
- is strategic and long-term,
- uses strategies to develop two-way communication with key audiences, and
- adds value to the corporate, brand, product and service positioning of the organisation.

Most importantly, the process inherent in the corporate image management approach inculcates the desired values throughout the organisation so that the attributes broadcast through strategic design are supported, true and consistent. In other words, corporate image management ensures that the promises made (implicitly and explicitly) are backed and delivered by the entire organisation. This is extremely important for decentralised management structures and operations, as these require an image umbrella that works both globally and locally.

Corporate Image Management as a Marketing Discipline

The corporate image management approach does not end with a set of deliverables by the outside resource (ie the consultancy firm). It has an in-built monitoring process that constantly evaluates how well the organisation is living up to its image commitments, and assesses whether the corporate image platform needs to adapt to changes in the market environment.

There may not be a need for the organisation to overtly promote its image platform and internal values to any or all of its key external constituents. For one thing, the first key audience is in fact the organisation's own employees. These folk need to fully understand and agree to the desired values and attributes of the organisation. The image platform and internal values are best communicated to external audiences through the actions of the organisation and its employees, actions that will be noticed and commented upon.

Can a corporate image be developed without an expensively executed communications campaign? Of course. Look at the solid reputations created through the behaviour of the most reputable newspapers and magazines around the world: *New York Times*, *Washington Post*, *Financial Times* (UK), *The Age* (Australia), *Australian Financial Review*, *The Economist*, *Newsweek International*. Or consider the solid corporate image of NASA, created by years of successes and overcoming failures and not by any multi-million dollar advertising campaign. The same holds true for countries. Japan created a country-wide image of quality manufacturing and product excellence through solid execution and a focus on product output over a period of 15 to 20 years. Meanwhile the generals in Burma not only changed the country's name to Myanmar, but also managed to devastate both the nation's economic system and its international reputation in practically no time at all.

The approach for implementing this corporate image management philosophy is summed up in the Japanese word *kaizan*, which means 'continuous improvement'. It is best illustrated by the personnel chief of a major Japanese car manufacturer who was quoted in *Fortune* magazine as saying, 'Our current success is the best reason to change things'. The risk with the one-off design approach is the tendency to rest on one's laurels. With the corporate image management approach, your organisation will never be shocked or surprised by a new entrant to the market or by a failure to deliver. You will notice immediately should any part of the

Corporate Image Management

organisation stop delivering upon the implicit and explicit promises in your corporate image.

If Texaco had practised the corporate image management principles outlined here, one doubts that several of its senior executives would have participated in racially insensitive discussions. The company may have written policies against such activities, but the internal beliefs and value systems of the organisation apparently condoned them anyway. From an external communications standpoint, Texaco was still positioned as 'You can trust the star' (a reference to its star-shaped logo). Only after a racially biased executive discussion was tape-recorded and released to the media did the company realise that it had not properly monitored the acceptance of its diversity training programs and policies. Employees can be both your biggest asset and your greatest liability. As in the Exxon case, it will take quite a while for this once-trusted star to shine brightly again.

The design approach to corporate identity has served Texaco well for a very long time. The company has a consistent look and feel to its service stations across the country, a well-designed logo and positioning tagline, and has created its own marketing niche through its external communications programs. What it hadn't done was to understand that the actions of its employees could not only harm its positioning excellence overnight, but could also damage its relationship building efforts with key audiences: service station franchisees, socially conscious corporate accounts and suppliers, shareholders, customers, and the general public. What black-owned business, black-majority school district, or African-American individual wants to develop a mutually rewarding relationship with Texaco today? Whatever the number, it is certainly a lot less than it was a year or six months before this sad incident was made public.

What can be learned from this lesson? For one thing, if your employees think your desired values are funny and that training in them is a waste of time, the chances are that they do not share the organisation's beliefs. If the deep-seated beliefs and values of the staff do not match the desired values of the executive management, then there is no way that management can expect the actions and activities of the staff to project the desired strategy. People do not easily change core beliefs and values. Either the organisation is going to have to rethink its desired set of values, or it is going to have to change the composition of the staff.

For the last two years I have watched and helped a major Asian government institution try to change its people management principles and practices. Part of this process has included a change in the way performance appraisals are conducted within the organisation and a change in the methodology for ranking candidates for promotion and salary increments. For the first year, despite the fact that almost 90% of the senior management staff underwent a four-day training course in this new system and new methodology, very little changed. Rankings were still based on personal judgment and favouritism, not on the quantitative methodology as instructed. The managers had undergone the training, but had not adopted the new process into their individual value systems. After the second year, however, as the training cascaded down to the third and fourth level supervisors, and as the CEO made several high-level executive switches, the new methodology began to be implemented. It took longer than expected, but then serious change often does.

Senior managers know that they cannot dictate policy changes and expect them always to happen without resistance or hesitation. Hence, they monitor changes in policy or corporate image closely for extended periods to understand what, if any, problems occur in implementation. Sadly, they generally assume that either:

- the external communications have worked wonderfully and the new corporate identity has been positively received by the intended audiences, or
- the external audiences haven't quite understood the new identity yet, but it's still early, so let's give them bit more time. After all, it's time to get on to the more serious issues of management.

Unfortunately, in the era of relationship marketing and partnering, such assumptions are a sure road to corporate image and marketing tragedy.

Adding Value

With the design approach to corporate image, the value added into the equation comes from the positioning advantage given to the corporate or product brand by the identity. Often this is merely a greater awareness of the existence of the organisation or brand. While brands are unique and timeless and, unlike mere products, cannot be copied, positioning statements or platforms for brands and corporate images can easily be

Corporate Image Management

usurped by competitors using a clever positioning consultant. This is even easier when the positioning advantage created by the corporate identity is not fully supported with sufficient marketing communications tools and programs.

With the corporate image management approach, the process creates added value to the organisation by identifying and leveraging a set of corporate culture attributes and by providing the staff with a sense of belonging to something worthwhile. By linking the internal attributes to staff action and organisational activities, the organisation is better able to obtain and maintain a universal recognition of a true (not manufactured) corporate personality.

With this holistic approach to continually managing the corporate image, the organisation is more likely to:

- shorten and simplify the buying decision process for its customers,
- create rationales and emotional criteria for repeat purchases,
- create rationales and emotional criteria for product and brand loyalty, and
- help prevent customer attrition.

Organisations can develop repeat buyers into habitual purchasers by delivering a consistent level of product quality, positioning and service. Across the world, the most common complaint is that there is not enough time in the day or enough days in the week, and so many people do not have time for comparison shopping. As long as the corner laundromat continues to be convenient and to provide a consistent level of service and quality, you are likely to use it. When it stops delivering one aspect of the equation (ie becomes unfriendly, makes an error, changes business hours) you are likely to begin thinking about an alternative service provider. As your perceived image of the outlet changes, you will become more susceptible to offers from similar providers, even if these outlets are not as convenient. And, if by chance you come across one that is even more convenient than the current outlet, the decision to change is made rapidly.

This same process is followed by customers the world over, whether for small ticket items like dry cleaning or major purchases such as cars, air travel and insurance policies. If repeat business from a solid customer base is crucial for tomorrow's marketing success, then managing customer attrition becomes a critical concern. Any dialogue marketing program should aim to prevent customer attrition as well as encouraging larger or more frequent purchases. Take this a notch higher, and a successful relationship marketing strategy results in reduced customer attrition.

In the end, the greatest added value a corporate image management program can provide to the organisation is a solid platform for developing and implementing a relationship marketing strategy with both employees and customers. A successful corporate image management program and philosophy will prevent a scenario of indifferent staff serving indifferent customers. If you have either—indifferent staff or indifferent customers—you have one of the components likely to lead to marketing failure in the coming age of dialogue excellence, relationship excellence and partnering excellence.

An organisation with a sound, stable corporate image will find it easy to recruit the human resource talent it needs to execute strategies and implement winning programs. Recruiting costs decrease for organisations that include employees and potential employees in their corporate image management processes. In fact, the best-qualified people often come to these companies first when looking for employment opportunities. As part of their compensation packages, they seek the 'psychological income' that comes from working within an organisation that they respect, that shares their values and belief systems, and that builds relationships with employees.

It is fairly easy to tell when a company is well perceived by its employees. Here's my own litmus test: ask someone 'What do you do for a living?' If they respond, 'I'm a software engineer', you'll know they probably identify with their job function first, not with the organisation. However, if they respond, 'I work for IBM', the statement tells you that they probably have a close and deep-seated bond with the organisation.

An organisation that achieves the latter does not have to worry about having indifferent staff. These organisations have created an ethos, a corporate essence that is enthusiastically exuded by its employees. IBM employees used to be said to have 'IBM blue in their blood veins'. Tommy Lasorda, the Hall of Fame baseball manager, claimed to 'bleed Dodger blue' in reference to the baseball team he spent most of his career leading. Singapore Airlines established a service standard that 'even other

Corporate Image Management

airlines talk about', at least according to its advertising campaigns. Even if other airlines did not in fact sit around and discuss SIA, the airline's staff and customers certainly did. There was an 'SIA way of doing things', particularly on board its fleet of immaculately kept planes. At Magnavox, the advertising slogan 'Where quality goes in before the name goes on', created one of the first in-depth corporate-wide cultures of product quality in the United States.

Almost all new employees have positive feelings about their organisations immediately following their recruitment. The companies that practise what they preach and create identifiable images for their employees to believe in are those most likely to convert this initial employee enthusiasm for the organisation into long-term loyalty.

Companies who state that 'employees are our greatest asset', and then brag in their annual reports about the size of recent staff reductions, are sending messages that what is said is not necessarily what is done. As an investor, one has to wonder about companies that take pride in reducing staff. Who wants to invest in a company that is reducing its greatest assets? Many organisations seeking growth used the re-engineering process to reduce staff numbers, only to discover that corporate assets need to be used more efficiently, not whittled away. No wonder such organisations rarely include trust as a key component of their corporate images.

The last value-adding attribute of the corporate image management process concerns global image management. In today's global market place, even if your organisation does not operate on a global basis, one or more of your competitors might. The importance of having a congruous and compatible corporate image across the organisation and across the globe is readily apparent. The corporate image for a global company can no longer be a collection of bits that are pieced together only at the macro level. IBM must be IBM in Malaysia as well as in the US. Indonesia's state-owned oil and gas company Pertamina cannot act differently in overseas markets than within its home base. The corporate image must be consistent throughout the organisation. Otherwise, the corporate image becomes confusing and projects different versions and definitions of who it is and what it does.

As an adjunct to the market aspects of globalisation, companies are now competing on a worldwide basis to hire the best and the brightest. Tight labour conditions in some markets exacerbate the problem. The talent pool is no longer confined by domestic borders and international boundaries. Here again, the corporate image management program is essential in developing the organisation's ability to integrate cross-cultural teams and partnerships. Note I said to integrate them, not to manage them! The concept of managing something connotes limitations and keeping things within defined parameters. That's fine for intangible concepts like the corporate image. But people, particularly those in cross-cultural arrangements, need to be able to open up and bloom, and not be managed into boxes. Mushrooms need dark quarters and close supervision (management) to grow. Flowers need open air, sunshine and room to grow. People are flowers, not mushrooms.

Understanding the Corporate Personality

Like individuals, organisations have personalities. These personalities reflect upon, and are reflected within, the corporate image perceived by the organisation's diverse audiences. Understanding the corporate personality is only a superficial consideration in the design approach to corporate identity. The corporate image management approach, however, defines in psychological terms what an organisation's culture is all about, and how it relates to important audiences; it is one of the foundations required for building relationship marketing excellence.

What comprises the corporate personality? What elements and environmental factors determine whether, and how, a corporate spirit, ethos, or soul develops? How are sets of systems, practices, habits, methods, beliefs, values, codes of conduct, and regulations fashioned and maintained from year to year, despite personnel turnover, changes in corporate size and structure, and even changes in corporate name, leadership and ownership? In other words, what makes Compaq be Compaq? What makes Hoechst Chemicals consistently the same worldwide, across its many divisions, manufacturing locations, and local employee cultures?

Does the corporate personality really matter, other than to a handful of university professors and researchers with nothing more substantial to talk about? It certainly does. The corporate personality enables the organisation to react to changes and challenges as a single unit. This can only happen if the principles, values and beliefs that influence and impact on decision-making have been uniformly spread and internalised

Corporate Image Management

throughout the organisation. It also enables the organisation to 'speak with one tongue' in its communications and interactions.

Organisations with succinct corporate personalities operate in an exceptionally unified manner, despite their composition of numerous individuals all with unique personalities, cultures, beliefs, backgrounds, experiences and motivations. This is extremely important in today's environment, where companies are merging with one another or forming partnerships with other organisations. Mergers, partnerships, working arrangements and joint ventures all require the right fit between compatible corporate personalities.

Without a succinct corporate personality in place, employees must rely on their own individual personalities and backgrounds. If there is no culture or corporate guideline that says 'This is how we do things here' or 'This is how we handle these types of situations at XYZ company', the employees are left to their own make-up in deciding how to proceed in a given situation.

Fortunately for organisations, people like to belong to groups. As social animals, people like human interaction and group identification, both of which come from being a part of a bigger whole. Individuals who start to work from home often cite the day-to-day, face-to-face interaction with other group members as the thing they miss most. The human psyche has a strong need for group association and group identification. Plus, groups provide additional protection (from wild animals or bosses) that the individual members cannot achieve on their own.

The key for today's advancing corporations is to turn such group association into group loyalty and shared enthusiasm, along the lines of success that sports teams have with their devoted fans. The human psyche reacts positively to a strong emotional pull, whether it is from a favourite sports team or the company vision statement. Companies that develop the 'family feeling' sense of pride, enthusiasm and loyalty in their employees are well on the road to having definable corporate personalities. These can be highly leveraged during the building of customer relationships and corporate partnerships.

The corporate personality, of course, does not need to be based on long traditions. In fact, sometimes the traditional ways of identifying opportunities and solving problems need to be changed radically to allow the organisation to progress. However, an internal culture is required that meets and combines the organisation's requirements for efficiency and consistency with the basic need of employees and customers for emotional bonding and group identification. This combination, in turn, must enable the organisation to meet the challenges of evolving markets, new technologies, changing competitor sets, increasing customer demands, revised government rules and regulations, and the forces of globalisation.

It will be essential for the most successful corporations of tomorrow to create and sustain such an internal culture. This will combine the self interests of the organisation with the employees' needs for a sense of community, family-like spirit and the feeling of belonging. In other words, it will create a corporate culture if not to die for, then at least one with which to become emotionally attached and bonded. The result will be a distinct, defined corporate personality to replace the artificially conceived corporate identity as the key corporate positioning differential.

Creating Benefits

The macro environmental changes mentioned above will force organisations to face an array of opportunities and challenges. Those that forge and preserve lucid and exclusive corporate personae will be best equipped to maximise the opportunities and capitalise upon the challenges. The equation is quite straightforward:

- distinct corporate personalities create winning corporate cultures,
- winning corporate cultures result in distinct corporate images,
- the continuous management of the corporate culture will provide the foundation for successful dialogue and relationship marketing techniques,
- relationship and partnership marketing strategies will provide the winning formulas for the next two to three decades.

The bottom line: managing the corporate image will be the most important marketing discipline in the coming years. A well-managed corporate image will:

- provide the road map, direction, drive and corporate energy to achieve the broader and identifiable goals for the organisation,

Corporate Image Management

- enable the organisation to balance the contradictory and sometimes conflicting needs of itself and its staff,
- enable the organisation to balance the contradictory and sometimes conflicting needs of itself and its customers,
- allow management to rely less on internal structures and more on their staff to use the right processes to implement strategies for dealing effectively with the unexpected,
- value multicultural teamwork and staff diversity,
- allow project teams to form, accomplish assignments and disband without creating stress and staff turnover problems,
- create an environment where knowledge and skills are continuously upgraded, and
- create an environment of flexibility where change is encouraged, handled with skilled and not feared or avoided.

In short, management of the corporate image goes hand in hand with the development and management of the organisation's corporate strategy. The key here is that the corporate image management process forces you to continuously define the singular message that describes how the organisation is different (and better) than its rivals. Unlike the design-driven corporate identity process, however, the unifying message derived from corporate image management practices will be equally valid to all key constituencies, not just to customers and competitors. Better still, the external projection and communication of the principles, values and beliefs underlying the corporate image will be based on individual and collective action, not on a shrewdly created positioning tagline.

Corporate image management: the marketing discipline for the 21st Century. Need we say more?

Chapter Eight

Corporate Image as a Strategic Weapon

What process does someone with only limited knowledge or experience of products go through when they need to make a purchase decision? Let's use wine as our product category of choice, because most people have only limited knowledge of the choices available and are unfamiliar with the criteria that differentiate wine styles or wine makers. The selection process is complicated by many factors: the need to match wine style with food choices; ambiance; suitability and acceptability to the diners. Add to this the knowledge that the choice may reflect upon the person making the selection and the decision becomes more difficult and complex. The goal for anyone faced with the problem of wine selection is to choose an appropriate bottle at an acceptable price, two criteria that change as the situation changes. The buyer must rely on:

- previous experience or familiarity with the products proffered on the wine menu,
- suggestions or recommendations by the wine steward or waiter, and
- perceptions of the wine regions, bottle labels or grape varietals on offer.

If unfamiliar with the wines in stock, and in the absence of reliable help from the waiter, the buyer must rely totally upon perceptions of the products on offer and the ratio of price to image.

For years, the public image of France as a quality producer of wines was strong enough for French wines to win many, if not most, of the marketing

Corporate Image Management

battles described above. Today, equally strong images for Australian and Californian wines have made the purchase decision-making process more difficult for the average wine consumer. Fortunately, the quality of wines from these and other regions (eg South Africa, New Zealand and Chile) is sufficiently high that our hypothetical wine buyer can hardly go wrong these days. Even so, the reputations of labels such as Penfolds Grange from Australia and Château Margaux from France allows them to command premium prices vintage after vintage.

If anyone doubts the power of the corporate image as a strategic marketing weapon, they should study the relationship between wine prices and the public perceptions of the names found on the labels of the premium priced bottles. Wines made directly across the road from one another from grapes grown on similar soils, in the same climate, at the same time, and harvested in the same manner can differ by anywhere from 10% to 500% in pricing.

For the past two to three decades, the basic principles of marketing have been taught as: product, price, promotion and place. These four 'Ps' of marketing have been the basis for success during the eras of product excellence, positioning (promotion) excellence and service excellence. For some products, but not all, distribution excellence (place) has also become a key success factor.

While their importance is still undisputed, the formula of the four Ps is now only partly accurate. Formerly considered merely as part of 'promotion', the image perception of a company, brand or product has become ever more important in the marketing success equation. For proof, consider the immediate global success of numerous branded goods and corporations whose names did not exist prior to their brand creations: Adidas, Kenzu, Nike, Compaq, Motorola, Nokia, Kodak, Pixar, etc.

As argued elsewhere throughout this book, the corporate image will continue to take on even greater significance as organisations move towards excellence in relationships and partnerships. The new equation for marketing success is:

> 4Ps + Image = Success.

Alternatively this can be thought of as the five Ps of marketing, with Perception (with a capital P!) joining the ranks of product, price, promotion and place.

Already, the effects of a fuzzy or indistinct corporate image are apparent in troubled brands (Perrier, Exxon, Texaco) or organisations beset with public persona problems (AT&T, Walt Disney, Time Warner, BHP, Kia Motors). The business literature is full of articles on the decrease in company loyalty by employees. Who can blame them, as the middle managers and the line staff have been the ones most hurt by various re-engineering program? At the same time, the executive office crews have reaped enormous wealth by collecting stock options during the recent six-year bull run on global stock markets. Consumers are more confused than ever by tactical promotional activity being applied to their favourite brands. Examples are changing brand positioning, the proliferation of new products, and the effects of coupons, and price discounts. Several surveys have shown that some of the heaviest users of coupons are consumers who would have purchased the product anyway without the incentive of a price discount.

Corporate Image as a Strategic Weapon

These problems have yet to reach their full extent for the elementary reason that we have yet to fully enter the era of relationship marketing. Customers, for the most part, have yet to cry out for 'relationships'. However, from observing customer buying habits, as we will discuss below, it seems that many customers are both willing and capable of entering into long-term relationships with their product and service providers. On the other hand, with the *Fortune 500* list changing in composition by approximately 30% every five years, customers have a right to be hesitant about forming long-term relationships with corporate entities. When the list of the 500 largest companies in the United States changes by one-third during any five year period, can the turmoil and change among smaller firms and organisations be any less?

Competitors can mimic a product. Competitors can create their own market positioning and branding strategies that can shove an established brand and corporate identity aside. When Ford Motors established a market beachhead based on a position of price, General Motors came along and won market share by focusing on a position platform featuring choice. Competition can even copy manufacturing and distribution methodologies. When Compaq Computers was faced with market share losses to both Gateway 2000 and Dell Computers (two firms that created a marketing niche by producing customised personal computer configurations), it announced the start of its own direct marketing and customised, build-to-order configuration activities.

Corporate Image Model

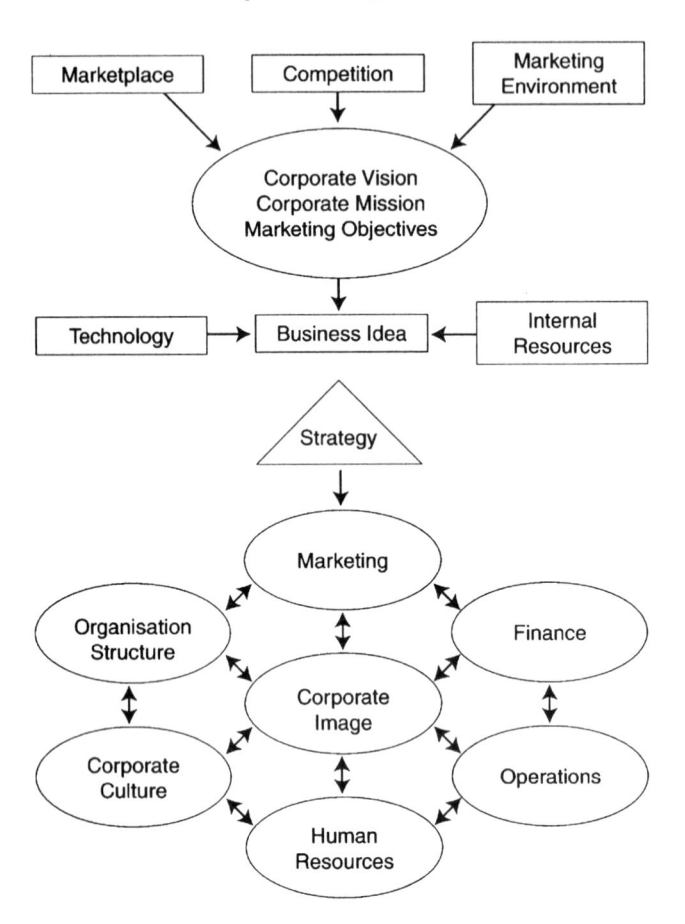

```
    Marketplace      Competition      Marketing
                                      Environment
         \              |              /
          \             v             /
           \     Corporate Vision    /
            ──> Corporate Mission <──
                Marketing Objectives
                       |
                       v
    Technology ──> Business Idea <── Internal Resources
                       |
                       v
                    Strategy
                       |
                       v
                    Marketing
                   ↕   ↕   ↕
    Organisation            Finance
    Structure
         ↕     Corporate      ↕
               Image
    Corporate               Operations
    Culture
                   ↕   ↕   ↕
                    Human
                    Resources
```

The corporate image management model approach inculcates the desired values throughout the organisation so that these attributes are communicated consistently within the organisation and through corporate behaviour patterns.

The corporate image is the very heart and soul of the organisation, impacting every functional operation and every strategic direction planned by management. If the organisation's strategy is the fulcrum for its success, then the corporate image is the very foundation and glue which holds the strategy together.

Competitors can mimic every aspect of an organisation's strategy—but they cannot copy a well-defined corporate image. Hence, the corporate image can be the best strategic weapon for any organisation to use to gain competitive advantages.

Corporate Image as a Strategic Weapon

The one thing that competitors cannot copy is a well-defined corporate personality.

In the past, I have taught sales managers the marketing and sales philosophy that 'Customers buy on price only when they cannot perceive sufficient differences in quality, service, convenience and value between competing product or service offerings'. In the future, I will have to change this to 'Customers buy on price and change brands until they locate an organisation or a product that meets their own relationship requirements for quality, service, convenience, value and image association. As long as these are delivered consistently, the customer will become a repeat and loyal buyer'. The corporate image is a strategic weapon in helping customers identify those organisations that are capable of delivering these relationship requirements.

Coping with Change

When an organisation faces rapid change, whether from external or internal forces, its employees are subject to high levels of confusion, stress and anxiety. The bonding links to the organisation become stretched as individuals question whether the direction of change is compatible with their beliefs and value systems. If not, their willingness to continue associating with the organisation, and fully committing to its revised ethos or persona, is highly questionable.

On the other hand, a corporate personality characterised by taut and strong emotional bonds by the collective staff is more likely to persevere through periods of immense, abrupt, unexpected or fast-paced change or other difficult times. These types of organisations are better positioned to handle change in a unified and precise manner, with the individual units and employees acting and functioning in unison for the common good and towards a common objective.

The corporate culture, as personified by the corporate image, can also be used as a strategic weapon for internal non-marketing purposes. Patterns of behaviour within an organisation are often difficult to observe and even harder to break. The corporate image reflects to both customers and employees the internally shared and embedded assumptions, operating procedures, system flexibilities, response behaviour patterns, and

Corporate Image Management

organisational structure. At times of rapid change, the corporate image, as perceived, lived and enacted by the employees, is one of the most strategic tools available to management. It can be used to prevail upon the staff to function in the required manner—and to believe in both the ultimate destination and the direction being taken to cope with the agents of change. The stronger the shared experiences and shared enthusiasm by group members, the stronger will be the corporate culture and the resultant corporate image. This is analogous to the sports franchise, whose loyal and dedicated fans share the play-by-play of the contest, the experiences of the final result and, when championships or major victories occur, the enthusiasm and joy of high-level achievement.

One component of the corporate culture that has changed in recent years is that the staff, in most markets, have greater choice in determining their length of stay and association with the organisation. While retrenchments and down-sizing have had copious negative consequences for those directly impacted, temporary unemployment no longer has a social stigma. Nor is it necessary to be completely loyal to one's corporate employer. More than at any time in history, employees have a choice in whether they continue the shared experiences and enthusiasms of their current workplace group, or seek entrance and acceptance into an alternative organisation. In his book *New Rules*, John Kotter suggests that one of the worst possible career plans for a new graduate in the USA is to contemplate taking an entry-level position in any organisation with the idea that he or she will be employed there continuously for the next 25 to 30 years. I concur with his thinking and highly recommend his book, not only for those working on their own career development plans but also for those who wish to think about current business trends that are having an impact on the use of the corporate image as a strategic management tool or strategic marketing weapon. In either use, the corporate image is one of the crucial factors determining how the organisation will cope with change.

Image Association

Customers too have a need for group associations. This has long been a foundation of the branding principle: develop brand characteristics for the product's buyers to identify with. In the battle of the cola wars, soft drink buyers and consumers have either been 'part of the Pepsi Generation' or were seekers of 'the Real Thing'.

Image association is much like word association. What word comes to mind when you read the name Volvo? How about BMW? For the first, undoubtedly it is safety that comes to mind for most people. For the latter, the range is broader and would include performance, style, speed, and other associations.

What do these branding positions tell us about the respective *companies* behind the brands? Unfortunately, very little. Positioning is a result of product branding and the design approach applied to corporate identity. Positioning is like seeing a message on a billboard: there is not enough time or space to provide many details. This is why I advocate that the consumer can have loyalty to the Volvo or BMW brands, but is currently unlikely to develop an entrenched relationship with either company.

Positioning and design strategies do not furnish sufficient information for customers to form adequate judgements and *perceptions* of the company. Positioning is a one-way projection of an image that is completely understandable only to the sender. Perception results from two-way communications between the organisation and the receivers. Perception is based on deeper criteria because the recipient is seeking a greater understanding of the projected image, which leads to discernment and engagement.

Organisations that develop meaningful personalities will also be on a constant lookout for opportunities to differentiate themselves, and to further entrench the corporate character, across both management practices and design applications. Observers will notice a consistency in the application of architecture, interior design, plant and office layouts, customer interaction areas and other work area environments. These will be applied, as much as feasible, across all worldwide locations as well as within the organisation's sites within one city, country or other geographic region. When design styling is used to boost distinctiveness, and to reinforce the corporate personality both visually and functionally, the organisation creates further opportunities to be clearly understood by its important audiences, both externally and internally.

Corporate Image Management

Branding Strategies

Organisations have three choices from which to select a corporate branding strategy:

- mega brand,
- dual brand, or
- product branding.

Firstly, mega branding occurs where the organisation's name is also the brand name for the majority of its products and product lines. Examples are Kodak, IBM, Fuji, Coca-Cola, and Sony. While mega branding can be the most powerful corporate branding strategy, with the most powerful rewards, it can also lead to the greatest risk. The biggest risk is that a failure or problem in one product line may be projected to the other products, which could be disastrous if the key corporate brand is hurt. For instance, a failure by Kodak with digital cameras or photocopiers could be cataclysmic for their core film products.

Even mega brands can resort to the occasional product branding strategy, as Sony did with its successful Walkman and Discman products. This Japanese consumer goods marketeer has a firm grasp on the intricacies of mega branding, for it closely linked the corporate mega brand with both of these product brands by using the terminology *Sony* Walkman and *Sony* Discman. Like many other highly successful products, the name 'walkman' has become a generic term used by consumers to describe all portable radio and tape players (a fate suffered similarly by other brands that dominated their respective product categories, such as Xerox and Kleenex).

In situations where the company is the brand, management of the corporate image becomes even more essential and significant. Any serious missteps at the corporate level, such as in the Perrier case, result in an immediate and consequential impact on the marketing and sales results for the core products. Minor blunders, such as the Pepsi associations with Madonna, Mike Tyson and Michael Jackson, do not have the same repercussions and thus make for easier recovery of the corporate image.

Secondly, dual branding takes the form of the corporate name being combined in a variety of ways with a range of product names. This is found most often in the fast moving consumer goods industry. Companies like

Nestlé, Heinz, Fraser & Neave, and Danone market a diverse range of products using various naming systems to link the product names with the corporate identity. In the case of Nestlé, the company produces Nestlé Crunch candy bars, Nestlé coffee and associated products like Nescafé. Because of the sheer multitude of products carrying the corporate name, product names and hybrid brandings, it would be more difficult for a problem in any one product to have a serious impact on the organisation's overall corporate image. The corollary is that the positive attributes of the corporate image cannot be fully leveraged in support of the individual products and brands.

Thirdly, organisations that use the straight product branding approach often have competing brands in the market battling for shelf space and market share. Examples include Unilever, Proctor & Gamble, Colgate and several of the cigarette companies. No attempt is made to link the product brands with the corporate mother brand. In fact, these companies will make serious attempts to completely dissociate the product brands from the corporate name, partly to make consumers think that particular product categories (eg toothpaste) have keener levels of competition.

There is no single method of associating product brands with the corporate image personality that is intrinsically better than the other two. However, as shown above, customers are more likely to forge emotional bonds and relationships with organisations displaying distinctive corporate personalities and unique corporate images than with product brands. So, for organisations that feel that future marketing success will come partly or mostly from relationship marketing and partnership marketing, the mega or dual brand methodologies would make greater sense and provide a far greater payback.

The other risk to the straight product brand is that these brands have to stand on their own, without support from any invested communications in the mother brand. This can be difficult when you consider that supermarkets stock upwards of 30,000 different items and some studies show that only about one-third of all consumers arrive at the supermarket with a prepared shopping list. Further, a survey by Hanigan Consulting of New York once asked 250 MBA students what products were made by the top 200 American firms. The students reportedly only knew the business lines of about one half of the companies, with some even thinking that PepsiCo made Coca-Cola. A great deal of educational effort will

Corporate Image Management

have to be spent by marketeers of consumer products to establish the criteria for forming brand relationships (see below).

Secondary Identifiers

Another form of corporate branding is the use of a secondary identifier, usually an image, icon or other mnemonic device, that becomes associated exclusively with the parent or product. Two of the best examples are the Marlboro Man created by Leo Burnett Advertising for Philip Morris, and the Singapore Girl, created by Batey Advertising for Singapore Airlines. In a similar vein, but not nearly as successful, is the black and white 'cow patch' box designed used by Gateway 2000 to ship its products to customers. The Marlboro Man came to represent the rugged and self-confident (or self-imagined) characteristics of the supposedly typical Marlboro smoker. In contrast, the Singapore Girl came to represent both the product and the corporate image of Singapore Airlines (and, to a small degree, even the island state of Singapore itself).

The Singapore Girl was created in 1973, shortly after Singapore Airlines was formed by the division of Malaysian-Singapore Airlines (MSA) in October 1972. At the time, SIA management struggled with the question, 'How many ways can an airline differentiate itself?' SIA had retained most of the international routes operated by MSA and immediately began to aggressively modernise and upgrade its fleet. It also employed top notch pilots and engineers and rapidly developed a world-class maintenance operation to go with its modern jet aircraft fleet. However, SIA management felt that something more was needed for the airline to catapult into world's top ranked airlines (the combined MSA was the 57th largest airline in the world in 1969).

The product differentiation SIA focused on was innovation and in-flight service. It introduced 'hardware' improvements to its product and service offering. For example, it was one of the first Asian airlines to fly the new Boeing 747 'jumbo jets' that it placed into service in 1973; it started supersonic Concorde services in 1977 in a joint venture with British Airways; it introduced live musical entertainment on flights between Singapore and Sydney for two months in 1976; and added fully reclining 'snoozer seats' to First Class in 1977. In 1980, SIA put adjustable headrests on all Economy Class seats, making its long-haul flights less stressful and more comfortable for the 'back of the bus' passengers.

Corporate Image as a Strategic Weapon

On the 'software' side, SIA management decided to create a cabin crew that would reflect the Orient's cultural traditions of hospitality and service. Added to this were the charm and grace of Chinese, Malay, Indian and Eurasian stewardesses costumed in a Pierre Balmain specially designed version of the beautiful and elegant Malay *sarong kebaya*. In addition, the relatively unknown SIA decided to use only young adults to comprise its cabin crew, even though older and more experienced stewards and stewardesses might have inspired greater confidence in its passengers.

Here's where the corporate image management process can be shown to give clear directions to management in the formulation of policies and procedures. In order to maintain the image of a youthful cabin crew, applicants for stewardess had to be between 18 and 25 years of age. Additionally, SIA offered only five-year contracts to its female cabin crews, which could be renewed by mutual agreement. However, retirement age for stewardesses was set at 35 and usually only those who had attained chief stewardess or senior chief stewardess were kept on duty until that age. Applicants for flight steward had to be between 20 and 25 years of age and retirement was set at age 40, unless a promotion to the rank of chief steward or higher had been attained by that age.

The SIA cabin crews went through eight weeks of ground training and six weeks of flight training before they were qualified to start working as operational crew members. The ground training included personal grooming, poise and personal conduct sessions. Rules imposed on cabin crew staff included specifications on the use of make-up, wearing of jewellery and hair styling. SIA even required all crew members to have their teeth checked and cleaned twice a year at the company dental clinic.

The objective of these rules and procedures was to ensure that the onboard experience of passengers lived up to the image of the Singapore Girl depicted in the airline's wonderfully produced advertising: gentle, courteous, graceful service accompanied by warm smiles, attention to detail and the meeting of individual in-flight needs. The Singapore Girl was created and managed to be the public persona of Singapore Airlines and remains the carrier's icon a quarter of a century later. By managing this image, including its public projection and in-flight execution, SIA has had a strategic marketing weapon to help make it the ninth largest airline in the world by 1979. It remains in the top 10 ranks today and receives regular rewards and accolades from industry surveys (though its image

Corporate Image Management

gap advantage over other airlines has closed significantly in recent years, as discussed earlier).

Environmental Identification

The environmental movement is one area that organisations seem keen to associate with these days. Except for a handful of truly exceptional cases, these efforts should not be thought of as the kind of strategic corporate image management practices we are discussing here. Rather, they are more akin to the positioning strategies undertaken by other corporate sponsorship activities.

There is nothing wrong with an organisation wanting to associate with the green movement, but management should not be confused that such marketing activities are anything other than tactical promotional campaigns. In a study of US consumer attitudes released at the end of 1990, 47% of those polled said they believed green advertising was basically a gimmick. Only 32% took green advertisements at face value as a reflection of genuine corporate concern over the environment.

The Body Shop is one of the few organisations that has thoroughly integrated an interest in environmental protection into its global operations and corporate image. The firm fended off a journalistic attack on its environmental credibility a few years ago that, had the charges been more fully substantiated, would have blown a huge hole in its corporate image and possibly could have led to its demise. Instead, the company continues to thrive and grow by adding more franchise outlets throughout the world. Consumers who place a premium value on support for environmental protection receive two benefits when they make purchases from The Body Shop:

- comfort in knowing that the products have not been tested on animals and are made from the most natural ingredients and processes, and
- personal self-actualisation or social benefits from being associated with individual support for environmental causes.

The HongkongBank 'Care for Nature' MasterCard is an affinity program in Malaysia and Singapore that allows cardholders to associate themselves with support for nature. In this program, a small percentage of each cardholder transaction goes into a special trust fund, managed by HongkongBank, which is used to fund special environmental activities within each community. While this program has been very successful, as have many other environmental affinity programs around the world, the product linkage with the environment does not translate upward to the HongkongBank corporate image. HongkongBank is perceived as neither more nor less environmentally friendly than other international banks as a result of this particular credit card affinity program. The environmental association benefits are received by the cardholders, not the card issuer.

Wayward Attempts

Two of the most frequently seen wayward attempts at projecting corporate images are organisations that:

- try to be too many things to too many people, and
- are so vague that their images become meaningless.

An example of the latter is the mission statement advertised in a major international publication in 1991, that the organisation stated was developed as part of a strategic review undertaken in 1990. This mission statement is reprinted below, with slight modifications to protect the identity of the company.

> 'Our goal is to create long-term value for shareholders by producing superior sustained returns.
>
> The core of our business will be satisfying customer needs for our products and services. In addition, we will offer related services where they support those needs. We will have a global capability, aiming to be a significant operator in attractive markets.
>
> We will focus on the needs of customers by providing those products and services that meet our customers' requirements for quality, and by controlling our costs so that we can offer customers maximum value.
>
> We will also strengthen our access to customers through effective means of distribution.
>
> To enable us to achieve our goal we will foster an environment in which all our employees can play their full part. We will do this by promoting the corporate values of financial strength and stability, integrity and dedication, teamwork and effective communication, innovation, personal development, planning, accountability and rewards linked to performance.'

Corporate Image Management

This statement provides little in the way of uniqueness to this particular company. It could just as easily be transposed to any of its competitors, or to any organisation in any other field, and have just as much applicability. As such, this mission statement has only marginal value, if any, as a strategic marketing weapon for this organisation. After all, if your strategic weapon can just as easily be copied, modified or used by a competitor, then how strategic can it truly be? While it has all of the fabulous buzz words from the early 1990s, it hardly helps either employees or customers have a greater, deeper understanding and appreciation of this particular company.

On top of that, what is the mission of this organisation? Is it the first line: 'to create long-term value for shareholders'? What determines this value? Market capitalisation? Share price? Dividend payout? Or is the mission 'satisfying customer needs for our products and services' as stated early in the second paragraph? If the former, what kind of relationship would customers want with this organisation, one that admittedly puts the interests of shareholders ahead of customers? If the latter, then why is the focus in the fourth paragraph on 'effective means of distribution', rather than on convenient means of access for customers?

These are the troubling questions that senior management must constantly ask about their organisation. The questions also need to be asked more frequently from the customer's perspective and the potential partner's viewpoint, than from the organisation's.

The Future of Money

The global credit card and charge card markets, like many other industries, are becoming more competitive on a daily basis. Like many fast growing markets, the credit card industry faces two choices. These are either to fragment into separate industries offering separate payment choices to cardholders (such as a more distinct separation between charge cards and credit cards) or to consolidate into an even larger and more important industry called the card payments industry.

As one of the leaders of the credit card industry, MasterCard International has been taking a long, hard look at the inevitable evolution of the global payments industry. In the eyes of the senior management at MasterCard, the opportunities for enormous growth lie with a consolidation strategy. This would respond to cardholder needs for all three types of payment options: pay-now (debit cards), pay-later (credit cards) and pay-before (pre-loaded cards that replace cash at the point of transaction).

In line with this strategic thinking, senior management realised in 1994 that MasterCard International would have to undergo significant internal change, a realignment of both short-term and long-term priorities, and the alteration of the corporate culture if it was to be perceived by its key audiences (banks, merchants, co-branding partners, cardholders and consumers, governmental agencies, technology partners and others) as being capable of affecting the future of the card payments industry. In short, MasterCard would need to change its corporate image from the second-largest credit card association in the world to a critical and quintessential global partner for the future.

As an association owned by its member financial institutions, MasterCard faces a different set of managerial challenges than executives at publicly listed or privately owned corporations. In addition, MasterCard has two distinct and separate sets of customers with which it needs to develop long-term relationships. The first set is the issuing banks, which are both owners of the association and participants in the MasterCard franchise. In this age of duality, many of these banks also issue Visa credit cards. There is tremendous pressure on both credit card associations to change their by-laws to enable the banks to also issue cards with the American Express brand. Representatives from the issuing banks sit on the various global and regional boards of MasterCard International, which must approve the investment strategies and growth plans put forth by the professional managers at MasterCard. Thus, it is extremely important for these member financial institutions to believe that MasterCard has the managerial talent and employee skill sets to lead the evolution of the global card payments business.

As for consumers and cardholders, the MasterCard points of differential need to be built into and communicated for all three of the association's key brands—the MasterCard credit card, the Maestro point-of-sale debit and deposit access card, and the Cirrus ATM card. Both Maestro and Cirrus cards are directly linked to the cardholder's deposit or cheque account, and thus have become known as deposit access cards. Cardholders have a different set of relationship criteria from the banks, as they are

Corporate Image as a Strategic Weapon

Corporate Image Management

more concerned with convenience, secure access to their credit or deposit account facilities, and global acceptance whenever and wherever they choose to use their plastic payment cards (including non-physical points of interaction such as ordering over the telephone or Internet).

An interesting phenomenon is that many cardholders, perhaps even the majority in some markets, actually feel that their relationship is with MasterCard, rather than with the issuing banks. One can see this being portrayed by the popular media. For instance, in the film *It Could Happen to You* the lead female character, portrayed by Bridget Fonda, calls MasterCard to check to see if they will issue her a new card. In actuality, of course, MasterCard does not issue cards directly to cardholders. The cards are issued by banks or other financial institutions, who have purchased the right to market the MasterCard branded cards as franchisees.

While this attests to the strength of the MasterCard brand, it poses problems for the issuing banks, who often consider the credit card to be a parity product that *they offer* to their customers as part of the customer's total banking relationship. In truth, the banks do indeed 'own' the strongest relationship with the cardholders, the direct bank to cardholder relationship. Unfortunately, many banks have failed to fully leverage this relationship, making them less than completely prepared for the coming era of relationship marketing.

The strength of the MasterCard credit card brand was a minor irritation in the development of a new corporate image position. Previously, when customer needs were sufficiently met by pay-later credit cards, MasterCard International could effectively rely on the mega brand strategy. However, as the importance of the pay-now debit cards and pay-before pre-loaded stored value cards became greater, MasterCard was locked into a product branding strategy that encompassed its Maestro and Cirrus brands. The challenge facing this forward-thinking association in the mid 1990s was how to establish a distinct point of differentiation for the mother MasterCard corporate brand, without causing confusion or deterioration to the MasterCard credit card product brand. The new corporate image strategy would also have to be flexible enough to encompass any future product branding strategies. In particular, they plan to introduce the smart card (a single plastic card embedded with an integrated circuit) that could offer multiple functions (credit, debit, prepaid, loyalty, discounts, etc).

The association identified the following factors affecting the brand personality of the MasterCard credit card product:

- product benefits
- service delivery
- issuing bank
- branch network
- franchise association
- card design
- merchant outlets
- price
- history
- competitors
- users' needs
- advertising
- promotions
- point of sale displays

Senior management aimed to develop criteria for the corporate brand that were distinct from the usual factors cardholders used in determining the credit card brand's personality and yet were capable of enhancing all of the association's brands (MasterCard, Maestro, Cirrus). At the same time MasterCard needed a unique set of attributes for the corporate image (brand) that would be relevant to its distribution system (the issuing banks), its acceptance channel (merchants), and its end users (cardholders and potential cardholders).

In 1996, after two years of numerous internal changes to its organisational structure, and several major technology-related investment projects, MasterCard International took a giant stride forward in creating a fresh perception for the association as a leading player in the future evolution of the card payments industry with the introduction of its new corporate image positioning platform: MasterCard—The Future of Money™. The new positioning platform was first communicated internally before it was exposed to banks and consumers via advertising and other marketing communications materials.

One of the technological investments made by MasterCard International that reinforces their commitment to being the future of money was its

Corporate Image Management

purchase in late 1996 of a majority stake in Mondex International. This UK-based technology company has developed the world's most advanced chip platform for the payments industry, with more banks signed up to participate in the Mondex electronic cash program than in any other chip-card system. Mondex is an electronic cash payment smart card that brings together the advantages of paying by cash with the convenience of paying by card. Mondex is unique because its technology platform allows for transfer of electronic cash between customers without the involvement of a central computer system.

'Using Mondex as our strategic chip operating platform provides MasterCard with the best possible opportunity to leapfrog other technology, and to offer banks and consumers the most sophisticated, best-tested product on the market, not only today, but for the future', explained Mr James A. Cassin, President, MasterCard Asia/Pacific. 'In the future, the need for chip-based cards will be driven by the need for better security and an increasingly sophisticated product offering for both banks and consumers', he added. All MasterCard member institutions will have the right to apply for a licence to issue the Mondex electronic cash product in the regions where they operate.

Taking this technological leadership a step further, MasterCard International and Mondex International joined six of the leading smart card manufacturers and silicon manufacturers from the United States, Europe, Asia and Australia to form a consortium in 1997 to develop an open industry standard for chip card applications. The consortium, called MAOSCO, includes Dai Nippon Printing, Gemplus, Hitachi, Keycorp, MasterCard International, Mondex International, Motorola and Siemens. The role of the group is to drive the adoption of MULTOS (multi-application operating system), that uses the proven Mondex security architecture to allow applications to be dynamically and securely loaded onto smart cards as the industry's operating standard. If this group is successful, MULTOS will be to the smart card industry (for financial and non-financial transactions and applications) what Windows is to personal computers.

In a related move, MasterCard International has been playing a fundamental leadership role in making the Internet safe for shopping and electronic commerce transactions. On 30 December 1996, a MasterCard cardholder in Denmark bought a book over the Internet in the first secure

Internet transaction using the Secure Electronic Transaction (SET) standard. SET is an open, free and non-proprietary global specification jointly developed and endorsed by leading electronic commerce players including MasterCard International, IBM, Microsoft, Netscape, GTE and others to safeguard consumer shopping on the Internet.

All of these technological advances and investments by MasterCard would have been unheard of from a company that merely thinks of itself as being in the credit card business. All, and many others, however, are extremely important for an organisation that has visions of participating in, and leading the development of, the future of money. Again, we see from this example that true corporate image management goes beyond the realm of logos, symbols, colour schemes and clever positioning statements. True corporate image management, as in the case of MasterCard International, becomes the organisation's playbook for who it is, what it is, and where it is headed.

Relationship Building

Building relationships with customers and business partners requires a different set of discipline skills than simply creating a unique selling proposition (USP) for a brand or a unique identity (name and logo) for an organisation. The criteria for relationship building between individuals and organisational entities is much like the criteria people use in determining what kinds of relationships they desire to develop with other individuals. At a minimum, they include:

- knowing you,
- understanding you,
- being able to communicate with you,
- being convinced that you listen to me, and
- being able to rely on you.

If I were to re-write that McGraw-Hill advertisement found at the beginning of Chapter Four, my copy platform would be:

> 'I don't really know you.
> I don't know what your company stands for or represents.
> I don't understand who or what your organisation is.
> Will I be able to communicate with you?
> How can I be assured that you will listen to me?

Corporate Image Management

How will I know that you will hear and understand my needs, my concerns?
How close are the values of your organisation and its people to mine?
How can I know if I can count on you and your organisation?
Will my loyalty to you be rewarded and returned?
Now—why should I consider having a relationship with you?'

Loyalty lies at the heart of any relationship, be it between two people, two organisations or an organisation and the individuals with whom it interacts. A high degree of loyalty will be as important between business partners and between customers and their product/service providers as it is between lovers. This is not a new concept for it has existed for centuries in the relationships between people and their respective religious institutions. Once the bounds of loyalty or trust are broken between the religious institution and a portion of its followers, a dramatic fallout in believers ensues (witness the creation of various church movements as offspring of a larger movement: the Lutheran Church as a 'corporate spin-off' from the Catholic Church, and the recent demise of Jerry Falwell's movement after his criminal conviction). The newness of this thinking is in its application to the corporate and business world as a recipe for future marketing success.

Brand loyalty is a function of brand characteristics and heavy brand promotion activities. Corporate loyalty, either by employees or customers, is found on a higher plane, with the bonding criteria being more emotional and personal than straightforward identification. For instance, loyalty to Coca-Cola (the product) requires some sense of identification with the brand. On the other hand, loyalty to Northwest Airlines (the company) requires a higher emotional decision, perhaps based on the consistent service delivery or perhaps in appreciation of their community service efforts such as their annual support of the Toys For Tots campaign.

From an employee perspective, corporate loyalty is a linkage through belief in the organisation and its future. For a customer, corporate loyalty transcends into the realms of trust, confidence, reliability, and interactions consistent with the perceived corporate image. These are relationship building, relationship enhancing, and relationship stabilising criteria, all of which are corporate characteristics and traits best projected by organisational action. If the business relationship, however, is simply based on a desire to collect frequent flyer miles from the Northwest Airlines WorldPerks program, then this bought loyalty will have little to do with devotion, faithfulness and fidelity.

Corporate Image as a Strategic Weapon

Customers will not build long-term, faithful relationships with a corporate identity. There is not enough substance attached to a corporate identity for the deeper emotional bonds that determine a true relationship and that provide something for the consumer to grip and cling to. Creating mutually rewarding relationships with customers will require organisational actions and corporate personalities that attract, foster and retain emotional bonding agents. These actions and personalities are best derived from a planned and managed corporate image process.

Relationship building is nothing more than the sowing of the seeds of loyalty, allegiance, and fidelity through consistent product and service delivery, and the consistent projection of a unified and coherent corporate image by the actions of the organisation and its employees.

A relationship will be determined by the willingness of the customer to rationalise repeat purchases or interactions using a higher scale of (mostly emotional) attributes. The top two hierarchical needs identified by Abraham Maslow, esteem and self-actualisation, are relationship building influences. Brand identification by customers is a lower hierarchical need, found mostly in satisfying the need for social recognition and a sense of belonging. One reason that branded clothing has been so successful is that people can more readily achieve social needs within their chosen peer groups by being able to show off the label names on their clothes. Customer rationalisations based on the satisfying of self esteem needs will easily counter concerns about pricing and convenience in the purchase decision matrix.

When customer needs change, who will they approach first? Most likely organisations with which a positive relationship has already been established. The problem many firms have is that they define the relationship in terms of product ownership or product usage. This is a product relationship, not necessarily an organisational relationship. For instance, just because I have a cheque account with a particular bank does not mean that I necessarily have notions of a relationship with that institution. If I, the customer, do not perceive a relationship arrangement, then I will have no emotional bonds that direct me to open a mortgage account or a credit card account with that bank. In fact, single product ownership with a multiple product organisation is a greater identification of the lack of a relationship, from the customer's perspective, than an indication that a relationship exists.

Corporate Image Management

Product relationships are less emotionally driven than corporate relationships. Additionally, product relationships are not automatically transferred to the organisation behind the product or service. My personal, unbreakable loyalty to Coca-Cola the soft drink is because I like the taste and I'm satisfied with my experiences of the product. It has little or no bearing on my perception of Coca-Cola the company or its corporate image. The same holds true for drivers who love their Oldsmobile cars, but who have no perceived relationship with General Motors.

The non-transferability of the relationship from a product to the corporate entity is true more for product firms than service establishments because it is harder for them to separate the service component from the overall corporate image. However, attempts to form service conglomerates have been notorious for failing to link the corporate images across independent and unattached organisations—as UAL found out in the 1980s when it tried to combine United Airlines, Hertz and Westin Hotels into the ill fated Allegis. To say that they were less than successful would be too kind. While there may have been some customer synergies within this strategy, there was certainly no unifying corporate image foundation that could have become a strategic marketing weapon for success.

In a similar vein, Hilton is (at the time of writing) attempting to take over ITT for its Sheraton properties. Is this a good match? This is doubtful from a corporate image management standpoint, as the two international chains have little in common except for two well-known product brands and a wide portfolio of respective hotels across the globe. A management policy of keeping the two chains 'separate but equal' would undoubtedly have the same success as the racial segregation policies of the US South that coined this phrase.

What if the managers of the Hilton wanted to create a new corporate image for the combined entity? First, they would be throwing out the existing values of both the Hilton and the Sheraton names. Secondly, why would they toss aside the Sheraton name, when they will almost certainly be paying a premium over book value to ITT's shareholders (if the takeover is successful) based partly on the value of the Sheraton brand name? On the other hand, both the Hilton and the Sheraton brands could be perceived as 'tired' and in need of revitalisation. Nevertheless, such a challenging attempt at creating a new corporate image would need to be based upon the internal attributes of the combined organisation through subsequent actions. If done correctly, however, the nature of corporate image as a strategic marketing weapon would enable the combined group to leapfrog to the top of the hotel industry by developing strongly branded relationships with key customers (travel agents, frequent individual travellers, infrequent travellers, conference organisers) and other key targets (Wall Street, shareholders, regulators, property investors).

The merger might look good from a financial accounting perspective. It might look good to Hilton's management and board as a strategic initiative. The question remains, does it make sense from a corporate image perspective? Let's hope Hilton's senior managers have a positive answer to this if they are eventually successful in their takeover attempt.

Image as a Strategic Weapon

As we move into the era of relationship marketing and partnership marketing, organisations will need to add the fifth P of marketing (Perception) to their marketing formulas. It makes no difference whether you call this Perception or Image. The important criterion is to remember to view the corporate image from the perspective of the customer, the prospect and the other key audiences for the organisation.

In doing so, you need to look at all the external factors and at all of the organisation's internal behaviours. Do they tell the target audience 'We are worth the investment of your time, your emotions, your money'? Do they broadcast 'We are a worthy partner'? If not, your organisation is not ready for the exciting era of relationship marketing and partnership marketing.

Image management is not simply increasing the general awareness levels of your organisation. Image management means internalising desirable behaviour patterns so that the resultant external expression of the corporate character comes through individual and organisational action. The consistent delivery of these actions across the organisation will be the most powerful strategic weapon in the corporate arsenal for relationship and partnership building.

Corporate Image Management

This attention to corporate image management will enable organisations to devise meaningful and long-term points of differentiation, to cope better with sudden and unexpected change, and to create image associations that are relevant and desirable for its customers and other key audiences.

Corporate image management as a strategic marketing weapon is nothing less than the cutting edge of marketing and management technology for the 21st Century.

Chapter Nine

Managing and Marketing the Corporate Image

Corporate image management builds upon the company's strengths, identifies and corrects its weaknesses, and exploits untapped opportunities in the market by ensuring that the projection of the corporate image is consistently portrayed by corporate behaviour. To manage the corporate image thoroughly, all internal and external communications must be continually managed, particularly those related to corporate behaviour, corporate culture and marketing.

The corporate image permeates everything about the organisation. It's the platform, or the operating system, for how we perceive and evaluate every company, organisation, product, country, place, movement or religion. When used in a shallow way, the perception is based on corporate identity and results in stereotypes, either positively or negatively. When used with discernment, the perception becomes based on a higher platform of understanding, established through experiences with the organisation's behaviour patterns.

Customers are satisfied when their experiences of interacting with the organisation surpass expectations. However, the reverse is true also: dissatisfaction results when the experience fails to meet expectations. The first rule of corporate image management is to ensure that the organisation is structured and designed to deliver a consistent level of experiences to its customers. When a shortfall occurs, either through delivery errors or inconsistent procedures, the result is disappointment, discontent and a reduction in the perceived corporate image.

Corporate Image Management

As an example consider the decline of service in Singapore Airlines discussed in Chapter Six. The airline is facing some serious management challenges (one of which will be discussed in detail later in this chapter).

I have noticed that frequent flyers are not only commenting (complaining actually) about cuts in the Singapore Airlines service, but have also become more aware and vocal about all of the other little things that can go wrong. Complaints about disappointing food selection and quality, headsets that do not work, seats that do not extend back fully, and other minor irritations have reached a voluminous level never before experienced in my 18 years living in Singapore. Add to this the disappointing VIP passenger facilities which SIA operates at the Manila and Seoul airports and it does not take long to understand why the once shiny corporate image of Singapore Airlines has become tarnished in the latter half of the 1990s.

Remember Rule Number One of corporate image management: inconsistencies in corporate behaviour patterns have a direct negative effect on the perceived corporate image by those who experience it. The corollary is that the worst thing that can happen *is not* the loss of that customer, it's the probability that the dissatisfied customer will tell dozens of other customers and prospects about their negative experience. Not only does this help to invalidate the organisation's positive corporate image attributes (or reinforce any negative perceptions) with those hearing about the disaster story, it may also cause the organisation to lose other customers or prospects. The multiplier effect of a dissatisfied customer is a wrecking ball on the organisation's efforts to attain mutually beneficial relationships with other customers. Eliminating inconsistency in product or service delivery should be the singular most important objective for any organisation wanting to fully manage its corporate image and acquire long-term customer relationships.

A Five Year Horizon

Corporate image management strategies for most organisations should be built on five year horizons. This is far enough into the future to be of strategic value, but not so far that the values and desired behaviour patterns become meaningless 'Mom and apple pie' statements. A five year thought process also builds in the requirement for flexibility, something that is mandatory in rapidly changing and continually evolving markets.

Additionally, it is probably not realistic to predict more than five years ahead. Think back to 1993, did you know or expect:

- the rapid growth of the Internet
- the emergence of electronic commerce through personal computers
- the development of credit cards with microchips
- the development of an international, on-line debit card system
- the bull run on the world's stock markets
- NASA to successfully land a rover on Mars
- the demise and near death of Apple Computer
- the ease with which Bill Clinton would win re-election
- the ease with which John Major would lose an election
- the taming of inflation and inflationary expectations in the United States, Australia and elsewhere?

With the possible exception of the exploration on Mars, each of these events has probably had an impact on every major business, industry and organisation in the developed and developing world, yet none were foreseeable only five years ago.

Core Competencies

The changing world and the need for corporate image management practices are combining such that key managerial business skills now need to be entwined within the corporate culture. These core competencies are required at all levels of the organisation, not just within the top levels of the management ranks. And, unlike the current business focus on financial management, these skills are all related to people and communications. As such, they require a new set of internal and external measurement indices to be formed for both private and public concerns.

Since these activities are required throughout the organisation, they will be shared across divisions, departments, staff rank levels and geographical boundaries. Core competencies are usually thought of in terms of manufacturing prowess, research and development expertise, innovation, marketing capabilities, and human resource skills. These are the types of core characteristics that organisations currently attempt to imbue from top to bottom and from bottom to top. The 'softer' management skills of vision, leadership, planning, staffing, and controlling have been relegated to the top tiers of most organisations, creating top-down approaches that

Corporate Image Management

often lead to inconsistencies in product and service delivery (eg the current state of Singapore Airlines).

Now, however, with the understanding that everything the organisation does has a direct or indirect impact on its corporate image, it is necessary for these softer management skills to be distributed everywhere in the organisation. While senior management still determine these key activities, it is now critical that employees at all levels participate and fully understand how they affect the future growth of the organisation and the evolution of its corporate image.

Two benefits will accrue from this new procedure. Firstly, management will have greater ability to steer the corporate vehicle during times of rapid change because a unified corporate culture will be in place comprising those who have 'bought into' the strategic direction of the organisation. Secondly, the front-line staff will act as guardians of the corporate image and provide important feedback to management from customers and other key audiences when negative decisions start to impact the corporate image or corrode customer or business relationships. In the case of Singapore Airlines, one has to surmise that either the front-line staff are not comfortable in bringing up the 'minor complaints' of a handful of passengers complaining about inconsistent service delivery, or senior management has failed to recognise that such complaints are having a direct impact on the airline's corporate image.

To inculcate relationship excellence and partnership excellence across the organisation, firms should strive to include the following six critical core competencies.

Vision skills
An ability to:
- identify the desired destination
- determine the overall direction
- define intermediate goals and objectives
- predict industry and market environment trends
- design flexibility into plans and processes
- understand critical components of the corporate culture
- comprehend organisational strengths and weaknesses
- recognise external threats and opportunities

Governing skills

An ability to:
- quantify intermediate goals and objectives
- establish priorities
- establish guidelines for acceptable and unacceptable corporate behaviour
- select courses of intermediate action
- implement and monitor plans
- assign tasks to individuals, teams, groups
- allocate resources to achieve tasks
- ensure clear lines of cross-organisational communication
- resolve problems and organisational, directional conflicts

Staffing skills

An ability to:
- establish recruitment criteria and methods
- understand critical components of the corporate culture and apply these in hiring practices
- identify and satisfy training needs
- determine performance appraisal criteria and methods
- establish reward and compensation systems
- establish promotion yardsticks

Monitoring skills

An ability to:
- monitor and evaluate processes and procedures continuously
- review short-term and intermediate activities
- compare performance with desired direction
- receive continuous feedback from customers, colleagues
- integrate monitoring and feedback loops into plans and activities

Communication skills

An ability to:
- establish and maintain interactive, two-way communications with customers and business partners, including an active feedback mechanism
- create open, honest and cross-organisational communications channels which leapfrog hierarchy, rank, cultural, racial and all other language barriers

Corporate Image Management

- evolve corporate communications processes and channels (both internal and external) to involve global audiences as required
- resist the temptation to hide bad news or to tell partial truths about any situation

Leadership skills

An ability to:
- ascertain required leadership style for corporate culture
- inspire commitment and dedication
- stimulate team, family, and company spirit and effect an atmosphere of teamwork
- coach at all levels of the organisation: with subordinates, peers and bosses
- give credit, take responsibility
- share authority
- enact decision-making procedures
- live up to the ethical, moral and cultural standards explicit and implicit in the corporate behaviour patterns through personal action
- understand the organisation's role in the lives of its employees, customers, business partners, community
- nurture organisational relationships with employees, customers, business partners, community
- pledge the organisation to the consistent delivery of a meaningful, coherent and clear corporate image as a foundation for relationship building with employees, customers, business partners, community

Leadership skills have purposely been placed at the end of this list. They need to be impregnated into and permeated throughout the organisation as a way of illustrating its importance *at all levels of the organisation*. If leadership was placed in its traditional top of the list position, readers might interpret leadership as being a top management function only. This is definitely not the case when it comes to corporate image management and the need to build and nurture successful relationships.

I have also chosen *governing* over the traditional word *managing*, as the latter has too many inferences to control, top-down dictates, comparing performance with standards, producing job descriptions, and determining work tasks. I see governing as the way that social groups should be managed, and the workplace is nothing if not a true social grouping.

Committees and volunteer groups are governed. Task forces are usually governed. Organisations that have a reputation for being 'people oriented' are governed, not managed. Organisations entering the stage of relationship marketing need to be governed, not overtly managed, in order to create an atmosphere and climate that naturally attracts business partners and customer relationships.

Organisations that are excessively structured and highly managed rely too much on processes and procedures and their product and service offerings tend to be highly standardised. Those that are governed are less rigidly structured, and rely more on their employees than on tightly controlled procedures for decision-making. They are more willing to meet customised requests from customers and therefore have the capabilities to develop customer relationships. Organisations that are unduly managed emphasise financial returns, whereas those that are effectively governed emphasise the identification and satisfying of customer needs. And naturally, organisations that are managed rely on corporate identity positioning strategies for success, while those that are governed understand how to continuously manage their respective corporate images.

In the area of human resources, potential employment candidates need to be evaluated not only on their skills and experiences but also on how well they will fit, and how well their individual value systems mesh with those of the organisation. As teamwork and inter-departmental activities play increasing roles in the governed organisation, both current and new employees will need to be judged, coached and rewarded on their interpersonal and teamwork skills.

Each of the competency skills and activities outlined here must be proactively managed if the organisation is to project a consistent corporate image through its behaviour patterns and its communications activities. There have been many great business management buzzwords in recent years, such as synergy and globalisation, that have captured new trends or identified new opportunities. I suggest that corporate governors need 'employeeisation', meaning the process of inculcating the desired corporate image into every employee, in every division, department, region, or country. Rather than trying to 'think globally, act locally' as the proponents of marketing globalisation write, it would be better to 'think and act uniformly and consistently in the pursuit of creating customer relationships and business partnerships'.

Corporate Image Management

Benchmarking Corporate Image

Benchmarking is a formal process of measuring, monitoring and comparing an organisation's characteristics (such as operations, processes, products, services, employees and customers) against those of the top performing organisations in similar industries or markets. The goal is to identify what skill sets or core competencies enable the top performers to outperform all competitors.

When used as part of the corporate image management process, benchmarking should aim to uncover the secret ingredients that allow the most respected organisations to attain image leadership positions within their industries or markets. In analysing these secrets, the objective is not to determine which ingredients to copy, but rather to identify two processes. First, what is enabling them to establish win-win relationships with customers and partners, and second, what internal processes are resulting in a thoroughly inculcated set of behaviour patterns that reinforce the corporate image? If the benchmarking analysis finds that the image leadership reputation is based primarily on an identity position platform or strategy, then it will have identified a leader in a precarious position who is ripe for knocking off the top of the image totem pole.

By understanding the key criteria which form the foundation of the corporate image of your competitors, you are better placed to either implement your own strategies which will close the image gap, or use the information to help determine your desired corporate image and the resultant corporate behaviour patterns that are needed for its support.

Benchmarking is also a valuable tool for monitoring the strengths and weaknesses of one's own corporate image. If nothing else, this self-monitoring system forces the organisation to shift its focus outside itself, a very valuable process where the organisation is too internally focused. This marketplace evaluation also helps organisations to contemplate and maximise their capabilities, rather than simply trying to surpass last year's financial results by an arbitrary percentage goal. By identifying the areas and processes used by the image leaders, every organisation can develop its own master plan for hurdling past competitors and creating marketing advantages based on customer perceptions of its corporate image.

Singapore Girl

The Singapore Girl, created as the secondary identifier for Singapore Airlines, continues to be the single most important marketing asset of the airline. The Singapore Girl also happens to be the single biggest marketing problem and future corporate image management concern for SIA's executives. How can this be so?

The Singapore Girl celebrates her 25th birthday in 1998 as the renowned image and icon of Singapore Airlines. Her global reputation for grace, charm, hospitality and subtle service has already landed her in the famed Madame Tussaud's Wax Museum in London, where she became the first non-individual personality to be depicted and displayed in this 200-year old gallery. (As a side note, the Singapore Girl beat former Singapore Prime Minister Lee Kuan Yew, who served as the country's leader from 1959 until he stepped down in 1990, into Madame Tussaud's by five years.) From her creation, the Singapore Girl has represented both Singapore Airlines and the city-state of Singapore.

Today, because of the tight labour supply in Singapore and the greater attraction for female Singaporeans to establish careers in other industries such as financial services, hotels, medical, teaching, and accounting, Singapore Airlines is facing difficulties in attracting enough young Singaporeans for its cabin crew staff. While the company's corporate image management policies have been successful in ensuring that passengers are handled by a young, clean-cut, wholesome and efficient Singapore Girl cabin crew, these same policies have been a turn-off for career-minded female Singaporeans who don't want to be retired in mid-career at age 35. Rather than fly with SIA for a few years and then enter the local work force in their late twenties or early thirties, more Singaporean women are opting to focus on long-term career development from the time they leave school. As a result, passengers on board Singapore Airlines flights today are just as likely to be welcomed and served by flight attendants from home towns in Indonesia, Malaysia, China, Taiwan, Sri Lanka, India and elsewhere. This is probably the single biggest corporate image management challenge facing Singapore Airlines as the carrier celebrated its 50th birthday in 1997 and prepares itself for the 21st century (and note that it has nothing to do with graphics, logos or other elements of corporate identity).

Corporate Image Management

Singapore Airlines is in a tough predicament. The international airline industry is definitely one of increasing competition, rising costs, squeezing margins and global partnerships (the lead of which has recently been taken by the Star Alliance partners of UAL, Lufthansa, Thai Airways, SAS and Air Canada). Internal polices and procedures at SIA are causing the airline to deliver an inconsistent level of service (see Chapter Six) to its core First and Business Class passengers. SIA used to be priced at a premium of 10% to 15% above other carriers on the same routes, particularly for these classes—today it is sometimes the lowest priced option. The airline has even decided to buy passenger loyalty through the Passages frequent flyer mileage program as other regional and international carriers close the perceived service gap. And to top all this off, the Singapore Girl, the foundation and cornerstone of the airline's corporate image and persona, no longer necessarily comes from Singapore.

How SIA's executives and advertising agency manage the evolution of the Singapore Girl, and hence the future corporate image of Singapore Airlines, will be more important to the future marketing success of the airline than its decisions on routes, aircraft purchases, pricing, business partnerships and means of financing growth.

Situations like this are one of the clearest indications that corporate image management will be a critical marketing discipline for success in the next 10 to 20 years. The SIA example is but one of many similar corporate image management challenges being faced by leading organisations across the globe. One of the key purposes of this book is to warn that if you're not seriously thinking about the challenges and threats to your current corporate image, from both market environment pressures and internal procedures, then you should put this somewhere near the top of your list of priorities. The future success of your organisation may very well depend on how you and your people manage the corporate image.

Corporate Image Management

What's in a name? Corporate identity designers will tell you 'everything'. In some ways, that may still be true. But it's truer from the perspective of the organisation's management than it is from the perspective of the receiving audience. Your key customers, prospects, employees and others cannot have a relationship with your corporate logo or symbol.

What needs to be managed? Everything, for there is no department, unit or individual within the organisation—with the possible exception of the financial control department—that does not impact upon the corporate image and all other aspects of the marketing equation. I exclude this department if it is mostly charged with the responsibility of tracking and reporting financial information to management. Obviously, if it plays a role in pricing issues, or handles items which directly impact customers such as invoices and billing statements, then it too impacts the corporate image. *If it touches the customer, it's a marketing issue.* And, of course, *if it's a marketing issue, it's part of the corporate image management process.*

Managing and Marketing the Corporate Image

Marketing the Corporate Image

At every point of interaction between a customer and an organisation, there is an impact on the customer's perception of the organisation's corporate image. From the moment a customer determines that he, she or it (in the case of business customers) has a need that needs to be fulfilled, the buying process begins as the customer consciously and unconsciously develops a list of potential solutions. At each stage of the buying process, from shortlisting possible solution providers to the customer's post-purchase behaviour, there are numerous interaction points at which the organisation's corporate image can be used to create a point of competitive differentiation. They include the following points.

- awareness
- location
- purchase decision
- purchase order or physical purchase at retail
- delivery
- installation
- payment
- storage and transportation
- usage purpose
- return or exchange
- repair and service maintenance
- refill purchases
- update purchases
- disposal
- replacement purchase

Corporate Image Management

Since the customer purchase decision (or repeat purchase decision) process can be broken off or lost at any of these points of interaction, it is necessary for the organisation to project and integrate its corporate image into as many, if not all, of the points as possible. If the corporate image is to be based on service, then a high level of service quality must be integrated into each step, not only at the time of purchase, usage experience or after-sales support. An airline that bases its image on service must provide a consistent high level of service in reservations, at check-in, during baggage handling and connections, in post flight assistance, onward reservations, billing, and posting of frequent flyer mileage statements. It cannot afford only to provide passengers with good service during flights.

Corporate image marketing should not be confused with corporate image communications (especially paid communications activities such as advertising and public relations). As discussed in Chapter Seven, we often see corporate image marketing being nothing more than the projection of a new identity through advertising, use of a new identity system, or the introduction of a new corporate slogan or theme.

To repeat, in the new era of relationship marketing excellence and partnership excellence, it will be more important to create a solidified and integrated corporate image than to communicate a preferential image position. This needs to delivered with consistency and coherency by the entire organisation through its behaviour patterns.

Corporate Image Projections

One of the problems in relying on corporate image projections through advertising, symbols and slogans is that these elements are too susceptible to change and quick fix thinking. True, market conditions are constantly changing and there will always be a need for fast response, tactical marketing activities. The corporate image, however, should not fall prey to these responses; otherwise, it risks confusing customers, employees and other stakeholders.

Sears, Roebuck & Co is a good example of what happens when the corporate image is used as a tactical weapon. Once America's largest retailer, Sears changed in 1989 from its long-time image of being 'the place where America shops' to focus on providing 'everyday low pricing'. The concept was to reduce the company's reliance on sales to draw in customers.

Managing and Marketing the Corporate Image

The convoluted slogan used for this image change was 'Your money's worth and a whole lot more'. In the resulting consumer confusion, store traffic and sales volume both slowed. A return to sales discount advertising ensued shortly thereafter. A few years later, having dropped to third place in some surveys of shoppers on the criteria of providing superior service, Sears launched another new image platform. This time the slogan was 'You can count on me', which emphasised the reliability of its housebrands: Craftsman tools, Kenmore appliances and DieHard car batteries.

According to newspaper reports at the time, a Sears representative said that the organisation's key message was 'Sears is an organisation committed to product quality and total customer satisfaction both before and after the sale'. That's the kind of image projection that is really only believable through actual experience at numerous points of interaction, not through watching 30-second television commercials. Today, this former beacon and pioneer of the retail merchandise industry in the United States is no longer the largest retailer in the land. That spot has been taken over by Wal-Mart. And while Sears may still have its name on the Sears Tower in Chicago, the tallest building in the US, it is no longer owned by the company. Times change, but leaders do not necessarily have to be dethroned. On the other hand, changing the organisation's corporate image for tactical marketing reasons and confusing customers in the process is assuredly a quicker path to marketing failure than it is to marketing nirvana.

Perhaps the only thing more damaging to a corporate image changed through marketing communications is one hurt by the actions of the organisation or its employees. The Dallas Cowboys football team is one of the best examples of what can go wrong when behaviour patterns are not in line with the projected corporate image.

Once promoted as 'America's Team', the Cowboys have an image problem that no amount of advertising or crisis communications activities will fix. In recent years, some of its players have been suspended for violations of the National Football League's drug abuse policies. Others have been publicly accused of spousal abuse and sexual assault, and its head coach has been arrested at the Dallas-Fort Worth Airport for having a loaded gun in his carry-on luggage. Upon breaking training camp in August 1997, several of these highly paid professional athletes trashed the dormitory facilities of the university where the pre-season camp had been held.

Corporate Image Management

While some of the sexual assault charges proved groundless, and the coach's error was apparently the result of having forgotten that the handgun had been placed in that particular bag, the Cowboys have the appearance of a team in disarray. How many parents are likely to encourage their children to be fans of the Cowboys? How many are likely to purchase Cowboys-branded shirts, caps and other sports apparel for themselves or their children? How many fan relationships has the team lost as a result of these behaviours?

Do they dare still call themselves America's Team? Not as long as they remain the butt of jokes for their antics off the field. My favourite joke: if four Dallas Cowboys are sitting in a car together, who's driving? Answer: the police. This corporate image has been damaged directly by individual and organisational behaviour patterns. As such, only future individual and organisational behaviour patterns can restore or recreate the corporate image of the Dallas Cowboys. A new logo, new team uniforms or any other attempt at designing or projecting a new corporate identity would be insufficient.

Another institution that has done an almost universally poor job of managing its corporate image is Britain's Royal Family. If the House of Windsor was a publicly listed corporation, the value of its shares would have plummeted over the past five to eight years to a mere fraction of their peak value during the 'Wedding of the Century' in 1981 between Prince Charles and Lady Diana. The manner in which the Royal Family has handled its never-ending series of crises, from divorces through to the issue on whether its annual income should be subjected to income tax, shows this to be an organisation badly out of touch with its core constituency, the British people. For the country to have a serious discussion on whether the British monarchy is still required in this modern era tells the rest of the world that this institution is no longer meeting the relationship requirements of its 'faithful subjects'. Here again, no amount of marketing communications and advertising will rectify the image problem of the British Royal Family. They need a good consultant to advise them on how to identify what the British want in their monarchy, and then the Windsors need to 'reorganise' themselves and their actions to meet the needs of their customers. One thing is obvious: sticking to traditional ways and methods and being afraid to do the unprecedented will keep this institution on its current path of self destruction.

Symbols

For years, corporate identity practices have been used to create points of differentiation between competing entities. The objective has been to enable customers and other interested parties to make distinctions, which in turn would give rise to choices. As part of the corporate identity practice during this period of positioning excellence, there has been a strong belief in the power of symbols (logos, icons, call them whatever you will) and the importance of symbols in the communication process.

At one point, I used to share and practise this belief. Like others, I once placed great emphasis on ensuring that the corporate logo was always used properly and that no advertisement would be complete without the required corporate or brand logo (and in the case of television commercials, the all important pack shot in the closing frames). When I moved to Asia in 1980 I began to notice that many of the most successful Asian businesses did not rely heavily on the use of their corporate symbol in their marketing communications materials. At the same time, I also noticed that many of the leading Japanese firms did not even bother with a logo, instead using a specific corporate typeface to create a unique look to the company name. As I began to study these successful firms, and started to work with individual companies in South-east Asia on their respective corporate identity programs, I became convinced of the overriding importance of corporate image management as the harbinger of future marketing success.

These feelings were reconfirmed to me in an article in the *Asian Wall Street Journal* in December 1991, which ran beneath a headline proclaiming 'Logos May Undercut Corporate Image, Study Finds'. The gist of the article was that corporate logos may do more harm than good and wind up 'undercutting the corporate image'. The article was based on a study by the Schechter Group, who asked 900 consumers in the US to review 22 nationally advertised corporate and product brand logos and symbols. Unfortunately for this group of major advertisers, respondents were not very adept at recognising the symbols or knowing what products the logos represented. Even worse, many of the logos had damaging consequences to the corporate images they were supposed to be representing and enhancing. 'Half of the logos made consumers less likely to trust the company, and less likely to want to buy its products or to think of it as modern', the article quotes Mr Alvin Schechter, chairman of the strategic

Corporate Image Management

design firm that conducted the survey, as saying. He added, 'It's not that easy for a visual device to add anything to a company's image, but you certainly don't want it to drag the imagery down'.

In the study, 11 of the 22 logos were found to 'downgrade' the image of the companies they represented, according to the newspaper report. For example, when the AT&T logo was shown without the company name, one-third of the respondents reacted negatively to the symbol. However, when the logo and name were shown together, 80% of those surveyed had a positive reaction. The conclusion drawn by the researchers was that the AT&T logo, an abstract mark designed to depict a 'global supplier of communications', was a detriment, rather than an enhancement, to the overall AT&T image for these survey participants. A similar conclusion was reached for the 10 other symbols that received lower approval ratings in the survey than did the individual names of the companies.

Symbols are very powerful, but only when they come to truly represent some quality or characteristic inherent in the organisation that is appreciated and desired by its customers. It also helps when the logo has been used consistently over the years to represent a key trait of the organisation. Prudential Insurance has been using a rock as its logo for more than a century and the company has been living up to the characteristics that the rock represents. On the other hand, what does the centurion figure used by American Express represent? What corporate trait of American Express is reflected by this helmeted warrior, and is it the kind of trait that will encourage any kind of customer relationship with Amex? Sure, American Express has been using this symbol on its charge cards and traveller's cheques for decades, but unlike the Prudential rock it does not seem to have any significance in today's rapidly evolving payments and financial services industries.

Marketing a Changed Image or Identity

There is no doubt that changing times and changing conditions often call for a change in the corporate identity or corporate image. Royal Dutch Shell is a classic example of a corporate logo that has evolved through the years, adding new shapes and secondary colours to keep its yellow shell logo modern and in tune with the times. Even Singapore Airlines went through a slight modification and update enhancement to its corporate identity in 1987 on the occasion of the airline's 40th anniversary.

Sometimes, however, more than just slight modifications and alterations are required. In 1967, four California banks changed from the California Bankcard Association to the Western States BankCard Association (WSBA). This group opened its membership to other financial institutions in the western United States and launched its new credit card product as MasterCharge. In 1979, MasterCharge changed its name to MasterCard to reflect an array of expanded services and it became one of two nationwide bank card systems across the United States.

By 1989 MasterCard had become the 14th best known brand in the US, but there was much lower, although still significant, awareness of this brand outside the country. Additional research also indicated that MasterCard was viewed as a trusted and reliable brand and that its interlocking circles were widely recognised even without the MasterCard name. However, those same consumers also viewed the MasterCard brand as old fashioned, an attribute they mostly associated with the red and ochre colours of the brand mark. To make matters worse, an investigation into the organisation's own identity practices revealed that it did not use its brand mark clearly and consistently throughout the world, and that local acceptance marks often overshadowed the MasterCard brand mark in markets outside the United States.

Despite its relative strength in the US domestic market, MasterCard International undertook a large-scale corporate identity revamp in 1989 in order to ensure that the MasterCard brand would be instantly recognised and accepted everywhere throughout the world. Implemented over a three-year period, this new corporate identity system included a redesign of the company's well-known interlocking circles and a new universal card design format that gave all its credit cards a strong and consistent look around the world. Through consistent use of its new logo, MasterCard International was able to create a new global brand for itself, and unsurpassed global acceptance for its cardholders at merchants, restaurants, hotels, and other outlets everywhere.

Of course, that was back in 1990, during the era of positioning excellence. As described in the previous chapter, MasterCard International has moved from a focus on managing its corporate identity to today's emphasis on managing its corporate image. This change has been accompanied by another update and revision to the MasterCard visual identity projection, although this time the changes were ever so slight. Introduced

Corporate Image Management

in 1997, the most recent MasterCard logo now has only nine bars, instead of 22, within those famed interlocking circles. In addition, the word 'MasterCard' has been enlarged slightly and enhanced through the use of a drop shadow behind each letter. These are minor visual adjustments to a symbol that has come to represent global acceptance and secure transactions anywhere, any time. The big changes at MasterCard International are those related to its *Future of Money* positioning platform that is now being inculcated into its corporate culture and into its current and future strategic investment strategies.

I Love This Game

I am often asked which organisation I most admire, or which organisation I feel is doing the best job with the management of its corporate image. I'm glad when people ask 'which organisation', rather than which company or which firm. That's because my current answer is indeed an organisation, rather than a corporation, government entity or private enterprise. My vote for best managed corporate image (as of March 1998) goes to the National Basketball Association (NBA) in North America.

Basketball and soccer are arguably the two most popular sports across the globe. And while soccer may have more global participants and is watched by a greater number of spectators in an average year, the sport cannot hold a candle to the appeal and imagery of the NBA. Children on the streets from Adelaide to Anchorage, Beijing to Bogota, and London to Little Rock can be found sporting shirts, pants and caps emblazoned with the logos of the Chicago Bulls, Los Angeles Lakers, Orlando Magic and any of the other 26 teams in the NBA.

Unlike many of the other professional sports leagues, the NBA has done a stupendous job in preventing labour disputes from wrecking fan enjoyment of the game. It has also reacted promptly and correctly in disciplining its multi-million dollar athletes and in punishing unacceptable behaviour on and off the court. While the people managing Major League Baseball allowed a ballplayer who had spat on an umpire to continue playing in the 1996 playoff series while he appealed the league's decision to suspend him, Commissioner David Stern of the NBA wasted no time in benching, and keeping benched, a half dozen players on two teams who had violated the league's rules about coming off the bench during a courtside altercation. The action occurred during the semi-finals of the Eastern Conference in May 1997 and despite the full knowledge that the suspensions would likely have an impact on the final outcome of this particular Championship series, the league stuck to its guns and sent a stern message to all players that violations of the league's rules and policies would not be tolerated, under any circumstances.

While tolerating some of the crazy antics of the wild and weird Dennis Rodman, the league also wasted no time in punishing him for kicking a courtside cameraman in frustration and, later in the year, for his off-the-court publicised remarks concerning the religious beliefs of the population in Salt Lake City.

This is an organisation that truly knows how to market both its product and its image. It generates over US$1.5 billion in the United States from ticket sales, souvenirs and television rights and now has its sights firmly set on the lucrative international market. The league regularly holds exhibition games in Europe and Asia prior to the start of each season and sends one team to Europe to participate in the McDonald's Championship, a tournament that pits teams from Latin America and Europe against the best of the NBA. It even produces two shows, NBA Action and NBA Jam, solely for the international market.

Of all the athletes or other superstars in our lifetime, only a handful are recognisable by a single name—Pelé, Ali, Tiger and Michael. In a survey of 28,000 teenagers in 45 countries by the global advertising firm Darcy Massius Benton and Bowles, Michael Jordan was easily the world's favourite athlete, far ahead of Andre Agassi, Carl Lewis and Diego Maradona. Fortunately for the NBA, not only is Mr Jordan a world-class athlete with gravity-defying skills, he is also a great role model for kids of all ages (and their parents).

The NBA has been able to leverage the Michael recognition and fan appreciation factor into its image of a fast-paced, fun-filled, highly entertaining and well-managed sport. The entire wholesome experience, whether viewed live in the arena or worldwide on the hundreds of games telecast, is summed up in the NBA's tagline: 'I love this game!' Listening to NBA fans discuss their favourite teams, their favourite

Corporate Image Management

stars, or what's happening on other teams in the league, it is obvious that the NBA has developed a deep relationship with its best customers. It's no wonder that major advertisers such as Nike, Coca-Cola, McDonald's and others are falling over themselves trying to get on the NBA bandwagon.

How good is the corporate image of the NBA? I cannot think of anything they could be doing better, unless they work out how to extend the season from seven months to a full year without losing fan interest or wearing down the skills of its players. This is an organisation whose corporate image is so good, that one only wishes it would go public through an initial public offering. The NBA is certainly one shareholding I would be glad to have in my investment portfolio. Its image is one that any CEO would be proud to be associated with.

Managing and Marketing the Corporate Image

Marketing success in the future will depend on the organisation's ability to manage and market its corporate image. For organisations moving on to the era of relationship excellence and partnership excellence, there is no other choice.

Of course, you don't have to do both. You can always manage your corporate image, but not market it. That will mean that your organisation will never achieve the highest levels of success of which it is capable. It also means that relationships with employees will be far stronger than the organisation's relationships with its customers.

You can also market your corporate image, without managing it. The short term profits gained from this strategy will be quickly decimated once your customers start to receive inconsistent levels of corporate behaviour and decide to go elsewhere in search of more fruitful and rewarding relationships.

Or, you can do neither and let your corporate image develop and market itself, or have it remain hidden in the background of your marketing efforts. This strategy will enable you to remain stuck in the era of product and positioning excellence, which to some may seem like a great place to be.

However, the company that made the best slide rulers in the world found itself in the same position. It continued to make the best slide rulers right up until the day it went out of business…because it didn't realise that its core customer base of engineers had migrated to electronic calculators. If you let your corporate image go adrift, some other organisation will come along and show you the path to the corporate graveyard.

Managing and Marketing the Corporate Image

Chapter Ten

The Image Management Development Process

The corporate image management process is a circular, continuous five-phase process that can be applied at any stage of an organisation's development. Unfortunately, the process is usually marketed as a one-off 'corporate identity exercise' that CEOs resort to at times of turmoil, during periods of sweeping change, or when they desire to leave their mark on the organisation for future generations.

Corporate image management should not be an occasional stimulus that prompts the senior management of the organisation to regroup and analyse how to project the 'best' image for the organisation. It should not be a sporadic or irregular process of rethinking key issues facing the company, and then packaging a plan of action items bundled under an inflated 'mission statement' to be communicated *to* the people within the organisation by those occupying the plush carpeted private offices in the headquarters palace. It should definitely not be a series of temporary reactions to market conditions that do not change the primary value systems or conduct of the organisation.

The successive steps taken by Britain's Royal Family during the 1990s in response to the country's intermittent displays of vocal disdain are an example of the half-hearted and temporary measures which organisations should not use. When management starts to think 'our customers just don't get it', or 'if they really knew and understood us, they'd want to be our partner', the organisation has a corporate image perception problem that is not necessarily going to be repairable through marketing communications. More likely, the problem first requires internal procedures and behaviour patterns to change and be communicated through action, not a media campaign.

The Image Management Development Process

The consultants who come in and tell you that senior management needs to take time away from their busy schedules to participate in a short-term corporate identity exercise are wrong. This leads to the attitude that the corporate image can be fixed through an assigned task force that will tell the rest of the organisation what and how to communicate the corporate identity.

Corporate image management should be the driving force for a continuous thought and evaluation process for leveraging the organisation's strengths and corporate persona to evolve into the kind of organisation it desires to be. It is the constant need for self-understanding and systemic feedback from employees, customers, stakeholders and the marketplace that is at the heart of an authentic corporate image management process. It is also a never-ending process that must be integrated into all aspects of the organisation.

The five phases of the corporate image management process are:

- Preliminary Audit, Research and Evaluation
- Analysis, Strategy, Planning and Development
- Creative Exploration
- Refinement and Implementation
- Monitoring, Managing and Marketing the Corporate Image

This process helps to ensure that channels of communications within the organisation, and with all appropriate external audiences, are both fluid and multi-directional. Such fluidity helps to prevent miscommunication and better ensures that the organisation has a conscious and collective finger on the pulse of evolving market forces, marketing environment trends, changing customer needs and desires, and relationship development and maintenance requirements. Internally, the multi-directional and cross-organisational communications result in almost everyone within the organisation understanding and accepting the collective goals and knowing the importance of the path being embarked upon by the organisation. This becomes crucially important when the organisation begins to include partnering and external partnerships as part of its future growth strategy.

Corporate Image Management

The objective of the corporate image management process is to provide the organisation, on a continuing basis, with a cohesive corporate image management structure, corporate culture and a set of acceptable internal and external behavioural patterns. These translate into optimum competitive advantages, increased employee morale and loyalty and they help management map a future direction for the organisation.

Phase I—Preliminary Audit, Research and Evaluation

While a true revolving and circular process has no actual start or end point, the explanation of the corporate image management process needs to begin somewhere. Since so few organisations are currently practising this discipline, we will use a phased approach to this subject similar to that of corporate identity practitioners.

This phase begins with a thorough assessment of the organisation's market situation, existing corporate identity practices, organisational structure, and overall circumstances, including a comparative view of the corporate identity practices and resultant corporate image perceptions of competitors. The assessment is drawn from a detailed collection of all relevant information pertaining to the organisation and includes both visual elements and qualitative research findings. This evaluation also tends to uncover a wide range of corporate image related problems that would have otherwise gone undetected. Quantitative research may then be required to either confirm such findings or determine their validity.

This information gathering stage includes three key activities:

- a thorough visual audit of the entire organisation and all of its subsidiaries or associate operations,
- primary research in the form of in-depth interviews with employees, customers, stakeholders, opinion leaders, media, competitors, and many others, and
- a detailed examination of the visual competitive environment and the perceptions held by the organisation's key audiences with respect to these competitors.

The visual audit entails photographing all elements of the organisation's visible design and image management practices, including buildings, manufacturing facilities, warehouses, offices, customer purchase and service areas, customer waiting areas, interior and exterior signage, uniforms, product packaging, in-store merchandising hardware and software, furniture, fixtures, equipment, vehicles, and any other items that are observable by customers, prospects, business associates and potential business partners.

The Image Management Development Process

The corporate image management consultant will also want to collect a comprehensive array of corporate identity application media such as graphic standards manuals, promotional items, corporate gifts, sales literature, product brochures, annual reports, corporate print materials (stationery, business cards, computer-generated and other forms, compliments slips), recruitment and training literature, operations and procedure manuals, greeting cards, sales presentations, customer communications, press releases and all other marketing communications materials including print and television advertising. These materials should be subjected to a meticulous analysis by a team of experienced professionals specialising in the field of corporate identity practices, corporate communications or corporate image management. This is one part of the corporate image process that is best left to outside experts as their judgements are less influenced by internal considerations and past corporate practices.

The examination and analysis of these corporate identity applications form one component of the existing corporate image of the organisation. When completed, it should provide a summary to the organisation of how it is currently communicating itself to its various publics. At a minimum, this investigation usually yields a list of inconsistencies in applying design standards. It should also result in a list of image equities that can be built upon for the future. Lamentably, this is often where the analysis by the corporate identity practitioners terminates.

What is more important, from a corporate image management perspective, is that the organisation is comprehensively scrutinised to the extent that significant corporate behaviours and practices that impact on the corporate image are also revealed. To illustrate, here are some of the image damaging conditions discovered on corporate image management projects in which this writer was involved:

- A publicly listed manufacturing concern had a left a broken window pane unreplaced for a period of at least six months, yet it couldn't

Corporate Image Management

understand why the message on its new quality improvement initiatives were not believed by security analysts.

- A manufacturer preached a policy of treating all employees equally and putting customers first. Interestingly, the only reserved car park slot in the entire company was directly in front of the main entrance. The spot was reserved for the firm's CEO, who was transported around town in his chauffeur-driven luxury automobile. Both employees and customers had to walk carefully around his vehicle to enter the main lobby as there was not much space between the car and the front doors. Since he was dropped off at the front door anyway, there really wasn't any need, except for ego satisfaction, for his luxury car to be positioned at the main entrance. So much for equality among employees and consideration for customers.

- Companies like to place their logos everywhere, but it really isn't necessary. One company had its logo and name painted (by hand) on the 20-gallon waste containers placed around its manufacturing facility. The lids for these bins were locked and chained to steel pipes. We never learned if this meant that the organisation's management didn't trust the staff to not steal them, but we did convince them that it probably wasn't a good idea for customers and security analysts visiting the plant to see the company's name emblazoned so prominently on trash receptacles.

- One bank had only three branches in a given market, but was using four different advertising agencies to produce its marketing communications materials. It was little wonder that the various products and services on offer from this bank showed little visual resemblance to each other, though the corporate logo was consistently used in all materials thanks to a very detailed graphics standards manual.

- A retailer of fine watches prided itself on having available one of the most complete ranges of premium watches in its outlets. It couldn't understand why traffic patterns in its stores were below expectations, until it was pointed out that the glass doors to each store featured decals and labels for every credit card and discount card imaginable. Anyone paying thousands of dollars for a watch wasn't going to be enticed into the purchase just because they could use a discount card. Once the decals were removed and the aluminium frames around the doors changed to teak, both traffic levels and sales volumes increased in all outlets.

Often what needs changing or modifying is not how the corporate logo appears or is used, but several other aspects of the organisation's visual communications. Many of these go entirely unnoticed, until a proper and sweeping visual audit is conducted.

The Image Management Development Process

The second part of the initial phase comprises qualitative interviews with internal and external audiences. The internal interviews are conducted at all levels of the organisation, from front-line staff and backroom support personnel to senior management and the board of directors. The interviews with external audiences will include key customers, end users, joint venture or other business partners, shareholders or other stakeholders, suppliers, distributors, retailers, prospective customers and partners, government officials, senior media people and other outside influencers, competitors, and members of the general public.

The interviews focus on how the organisation is currently perceived by these key audiences and what perceptions are held about the company's directions for the future and its capabilities to handle or execute change. The objective is to gain an understanding of the market's perception of the organisation by its customers, partners and competition, and to contrast these perceptions with those held by various levels of its own employee and management staff. Another aim is to identify the internal will to change and to gauge the levels of acceptance for change. This will help to formulate organisation-wide acceptance of any resulting corporate image management changes.

While this research is qualitative in nature, the issues to be examined and discussed during the interview process are highly strategic in nature. The benefit of the one-on-one qualitative interview methodology is that it allows each respondent to focus on the most important points. Sometimes an evaluation of the relative time spent on different topics is as valuable as an analysis of the exact comments and statements made during the interview. An outside resource is essential for handling and analysing these interviews because of the extreme sensitivity of the topics to be covered during the discussions. Also, the consultant must ensure the complete confidentiality of each participant and must in no way reveal to the client any details or particulars that may link comments to any individual.

A sample of the types of questions that should be explored is shown below.

Corporate Image Management

Executives, Senior Management and Board Members

- What is the organisation's mission statement? Do you see a need for change? How?
- What are the two, five and ten-year plans for the organisation?
- Who are the company's key target audiences?
- How does the company market itself to these target audiences?
- What is the single most important marketing issue facing the organisation?
- What are the three most pressing marketing communications issues facing the organisation at present?
- How is the company organised? What changes would you make in the organisational structure if you could?
- Who really plays the role of marketing the organisation? What is his/her role in the strategic management process?
- How would you describe the organisation's corporate culture? What are the shared beliefs, expectations and values found within the organisation? How are these learned by new employees?
- Is there a corporate philosophy? If so, describe this in your own words? Does it need changing or updating?
- How would you describe the organisation's external image? It's internal image? Would you say that you are proud to be associated with these images? Do you see a need for change in the image? How?
- Are the activities, products, services and image of the organisation adequately communicated through the current name?
- What makes this organisation unique?
- Who are the organisation's main competitors? What are their strengths and weaknesses compared to your organisation? Are you likely to have different competitors in five years time?
- Why do people choose products or services from competitors instead of those offered by this organisation?
- Describe the organisation's change management system and how you feel personally about this system.
- What do the organisation's customers look for or consider before establishing a relationship with this organisation?

Customers

- What is your impression of the organisation's products and services?
- What are the strengths and weaknesses of this organisation?
- Would you care to be employed by the organisation? Why or why not?

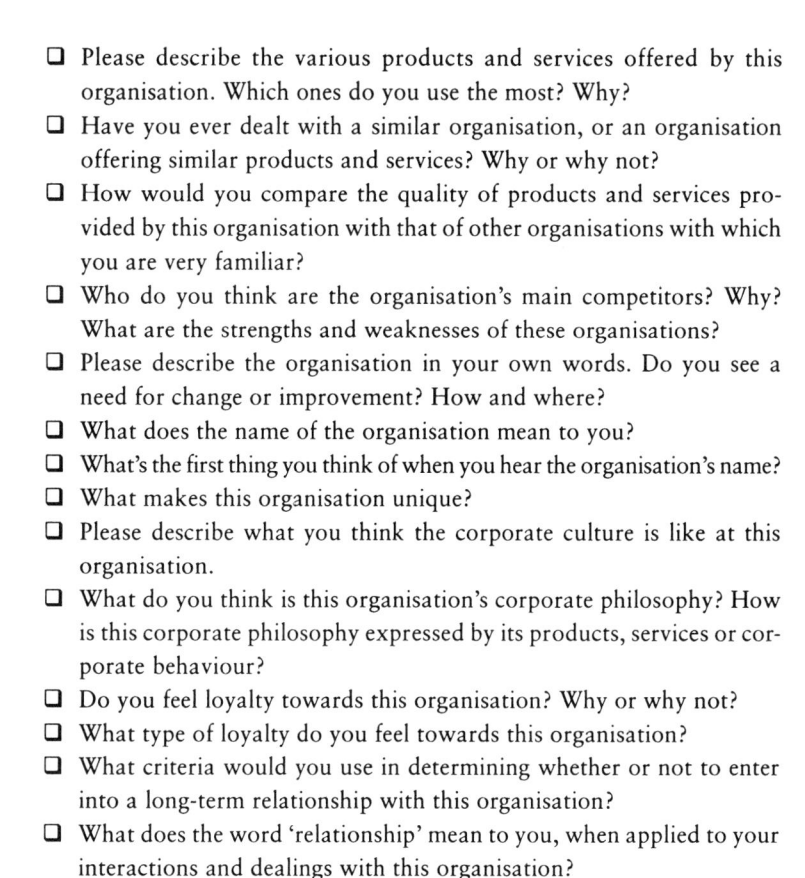

- ☐ Please describe the various products and services offered by this organisation. Which ones do you use the most? Why?
- ☐ Have you ever dealt with a similar organisation, or an organisation offering similar products and services? Why or why not?
- ☐ How would you compare the quality of products and services provided by this organisation with that of other organisations with which you are very familiar?
- ☐ Who do you think are the organisation's main competitors? Why? What are the strengths and weaknesses of these organisations?
- ☐ Please describe the organisation in your own words. Do you see a need for change or improvement? How and where?
- ☐ What does the name of the organisation mean to you?
- ☐ What's the first thing you think of when you hear the organisation's name?
- ☐ What makes this organisation unique?
- ☐ Please describe what you think the corporate culture is like at this organisation.
- ☐ What do you think is this organisation's corporate philosophy? How is this corporate philosophy expressed by its products, services or corporate behaviour?
- ☐ Do you feel loyalty towards this organisation? Why or why not?
- ☐ What type of loyalty do you feel towards this organisation?
- ☐ What criteria would you use in determining whether or not to enter into a long-term relationship with this organisation?
- ☐ What does the word 'relationship' mean to you, when applied to your interactions and dealings with this organisation?

The number of interviews required for this process to be effective is usually between 25 and 40, depending upon the size and complexity of the organisation or the anticipated likelihood by management or the consultants that a major corporate image change is required imminently. It is best if the interviews are conducted by two or more researchers or consultants, who then compare notes at the one-third point to see if any trends are developing or if the questionnaire needs adjusting.

This methodology will yield tremendous insights into the present corporate image of the organisation, as perceived both internally and externally. Because of the open-ended nature of the specific questions used, the feedback can be readily interpreted into specific observations and recommendations that can be actioned later in the corporate image management process.

Corporate Image Management

The last step of the Phase I procedure entails a visual analysis of the sales and marketing communications practices of all major competitors. As much as feasible, the same materials as those reviewed and analysed for the organisation itself should be included in the competitive visual analysis. Some of these materials, such as graphic standards manuals and sales presentations, may be hard to come by, but a great deal will be obtained effortlessly.

Once completed, a written report of the preliminary visual audit, research and evaluation should be delivered to the organisation's senior management by the corporate image management consultants detailing the findings and analysis. This professional assessment of the organisation's current image practices and its perceived internal and external images will provide management with a clear picture of the organisation's current corporate image. The other key deliverable in this phase should be a visual record (usually on 35-mm transparencies) of the organisation's current corporate identity practices and applications and those of its key competitors.

The Phase I process answers these key questions:

- ☑ How is the corporate image being portrayed and projected today?
- ☑ How is the organisation perceived by its key internal and external audiences?
- ☑ How does the image of the organisation compare with those of its competitors?
- ☑ How does the image of the organisation compare to the image desired by management?
- ☑ Will the current corporate image enable the organisation to reach the goals and objectives set for it over the next three to five years?

In short, Phase I provides the organisation with a snapshot view of where it is today, an important criterion when trying to decide where one wants to be in the foreseeable future.

Phase II—Analysis, Strategy, Planning and Development

Having established a reliable and relevant database in Phase I, the corporate image management process moves to utilising this information for strategic and tactical planning and development.

The Image Management Development Process

This phase begins with a review and critique by the external consultants of all the organisation's strategic planning and market development documents, processes and plans. This should include the corporate vision and mission statements, all corporate and divisional goals or objectives, organisational charts, multi-year strategic plans, annual marketing strategies and plans, technology investment plans, human resource staffing plans and any documents that reflect forward-looking thinking or planning by the organisation.

The corporate image management consultants should review these documents by assessing how well they integrate with one another, and how well the plans from separate divisions or separate subsidiaries match with the overall goals, objectives and plans of the corporate parent. The consultants should also identify any planning documents that have not been formalised and that create a gap in the organisation's total strategic planning process. The analysis and summary should take the form of a strategy report card and the issues illuminated in this document should be thoroughly discussed with the management team before continuing the corporate image management process.

Once the strategic vision and all the appropriate planning documents have been settled, the findings of the Phase I audit and research are applied to the strategic direction being planned by the organisation. Through a series of interactive sessions between the external consultants and the key managers within the organisation, specific and strategic objectives for the corporate image, marketing, and marketing communications can be developed that will form the platform for guiding future business and corporate image development.

In these interactive sessions, a range of potential marketing and corporate positioning strategies will be discussed and evaluated. For each alternative, a set of corporate image marketing strategies will be defined and reviewed. The objective is to define a corporate positioning strategy based on the organisation's key corporate attributes, as discovered through the research process of Phase I. Unlike the corporate identity model, the goal is not to define a corporate *image* positioning strategy. It is the organisation's strategic positioning that needs to be determined, thus allowing the corporate identity to be a true *reflection of this positioning*. Organisations entering into relationship marketing activities will not be able to live up to artificially created image positions. The days of developing

Corporate Image Management

strategic marketing advantages through clever image positioning are waning. Instead, it is the organisations themselves that will need to be strategically positioned, based upon the desired corporate characteristics and attributes that can be truly and honestly inculcated deeply and broadly within their specific corporate cultures.

The result of this corporate positioning strategy should be an agreed:

- corporate image mission statement,
- corporate image objectives,
- corporate image strategy,
- desired corporate attributes, and
- corporate positioning platform.

In order for each of these elements to be meaningful and relevant to the organisation's key internal and external audiences, they will need to be directly and closely linked to the organisation's key management strategies, as expressed through the:

- corporate vision statement,
- corporate mission statement,
- corporate philosophy,
- corporate values, and
- corporate strategic plan.

Often, as the organisation comes to grips with defining its new or revised corporate positioning platform or its corporate image mission and objectives, there will be a need to revise or revamp the existing corporate vision and mission statements. If, for whatever reason, any or all of these statements do not exist within the organisation, then they should be developed as part of the corporate image management process.

The corporate image management process is also an excellent opportunity for the entire organisation to inspect and ensure that the mission statements and marketing objectives of each subsidiary, division or associate company support the overall corporate vision and mission. As illustrated with the example of the broad-based Malaysian financial services firm discussed in Chapter Three, the vision and mission outlined by the CEO and senior managers of the parent company are not always reflected and supported in the strategic plans and objective statements of all the organisation's varied units.

At the conclusion of Phase II, the organisation should have a well-defined corporate positioning platform that is supported by the core attributes of the organisation, and a series of strategic image marketing objectives that will help to guide future business and corporate image development. Additionally, the organisation should have a unified set of vision, mission and value statements that can be uniformly applied across all segments of the organisation.

At this point, the consultants and the organisation need to address the issue of whether the existing corporate identity structure requires any changes, enhancements or even a total revamp. If so, these strategies should now be combined with a detailed analysis of the Phase I research findings in order to produce an overview of the organisation's total corporate image and image management system needs. This overview will be used to develop a detailed brief for the Phase III Creative Exploration stage. Incorporated into this brief should be a timeline and action plan upon which to base the development and execution of the corporate image management system.

Phase III—Creative Exploration

It is only in Phase III that the corporate image management process begins to take a serious look at making changes to the existing corporate identity system used by the organisation. In this phase, the tasks entail the creative exploration of design and nomenclature concepts that have been created in direct response to the strategic criteria established in the first two phases. As such, the strategic planning and marketing consultants take a step back and allow the graphic design teams to lead this project phase.

In many cases, the primary concern of senior management and the design team is to come up with a new or revised name. Together with the selection of a corporate symbol, choosing a name is one of the most subjective processes any senior manager is likely to experience. Unfortunately, there is no universal methodology or systematic approach to the development of names or logos.

The two most important criteria for a name are that it should:

- be easily memorable to the organisation's key audiences, and
- differentiate the organisation from others in its industry or field.

Corporate Image Management

As for symbols, the choices available to the organisation may include abstract, illustrative, logotype, computer-generated or other types of graphic designs. Where feasible, both the name and the symbol should include any positive image equities from the existing name and logo, if such equities were identified by a significant number of participants in the Phase I research.

More important than the name and logo selection is the decision on which nomenclature system to use. This can range from the unified approach, where every division or subsidy uses the corporate name, to the endorsed approach, where units are given their own names and identities, but are shown to relate to the parent organisation through the use of a phrase like 'A member of the XYZ Group'. The structure of the nomenclature system has major strategic implications for the organisation, because it determines how closely the various entities are aligned or associated within a single holding company.

Throughout this phase, the designers and the client engage in a series of interactive working sessions. In addition to evaluating alternative names and symbols, the teams explore typeface selection and colour palette combinations. The final shortlist of recommended solutions is usually demonstrated in prototypal applications such as corporate stationery, business cards and building signage. Once a decision is taken on the name and logo combination, along with typeface and colours, the designers must ensure that the proposed solution works equally well across all elements of the corporate image management system identified in Phase II.

At the conclusion of Phase III, the organisation should have an agreed creative solution that includes name, symbol, nomenclature system, colour palette and recommended corporate typefaces. In addition, an image platform should be developed as part of this phase, to provide a summary description of the new image to be used for briefing suppliers such as interior designers, advertising agencies and public relations consultants.

Phase IV—Refinement and Implementation

In the fourth and penultimate phase, all necessary refinements to the final design solution are made in order to complete the finished identity and image management system. This system encompasses the complete nomenclature criteria as applied to the organisation's divisions, wholly owned subsidiaries, joint venture operations and other applications. As part of this system, the designers should recommend secondary typefaces and the use of secondary or alternative colours.

The approved design is then applied to various client-directed media, such as vehicles, uniforms, external and internal signage and corporate stationery. The most important part of the implementation stage is the development and production of a graphics standards manual. This is a control document that should exhaustively cover almost all applications of the new corporate identity system in order to ensure consistency and integrity in all forms. The graphics standards manual, which will be discussed in detail in another chapter, should be widely distributed throughout the organisation and to all outside resources that are called upon to reproduce any element of the corporate identity system.

Before the new identity system is released publicly, the consultants and designers should ensure that all departments and individuals within the organisation are properly briefed and trained in the benefits and proper use of the image management system. Procedures should also be established during these training sessions for contacting the designers should questions arise or if further explanation is needed.

At the conclusion of Phase IV, the organisation will have received the master artwork for its new identity system, a series of applications within various media, and usage training in applying the new system. It should also have in hand a comprehensive and detailed graphics standards manual to ensure consistency in use across the entire organisation for future reference.

Phase V—Monitoring, Managing and Marketing the Corporate Image

Even though the graphics standards manual and the master artwork have been delivered at the conclusion of Phase IV, the corporate image process does not come to an end. To begin with, both the designers and the client need to monitor old materials and inventories of forms, stationery, corporate gifts and other items to ensure that these are expeditiously replaced as stocks dwindle. In addition, suppliers need to be monitored to safeguard the new corporate identity system standards.

Corporate Image Management

The marketing and strategy consultants now return to the forefront of the project. Unlike the corporate identity practices of the past, the corporate image management process cannot afford, and does not allow, the new corporate image to simply be projected through an identity system and marketing communications. Rather, the new corporate image, based on the strategies resolved in Phase II, needs to be *lived by the organisation*. This is the only way for the desired corporate image to be effectively *delivered*, instead of merely projected, by the organisation.

To assure the correct delivery of the corporate image, managers throughout the organisation (or governors of the organisation, as I would prefer to see), will need to concentrate on:

- *translating* the corporate vision, mission and values into realistic and understandable business unit objectives, corporate procedures and policies, and acceptable patterns of corporate behaviour,
- *balancing* contradictory demands and interests of employees, customers, prospects, shareholders, stakeholders and others, while *maximising* the communications flow within the organisation and between the organisation and its key audiences,
- *building* layers of trust within the organisation and between employee work groups, so that the corporate vision and mission can be the common goal of the entire organisation,
- *establishing* feedback mechanisms to optimise the flexibility of processes and procedures and minimise the response times of the organisation to customer needs, market opportunities and external change agents,
- *governing* work teams and multidisciplinary or interdepartmental task forces so that organisational, individual professional and personal goals and objectives can be attained through collaboration, open communication, team spirit and shared experiences,
- *training* and other continuous learning programs that teach flexibility, interpersonal relationship skills, and coaching techniques in addition to core job-related and task accomplishment skill sets, and
- *communicating* at all times, in all directions, with bosses, peers, subordinates, suppliers, external resources, opinion leaders, customers, prospects, business partners and all other key corporate constituents.

Managing and marketing the corporate image involves a great deal more than simply changing or refining the graphic and visual elements of an organisation. Instead, managing and marketing the corporate image focuses, defines, redefines and constantly adapts the interactions, experiences, and relationships of the organisation with all of its various constituents. *The result is that a well-managed corporate image provides and maintains a solid corporate culture, a firm basis for strong customer relationships, and the foundation for market flexibility—three criteria required for success in an ever-changing global marketplace.*

The Image Management Development Process

This process of corporate culture development and corporate image management should actually begin simultaneously with the Phase III creative exploration phase. This will give the organisation's managers time to evaluate how best to entrench the corporate vision, mission, values and philosophy into the organisation's culture. Through these procedures, management can utilise the corporate image management process as a successful catalyst for change (see Chapter Three for a discussion on this issue).

As highlighted in the previous chapter, the managing and marketing of the corporate image will be continuous and pro-active for the leaders of organisations entering the age of relationship marketing excellence. While the reader is certainly encouraged to read the previous chapter time and time again, the underlining principle of that chapter (and indeed of this entire book) bears repeating here:

> *If it touches the customer, it's a marketing issue. If it's a marketing issue, it's a central part of the corporate image management process.*

The corporate image management process is designed to give organisations greater control over the way they are perceived by their key audiences. This is mostly accomplished through the Phase V focus on monitoring, managing and marketing the corporate image on a continuous basis. Successful organisations in the future will be the ones that understand and implement the corporate image management process, and not the ones relying on the old methodology of positioning excellence through the projection of a manufactured corporate identity system.

Chapter Eleven

The Corporate Identity System

Ms Jenny Bigio, managing director of Write-Angles, a design firm in Singapore, has an interesting way of describing the importance of the corporate identity system to clients. 'Imagine', she says, 'wearing the same outfit to work all day, every day, year in and year out. An outfit that must differentiate you from everyone else on this planet. An outfit that defines your character, all facets of your personality in a clear, compelling way. An outfit that attracts and keeps the right people in your orbit. An outfit that is as uniquely yours as your thumbprint'.

'This is the essence of corporate imaging', she concludes. 'Like one's own DNA imprint, no two organisations are exactly the same. The corporate image manifests in a visual and verbal identity that is your mark of recognition. It's the "outfit" that is the expression of your organisation's unique personality.'

The corporate identity system is the visual representation and graphic style of an organisation, usually taking the form of a corporate signature combined with a corporate symbol or logo. These are used to visually and graphically distinguish the organisation from its competitors and to visually and graphically differentiate the enterprise in the global marketplace through a consistent use of typeface, colour palette and logo identifier.

According to the corporate literature of Lippincott & Margulies Inc., it was George Lippincott who coined the term 'corporate identity'. He used

The Corporate Identity System

the term to 'encompass all the ways a company identifies itself, from a new corporate name and logo to the colour of a factory building'. Today, practitioners of the art of corporate identity focus on the consistent projection of corporate identity elements throughout all applications in what is termed the 'corporate identity system'.

The key elements of the corporate identity system are: corporate legal signature, corporate signature, logo or symbol, strategic business unit (SBU) corporate signatures, nomenclature structure, typography, and corporate colour palette. The system may also include approved variations and alternatives, such as secondary colours, support typography, SBU logos or symbols, and special applications (for instance how to incorporate the system into joint ventures, where two or more logos need to appear together).

While we have given greater importance to the management and marketing of the corporate image throughout this manuscript, this should not be interpreted as an indication that the corporate identity system is not important. On the contrary, we feel that the corporate identity system is of the utmost importance in helping the organisation to project a uniform and consistent image to its various audiences. The corporate identity system is also critical for ensuring that the organisation achieves the marketing stage of positioning excellence, one of the three essential steps before the tiers of relationship excellence and partnership excellence can be seriously considered.

The corporate identity is the primary expression of how the organisation views itself, and is also crucial to the relationship building process. The organisation is saying to its customers, prospects or future business partners, 'This is who we are'. Whether they know who they truly are or not is one of the factors deciding whether the organisation's message is believed and accepted by its audiences.

While I believe that bonds between customers and brands can be created through product and service brand identity systems, I do not feel that the same applies to corporate identity systems. A corporate identity system may project levels of leadership, quality, care, community concern or innovative problem-solving solutions to customer needs, but authentic and deep emotional bonds created with organisations can come only through actual experience and interaction with the corporate entity.

Corporate Image Management

I have seen and read a lot of the sales literature from corporate identity design firms that discuss how their particular processes and design strategies help build emotional responses and bonds of trust between a company and its audiences. But when one looks closer at the examples these design firms offer, almost all are strictly product brands or for corporations that use the mega branding strategy. Corporate identity system solutions are great for product branding, but do little, on their own, to create emotional bonds and deep-seated levels of understanding and appreciation for the corporate brand. The exceptions to this are corporate identity systems for service firms, such as airlines and hotels, where the product brand cannot be separated from the corporate brand.

There is no doubt that a successful identity system does much more than simply create an identification for the organisation. At a minimum, the identity system should create something memorable and distinctive about the organisation, something that enables the organisation to stand out from the crowd. In the best executions, a corporate identity system will provide a unique positioning platform for the organisation, something that allows customers and others to develop a feeling of familiarity with the organisation. Familiarity, however, is but one step on the road to relationship building and organisational leaders should not be swayed that high brand and corporate awareness scores are the ultimate desired outcome for their investments in the corporate identity exercise.

Up until the present, the contrived niche positioning platforms carved out for clients by the strategic design and corporate identity consultants have been sufficient to catapult organisations into leadership positions on the rungs of the positioning excellence ladder. Today, however, the marketing battle has begun to move from the mind of the customer (in which the battles of positioning have and will continue to take place) into the heart and soul of the customer (where the struggle for relationship excellence and partnership excellence will take place). For future marketing success, the corporate identity system will need to be constructed from the core values, cultures, processes, procedures and visions of the organisation. In other words, organisations will have to move away from relying on corporate identity development and projection as a cure-all for their marketing problems to understanding how to incorporate the corporate image management process into their daily activities and strategic thinking. For many organisations, this will be a difficult and fundamental shift from current thinking about corporate identity and communications.

Shifting Sands

The importance of the corporate identity system becomes even greater when it is part of the corporate image management process. This is because the holistic approach of the corporate image management process requires the corporate identity system to be extended to areas not traditionally covered by the strategic designers and the identity design consultants.

Traditionally, organisations have delegated the design of products to engineers; the design of packaging to package designers or suppliers; the design of plants, offices and retail space to architects; the design of advertising to advertising agencies; and the design of corporate stationery to printers, local designers or other suppliers. Each of these design professionals will execute to the best of their ability, according to their understanding of the particular problem at hand. Historically, however, each designer would use his particular skill and craft without a knowledge or understanding of the overall corporate mission, positioning platform, or even customer base. Without knowledge of the organisation's long-term objectives or corporate positioning platform, the resulting solutions would be well designed, but often have no relevance or interconnectedness with the items being designed and developed by the other design professionals. Sure, the corporate signature and logo would always be used properly, and the corporate colour guidelines adhered to, but there would be no consistency in any other aspect (like the bank in Chapter Ten that had three retail bank branches and four design companies working on customer communications materials and product branding strategies).

By forcing the creative exploration and execution work into the third and fourth phases of the corporate image management process, the designers are compelled to base their design ideas and strategies on the Phase I research findings and the Phase II strategic contemplations and corporate image strategy decisions. At the same time, the design of the corporate identity system *must be extended beyond the mere development of the corporate signature, logo, typography and colour palette*. The corporate identity system must include specifics and guidelines on the quality of paper stock, key copywriting messages, projection of the organisation's corporate values, product branding criteria and the design of physical environments.

Corporate Image Management

To accomplish this, graphic designers will have to understand basic marketing principles, to be versed in the psychology of modern customer service, to develop an appreciation of the skills and qualities it takes to communicate on a global basis, and to be competent in several areas of architectural design and workplace layouts. Simply being seasoned in crafting artistically rich corporate symbols and award-winning logo designs will no longer be sufficient.

Customers and business partners want to experience relationships built on solid and substantial criteria. In the kingdom of marketing excellence based on positioning excellence, the projected corporate identity system is to be supported by the activities of the organisation. In this realm, designers create the image standard bearer that proclaims 'This is what we are telling you we are' and the organisation is asked to live up to this proclamation. In the kingdom of marketing excellence based on relationship excellence, the core values and culture of the organisation are projected through corporate behaviour patterns. Here, the designers must create a complete identity system that proclaims 'This is who we are, what we are and what we believe in, as you will find out through your experiences and interactions with us'. In this realm, the corporate identity system is a reflection of the organisation, rather than a fabricated image positioning and identity system.

Under today's practices, organisations often do not live up to their projected billing through their actual corporate behaviour patterns. Management's eye is too often on the quarterly financial numbers, the daily stock price swings, and the assurance that the corporate logo and colour palette are being used properly at all times. When the sands of the organisation start to shift, and the customer starts to experience inconsistent service delivery, the organisation is not structured (either organisationally or culturally) so that these changes are noticed and handled at an early stage. Like the shifting sands beneath a child's sandcastle, weaknesses in the foundation soon start to impact at all levels. The solution is not another corporate identity exercise or massive marketing communications campaign to convince customers of some newfound strength or unique position. The solution is to apply Phases I, II and V of the corporate image management process. The solution is to have the corporate identity system, and the projection of this identity, match the genuine nature of the organisation.

Environmental Identity

Rarely does the definition of the corporate identity system include the physical environment in which the organisation's products and services are presented to the public. In the world of corporate image management, even the distribution channels need to be considered when designing and implementing the corporate identity system.

Wherever customers can come into contact with the organisation's products and services, important information will be communicated about the market positioning of the products, services and the corporate image of the organisation. A high-priced branded good appears out of place if found in a discount store, and in this situation customers degrade their opinions of the product, rather than upgrade their opinions of the retail outlet.

The setting of customer expectations is an important part of the design of the environmental identity (as it is also for the entire subject of corporate image management). Banks, government institutions and doctors' offices are notorious for being inadequate in this area, particularly when it comes to the waiting time for service. Disneyland, on the other hand, has this issue down pat. In the queues for all its major rides, the amusement park places signs that indicate how long the wait will be from that particular point. There are usually two to four signs for each queue, depending upon the public demand for each ride, and the signs are spaced 10 to 15 minutes apart. In each case, the consumer usually reaches the entrance to the ride three to five minutes earlier than expected…because Disneyland has purposely set customer expectations for a longer period than is normally required at each signpost. The result: happy customers who wait for less time than expected. Does this have a positive impact on the corporate image of Disneyland and the Walt Disney Company? You bet it does.

Does this have anything to do with the corporate identity system? No, not under the old way of thinking, except that each sign must use the correct typography, corporate colours and proper corporate signature. But in our new way of thinking, not only is the Disneyland strategy a crucial factor in the corporate image system, but so too is the entire queue management system. Both the signage strategy and the queue management system are the results of a corporate image platform for Disneyland that probably says something like 'We will strive to surpass customer expectations at all times'. By setting the corporate image platform criteria first,

Corporate Image Management

and then designing all aspects of the corporate identity system to meet them, an organisation like Disney can live up to its corporate image through its corporate behaviour actions.

The corporate image of an airline is affected not only by its on-board service, but also by the look and feel of the aircraft interiors, the design of its ticketing offices, and the speed and efficiency of check-in facilities. The image of petroleum companies is affected by the cleanliness of their petrol stations, as well as the ease of using pumps, whether payments can be made at the pump islands or in another area, and whether or not their stations have car wash facilities. Many petrol stations are also mini-marts, with a range of non-petroleum products on sale such as drinks, food and other groceries. The image of petroleum companies may also be based then on whether they have entered the retail grocery and convenience store industries.

Environmental identity design is an important part of the corporate identity system since the environmental systems and atmosphere can either reinforce or tarnish the corporate image. Environmental design, however, should be more than the standard application of name, symbol and logotype to a retail, distribution, factory, warehouse or office environment. It should encompass all elements that contribute to the ambiance of a locale: lighting, fixtures, furniture, artwork, carpeting, interior and directional signage, as well as customer waiting areas, payment counters, self-service areas, selling and product information systems, queue management, traffic patterns and flows, merchandise return areas, storage areas for files and paperwork, storage areas for employee personal effects, and employee rest areas.

A strategically planned environmental identity, based on the corporate image platform developed during Phase II, is yet another important way for the organisation to manage and market its corporate image.

Corporate Identity as a Marketing Tool

A strong corporate identity (as contrasted with a strong corporate image) can be an important lever for organisations in supporting the marketing efforts of their products, services and brands. Creating powerful and positive perceptions about the corporate brand will always enhance the marketing and selling of products and services, particularly for organisations occupying unique niches within their respective industries.

The Corporate Identity System

The role and importance of the corporate identity, of course, depend on whether the organisation is pursuing a positioning excellence marketing strategy or one of the other marketing excellence strategies. For those engaged in marketing warfare in the trenches of positioning excellence, the strength and singularity of the organisation's corporate identity will be one of its most strategic weapons. For those seguing to the pursuit of relationship excellence, the corporate identity will need to represent authentically the organisation's corporate persona.

In the most competitive markets, product and brand advertising is often not sufficient to ensure success. This is doubly true when one or more competitors in the same industry has managed to develop a positive identity for the corporate brand through communications or its community service activities. An organisation with a healthy corporate identity amongst customers and prospects will be rewarded, because buyers will more willingly assume that it produces quality products and provides quality services to support its products. An understanding of this customer buying psychology has resulted in billions of dollars of corporate advertising, public relations and other corporate communication expenditures through the years. The firms most likely to benefit from communications of the corporate identity will be those that use dual branding or megabranding strategies.

In each case, the communications have tried to establish one or more aspects of the corporate character as another reason for customers to purchase products, services or brands from that particular organisation. The same holds true for non-profit organisations, whose corporate communications are designed to tell us why we should volunteer our time or donate our funds to support their particular cause. Without a doubt, the corporate identity is a valuable marketing tool, particularly as a technique for winning 'mind share' as a prelude to capturing market share.

One of the strategies for winning greater mind share is simply to create a memorable and easily recognisable name for the organisation. For instance, in the first half of 1997, a record 100 publicly listed companies in the United States underwent name changes. Of these, 57 were listed on the Big Board of the New York Stock Exchange, showing that large and

Corporate Image Management established firms are finding it necessary to change their corporate identities in order to meet changing market conditions. In doing so, one has to keep in mind who the key audience is for the name change. I have observed numerous name changes that appear to encourage recognition on Wall Street rather than in the minds of consumers.

On the other hand, an organisation with very strong and powerful product brands might hinder the customer buying process if it attempted to link its corporate identity with the brand imagery. One example is PepsiCo, which owns and markets several stalwart individual brands in addition to its soft drinks: Frito-Lay, Pizza Hut, Taco Bell, and KFC (the new name for Kentucky Fried Chicken). For PepsiCo, concentrating on promoting its individual brands makes more strategic sense than trying to link any of these to the Pepsi-Cola soft drinks brand. And, at the same time, it is doubtful whether PepsiCo could sell a greater number of soft drinks by linking its restaurants and snack food businesses in the minds of consumers to its drinks business. However, when one changes target audiences and thinks of the financial investment community, then PepsiCo may be better off promoting the totality of its businesses. This, of course, can be a difficult switch to make, since all individual and professional investors will also be part of the core audiences for each of the company's key brands. This difficult communications scenario may be one reason why PepsiCo is in the process (at the time of writing) of spinning off its restaurant businesses into a separate publicly listed company.

Uncontrollable Icons

One of the problems that organisations can face occurs when its corporate identity icon overshadows the corporate image, becoming something that can no longer be controlled.

Bill Gates, CEO of Microsoft, is an example of this corporate identity problem. His image, and the press that is generated on him and his views, eclipses all other components of Microsoft's corporate identity. He is inseparable from Microsoft and as his identity grows in stature and size, that of Microsoft diminishes. At this point in time, the corporate image of Microsoft cannot be managed or developed without taking into consideration the presence, role and image of Mr Gates. To me this is a most interesting and spectacular phenomenon, for Microsoft may be one of the few companies that has already climbed onto the ladder of relationship marketing. Yet, though the organisation delivers and executes in a 'Microsoft manner', the overwhelming image of the company is not related to its ubiquitous software products, but rather to the image and persona of its CEO. Perhaps only when he steps away from full time involvement with Microsoft will this organisation be able to project and deliver a corporate image based on the Microsoft culture, values and customer experiences.

Britain's Royal Family is in an even more challenging position. For all its pomp and splendour, and the legacy of a corporate identity system dating back hundreds of years, this organisation is more likely to be identified and associated with Princess Diana than with any other symbol or icon for the next couple of decades. Even in her death, the Princess of Wales will pose a troubling image problem for the House of Windsor, probably at least until the heir after Prince William. If Prince Charles assumes the throne, the story of Diana's troubled marriage and tragic ending will become front-page news all over again. The same will occur if and when either of her two sons assumes the throne.

The image of Diana, the beautiful but heavy-hearted Princess of Wales, will tower over any new or revised corporate identity the Royal Family can concoct. In many ways, Diana was a dreamed up fairy tale designed to improve the waning image of the Royal Family in the early 1980s. Beautiful, charming, and graceful, she became the ideal marketing icon for the House of Windsor, particularly after producing the required 'heir and a spare'. But, so powerful was this new corporate icon of the Royal Family that she soon began to outshine all other symbols of the British monarchy, including the Queen, the highly popular Queen Mother, and her husband Prince Charles, the next heir to the royal throne.

In the case of both Microsoft and the British Royal Family we see the potential problems that may occur when the communications of the corporate identity overwhelm the organisation's ability to deliver on the identity or on its ability to ensure that the corporate identity is a true reflection of the organisation. In each case, the corporate identity icon has taken on a greater life of its own, causing problems or damage to the organisation's future corporate image management capabilities. As in many other aspects of marketing and corporate image management, there are risks inherent in using the corporate identity, or one of the corporate identity elements, as a strategic marketing tool.

Corporate Image Management

The Corporate Identity Checklist

As we have emphasised throughout this book, there is a great deal more to the corporate identity system than name, signatures, logo, use of colours and choice of typography. Remembering that everything that touches the customer, or any other key audience, has a direct or indirect impact on the perceived corporate image, here is a partial list of items that the corporate identity designer must consider when designing the corporate identity system. These are also elements of the corporate identity system that should be evaluated during the Phase I visual audit procedure.

Corporate stationery

- ❏ Letterheads
- ❏ Continuation sheets
- ❏ Inter-office memos
- ❏ Compliments slips
- ❏ Samples of customer communications
- ❏ Name cards
- ❏ Envelopes
- ❏ Mailing labels
- ❏ Invoices
- ❏ Price lists
- ❏ Customer applications or order forms
- ❏ Customer name, phone and address change forms
- ❏ Customer statements
- ❏ Customer late notices
- ❏ Payment demands
- ❏ Payment receipts
- ❏ Purchase orders
- ❏ Purchase acknowledgements
- ❏ Delivery receipts
- ❏ Shipping papers
- ❏ Computer-generated reports
- ❏ Computer-generated customer communications
- ❏ Employment applications
- ❏ Press releases
- ❏ Payroll advices
- ❏ Company cheques
- ❏ Note pads
- ❏ Corporate gifts

- Proposals sent to customers or business partners
- Certificates used for employee or customer recognition
- Certificates used for employee training
- Training manuals and binders
- Safety manuals and binders
- Product instruction sheets
- Product installation sheets
- Nameplates (doors and desks)
- Long-service rewards and recognition
- Company vehicles
- Uniforms and other company clothing

Corporate literature
- Annual reports
- Quarterly reports
- Corporate brochure
- Corporate video or CD-ROM
- Press kits
- In-house newsletter or employee magazines
- Publications on staff guidelines, corporate policies
- Corporate invitation cards

Marketing and sales
- Product brochures and catalogues
- Sales leaflets and brochures
- Sales videos or CD-ROMs
- Sales bulletins sent to distributors, field sales staff
- Sales manuals
- Portable exhibits and displays
- Product displays
- Print advertising
- Television and radio advertising
- Direct mail
- Point-of-sale materials (counter cards, posters, store decals)
- Merchandising materials and retail sales aids
- Sponsorship materials
- Products
- Product packages
- Shipping materials

Corporate Image Management

Environmental elements

- ☐ Office layouts
- ☐ Factories and manufacturing plants
- ☐ Warehouses
- ☐ Show rooms and display areas
- ☐ Retail outlets
- ☐ Customer waiting areas
- ☐ Payment counters or areas
- ☐ Customer service areas
- ☐ Returned merchandise areas
- ☐ Queue management systems
- ☐ External and internal signage
- ☐ Directional signage (external and internal)
- ☐ Entrances and exits
- ☐ Car parking facilities
- ☐ Lighting
- ☐ Fixtures
- ☐ Furniture
- ☐ Carpeting
- ☐ Window blinds and curtains

Chapter Twelve

Implementing a New Corporate Image System

Implementing a new or revised corporate image system is both difficult and time consuming. It is not something to be delivered or implemented overnight. And, like many other strategic processes, senior management and others are likely to become frustrated at its slow implementation pace and tire of the new system before many others in the organisation have begun to come to terms with it.

For every corporate image program it is important to establish a prioritised roll-out plan that incorporates explanatory training sessions for all employees as well as honest, open communication structures complete with confidential feedback mechanisms. The corporate image program needs to be implemented gradually, as few organisations can afford to stop and close the doors one day and reopen them the next under a new corporate image umbrella.

The corporate image program should be planned to be implemented in stages, with the internal communications and processes coming first and the public announcements and displays following. While the Phase III creative exploration is in progress, the task force for internal corporate image change should identify how the change will be communicated to staff and which aspects of the public unveiling of the new image should be given priority. At the same time, the entire organisation should be taking inventory of forms, stationery, marketing literature, and other corporate collateral materials in order to prevent large restocking orders taking

Corporate Image Management

place just prior to the disclosure of the new image. This process usually yields two benefits:

- a number of forms and reports are identified that are really no longer necessary and thus can be discarded for the future, and
- tremendous savings can be realised by properly planning the replacement cycles for printed materials to coincide with the scheduled launch of the new corporate identity system.

To achieve the first benefit, every form and report in the organisation should be reviewed in terms of reason for its existence, actual use, function, and absolute necessity. In the case of one organisation in Singapore, the corporate image management consultant team and the client 'forms task force' identified over one-third of the forms being used at that time as either redundant, out-dated, no longer required, or better off being incorporated into one or more other forms. The total savings to the client amounted to tens of thousands of dollars on an annual basis just in reduced printing costs, not to mention the money saved in wasted staff time from filling and filing forms that had no real utility or value. Citibank in Singapore went through a comparable exercise with computer-generated management information system reports produced on a daily, weekly and monthly basis. Again, well over one-third of the reports were no longer required. By eliminating surplus reports the strains on the bank's space and its computer systems were reduced. The cost savings equalled three or four middle level salaries. These are the types of savings and benefits that come from the corporate image management process and that are not as easily discovered or revealed with the design-directed corporate identity exercise.

If the new corporate image platform is a result of a fresh or revised corporate vision, corporate mission, newly identified or defined corporate values, or any other changes to the corporate culture or to the existing organisational structure, then the organisation will need to invest in a change process operation. This may entail internal focus group sessions, multidepartmental and interdisciplinary task forces, off-site training sessions or other methods to cascade the changes from top to bottom. These techniques must also channel detailed feedback about concerns, disillusions, questions, anger, fear, uncertainties, disagreements, and any sense of unwillingness to enact the changes, from the bottom to the top of the organisation pyramid. (For more on managing change, see Chapter Fifteen.)

These sessions should not be planned as one-way communications meetings with a lot of razzmatazz and attempts to obtain immediate acceptance of the new concepts. Instead, they should be interactive and highly participatory meetings, whose main purpose is to elicit comments and feedback rather than achieve immediate acceptance and commitment. It's best to think of this the way you would handle moving your family to a new neighbourhood or a different city. You wouldn't just come home, pack the house, and take the family to its new abode and say 'This is it, I hope you like it and will commit to living here'. More likely you would sit down with each family member, explain the rationale for making the move, highlight some of the expected benefits of the new place, and inquire about each person's key concerns, fears, worries or expectations. This is the same process that the change agents in the organisation need to use with each and every staff member (and sometimes with key clients, customers, suppliers or other business partners). Acceptance and commitment will come soon enough. First the participants in the change have to:

- feel that they are willing participants in the change process,
- come to their own understanding of why the change is occurring and what it means to them, and
- identify for themselves the most relevant and important benefits to be gained from the change.

The early acceptors and adopters of the change will become key proponents of the new corporate philosophy and values, thus creating social pressure on others to jump aboard the change bandwagon. This will be the time to start thinking about how to rally all the troops around the new corporate identity flag and how to obtain their final acceptance and commitment to the new corporate value system, processes and structure.

While most executives understand the importance of sending frequent messages to customers and the general public, very few seem willing to apply this same technique to internal audiences. Time and again I have seen new corporate image platforms and corporate identity systems communicated to employees as a one-time event. There is the grand corporate announcement, accompanied by perhaps one explanatory article in the organisation's employee newsletter. And that's it! Hundreds or thousands of different individuals, each with their own level of commitment to and understanding of the previous corporate identity, are now fully expected

Corporate Image Management

to totally understand and accept something in one message that took hundreds of hours to conceptualise, formulate, verbalise and agree upon. Shocking, isn't it? Yet it happens so frequently that I have almost become immune to the insensitive nature of this type of thinking and action. However, its regularity has hardened my belief in the need for organisations to implement on-going corporate image management processes that will force senior executives to pay more attention to the manner and methods used to communicate strategic developments and initiatives to staff.

Only after all levels of the organisation have become thoroughly versed in the new corporate image platform and the new corporate identity structure will it be time to release the new image to the public. For some organisations, it may be best not to use advertising or public relations to announce the new image, but rather to execute and perform according to the new corporate guidelines. Allowing customers to experience the 'new us' is a more sagacious blueprint for success than using the marketing communications budget to tell customers about the 'new us'. Of course, it is a rare senior executive or CEO who is willing to spend thousands of dollars in shaping a new corporate image but who then does not want to go out and tell the world about his just-finished creation.

The unveiling of the new corporate image is a precarious juncture for the organisation. Getting this wrong is a hazard that is hard—sometimes impossible—to overcome. There is little margin for error, yet too often we see corporate image and corporate identity launch campaigns that are either rushed jobs or not fully thought through. One of the problems is that, a few weeks or months before the scheduled launch, the advertising agency or public relations firm is called in, given a short overview of the new corporate image and, if they are lucky, a one-page written brief. They are then asked to formulate a communication plan for the new image, often additionally hampered by a limited budget for execution.

Two major errors often occur during this process:

- the corporate image management consultants who have been working on the project for months are not involved in briefing the communications agency or in working closely with them in the development of the launch campaign, and
- the communications company is expected to fully understand all of the intricacies of the corporate image platform, the corporate values,

and the corporate vision and mission despite not being involved in the processes that led to them.

The words, feelings and emotions contained in these statements are often interpreted differently by the communications company to the definitions determined by the task forces working on these issues.

A further error is to tie the launch of the new image into some other major corporate event where the messages competing for attention will dilute each other.

As a result of seeing several corporate image launch campaigns go astray, I advocate having representatives of the communications company participate in the corporate image management process from the start of the Phase II Analysis, Strategy, Planning and Development stage. If not feasible, such as when the organisation does not have a current long-term relationship with a specific communications company, then the corporate image management consultants engaged for the project should be capable of handling the launch and post-launch communications activities on behalf of the client, either directly or indirectly in partnership with others. It takes active involvement in the determination process to be able to communicate and explain a new corporate image system credibly.

The final requirement for the pre-implementation stage is to fully brief all suppliers on the standards and guidelines for using the corporate identity system. Again, the corporate image implementation task force will need to develop a list of all suppliers to the organisation to be briefed: advertising agencies, public relations firms, printers, uniform makers, signage contractors, building maintenance contractors, and others. In some instances, a pre-launch briefing will also need to be held with the editors of local or industry publications. Not only does this alert them to the forthcoming news story about the launch, it also gives the organisation an opportunity to explain how it wants to be called in press articles. When I worked on the creation of a new capital investment company in Singapore a few years ago, the name agreed upon was PrimeEast Capital Group. Part of our pre-launch activities was to brief the local and regional business press that the firm's name was one word, not Prime East, Prime-East, PECG, or Primeeast—all variations that unfortunately still saw the light of day despite our best efforts. This just goes to show that no matter how well prepared you think you are for the launch of a new

Corporate Image Management

corporate image system, some things will always go wrong. This is a further reason for suggesting that the corporate image management process should be continuous and not a one-off event.

The Corporate Identity System Control Manual

There is no way to properly implement and manage a corporate identity system without a control manual. Without a control document, organisations will slowly and unknowingly build a disjointed and confusing identity and wind up with a perceived corporate identity out of sync with the stated corporate image platform.

This control manual is called the graphics standards manual. It contains guidelines and specifications on how the corporate identity system is to be implemented, with details on typography point sizes, spacing and format of corporate stationery and other documents, rules for using the legal and corporate signatures, and design guidelines for printed materials, uniforms, vehicles, signage and other applications. The graphics standards manual provides an authoritative means to help the organisation ensure standardisation and consistency in the presentation of the corporate identity system. It should be used by all departments that specify, produce or order materials that utilise any of the corporate identity system elements, as well as by all outside resources and producers that are engaged by the organisation for these purposes.

For ease of use, the manual should be divided into sections, such as: Basic Graphic Standards and Nomenclature Structure, Corporate Stationery, SBU Stationery, Special Applications, International Formats and Translated Materials, Vehicle Identification, Signage, and Environmental Applications. A technical supplement section should contain a grid scale presentation of the corporate signature, along with colour swatches to be used for matching colours on printed and finished materials. Most manuals also include an opening message from the CEO stating the importance of the new corporate identity system to the organisation and the need for a consistent projection of the system.

These manuals are usually produced in three-ring or four-ring binder formats and run anywhere from 30 to 100 pages in size. The binder format allows updates to be made easily and inexpensively. While these manuals are very technical in nature, they need to be designed and written so that they are easy to understand. It is best to have a minimal amount of text and to use illustrations of examples whenever possible. The knowledge and expertise of the users should always be kept in mind when the manual is being planned.

While the manual should attempt to cover every possible use of the corporate identity system, showing both recommended and inappropriate applications, the actual size of the manual and its contents will depend upon the budget provided. Since it is unlikely that every conceivable application can or will be covered by the manual, it should note that any situation not covered in the manual needs to be referred to the organisation's corporate image coordinator for explicit approval. This procedure provides the organisation with two benefits:

- it assures the continuity and consistency of the visual identity for all unanticipated situations, and
- it allows the manual to be regularly updated with new information and new applications.

In fact, the corporate identity graphics standards manual should never be thought of as being complete. It is a living and changing document and thus needs to be designed to be flexible and updatable. With the looseleaf binder format, updates and changes can be made quickly and easily, and there is no need to reprint the entire manual.

In bound manuals, it is impractical and difficult to replace or add a single page. Updates and changes will need to be collated and the entire manual reprinted as a second edition. For all updates and further editions, seek the input of the people using the manual. In order for it to work best, the corporate identity graphics standards manual should undergo regular reviews with the user base so that changes can be incorporated, which will make the guidelines easier and clearer to follow. Updated and revised manuals should also include photographs of actual applications to replace the artist renditions and drawings that are typical of first editions.

The Corporate Image System Control Manual

While the corporate identity graphics standards manual is great for helping to monitor and manage the visual identity of the organisation, it is not enough when it comes to monitoring and managing the corporate

Corporate Image Management

image. To achieve this, the control concept needs to be extended into the non-visual area of corporate image management. This document too should be produced in an easy-to-update format. It should include detailed explanations of the organisation's corporate vision and mission, SBU or departmental visions and missions, core corporate values, corporate business strategy, corporate image strategy, and corporate image objectives. Separate sections should be used for whatever subjects are most relevant to the organisation: codes of acceptable individual and corporate behaviour, internal communication procedures and methodologies, hiring guidelines, customer service strategy, corporate ethics policy, etc.

The corporate image strategy section should include a rationale for the name and corporate symbol, a brief explanation of why the corporate colour palette has been chosen, and a listing of the nomenclature structure for all SBUs, business unit, division and department names. This section should also detail the desired attributes that the organisation wants to become known for and a short, concise positioning platform that encapsulates the overall corporate image strategy. A set of core image strategies, covering approaches to external and internal communications, partnership development, implementation of technology and geographic expansion, is a further useful tool for explaining to employees how these will be linked to the development and projection of the desired corporate image.

The corporate image objectives section should cover the desired image objectives for each key audience: local industry image, international industry image, government, employees, shareholders, customers, the community, etc. This section will also highlight key points of competitive differentiation that will be used in corporate behaviour patterns with each key audience to ensure that these interactions are in keeping with the desired corporate image. The monitoring and feedback methods to be deployed should also be explained and highlighted in this section.

One other section I like to recommend to all organisations is called the 'corporate case study' section. Organisations use it to recognise employee behaviour that exemplifies the desired corporate behaviour patterns. This is not an 'employee of the month' section, but rather short case studies describing particular situations and detailing how individuals handled these predicaments or circumstances in line with core corporate characteristics or values. For instance, if a core attribute is innovation, then some of the examples should show how individuals have used innovation in various scenarios. Or, if a key value is honesty, examples of honesty being used in customer, internal or partnership interactions should be depicted. In one organisation, we called these situations OTEs, for Opportunities to Excel. These case studies must be real-life incidences and the employees should be identified both by name and, if appropriate, photograph. By including these small case histories in the corporate image system control manual, the organisation not only rewards outstanding behaviour by giving due recognition to the employees involved, it also creates a corporate culture that constantly reinforces corporate behaviour patterns that project the desired corporate image through action.

The manual should be distributed to all employees but not to external parties, although exceptions can be made for key business partners. Again, this is a living document and updates and changes should reflect changing market conditions and the fine-tuning of corporate conduct through customer, partner and employee feedback. Many leaders of organisations today complain that recent re-engineering and employee down-sizing have left their organisations without a database of historical precedents and background information on the 'XYZ way of doing things'. As the older generation of long-time workers leaves the organisation, this critical aspect of corporate history and culture is not being passed on to the current generation (many of whom see themselves as only temporarily employed by the organisation and hence not interested in past history and former glories). Using the corporate image management procedures to document these corporate methodologies and to inculcate their use by new employees is another unexpected benefit of this process.

The organisation should also arrange for all new staff to undergo some sort of corporate image and culture orientation program. Many companies have orientation programs, but most cover only basic issues: how annual performance reviews are conducted, corporate dress codes, overview of products and services, short overview of the organisation's history, and organisational structure. What these orientation programs need to include are sessions on the corporate image platform, how the corporate image objectives are to be achieved, and examples of how individual behaviour affects both the perceived corporate behaviour patterns and the perceived corporate image. The sessions should be interactive and facilitated by a senior executive or the corporate image coordinator, rather than a set of standard slides presented without interruption. The new

Corporate Image Management

employees should be asked to explain, in team groups, what certain core attributes or corporate values mean to them. The facilitator should take their meanings and shape them into the definitions that are used by the organisation. The same process of two-way involvement and interaction is required to obtain acceptance and commitment from new employees as that described for the existing staff base in the previous chapter.

Finally, your corporate image is defined by the experiences people have with your organisation. All the planning, slogans and fancy graphics in the world won't help if your delivery system and corporate behaviour patterns fail. New employees are probably the weakest link in the corporate image chain, since their newness to the organisation makes them highly susceptible to procedure and process errors. New employees, and current employees undergoing corporate culture or corporate image change, cannot learn how to maintain your delivery systems and how to enhance the corporate image through their actions from the corporate identity graphics standards manual. This is why a new, well thought out, planned and updatable corporate image system control manual is required for monitoring, managing and marketing the corporate image.

Having a Keeper of the Image

The successful continuation of the corporate image program will not be assured simply by having control manuals, procedures, and orientation programs (although they are each extremely important when implementing the new image). The most important factors for ensuring the on-going success of the corporate image management process are two-fold: top-management commitment and dedication *after* the initial launch phase, and organisation-wide commitment and dedication to monitoring the corporate image from the start of the launch period. The next most important factor is to have a single person holding a high-level rank within the organisation in charge of corporate image management.

I call this person the 'gatekeeper.' Their role is to constantly monitor both the software side (corporate behaviour patterns) and the hardware side (corporate identity applications) of the corporate image. This function also serves as the central feedback locale for both formal feedback (qualitative and quantitative research studies) and informal feedback (customer and employee suggestions, industry talk, media reports, investment analyst opinions, etc). This person should have enough seniority in the organisation to be able to recommend and effect policy changes.

Once the new corporate image is launched internally and externally, the gatekeeper's role is unlikely to be a full-time position, except in very large global organisations. The natural reaction of many CEOs is to place this function in either the corporate affairs department or the marketing communications department. Neither is necessarily a good choice. The gatekeeper is not just a guardian of the logo and other elements of the corporate identity system. They need to have a broader, organisation-wide perspective in order to fully monitor and administer the corporate image system. As the gatekeeper needs to be in touch with all SBUs, divisions, departments and units of the organisation, this function is best placed in the strategic planning unit, marketing department, or inside the offices of either the CEO or the Chief Operating Officer.

No matter where the function resides, it should not be delegated to a junior staff member. The entire organisation needs to see that a senior executive has taken ownership for the implementation and maintenance of the corporate image, and that management is committed to providing the necessary capital and human resources required to sustain the program. At the same time, the organisation also needs to witness that any incorrect or non-standard uses of the corporate identity system, as well as any noncompliance with acceptable corporate behaviour patterns, are rectified speedily and with authority by a senior executive. Such actions are the best way to communicate to the entire organisation the importance of adherence to the corporate image structure.

In the end, the success of the corporate image program requires the entire organisation not only to support the program, but to be fully committed and involved in its monitoring, management and marketing.

Chapter Thirteen

The Importance of the Corporate Image on your Communications and Audiences

Marketeers and marketing professors have long spoken and written about communications as being the lifeblood of the marketing process. All four key elements of the marketing process (product, price, promotion and place) are driven by the organisation's ability to communicate effectively and convincingly about these factors.

Through the years new forms of marketing communications were devised and field tested: advertising, public relations, promotions, coupons, sponsorships, direct mail, telemarketing, Internet web sites. The primary purpose of these activities has been, and still is, to inform the targeted audience about certain characteristics or properties of the organisation, product or service. As such, the majority of worldwide marketing communications expenditure still remains in one-way communication activities, with messages being sent by the marketeer to the intended audiences. The response mechanism used for this type of communication process has largely been sales figures. If product unit sales rose immediately after the marketing communications efforts appeared, then the campaign was considered to have some level of success. As this puts a great burden on the designers and implementers of all forms of marketing communications, another school of thought—the importance of raising awareness as a prelude to sales—entered the marketing scene. The argument here is that potential customers need to become aware of the product or service first, particularly for considered and expensive purchases. The response mechanism in this case is broadened to include pre- and post-campaign awareness research studies, telephone enquiries, customer traffic flows in retail showrooms, direct response requests for additional literature or more information, and the number of 'hits' on the web site home page. All of these remain valid measurement devices for tracking the return on marketing communications expenditures for organisations trapped in the trenches of positioning excellence warfare.

Moving forward, the marketing communications process will take a giant leap for organisations entering the relationship excellence marketing arena. These organisations will quickly learn that marketing communications needs to be a two-way, mutually beneficial umbilical cord to their relationship partners. Marketing communications in the future will need to be highly connective and mutually bonding. By adding the 5th 'P' of Perception to the marketing equation, organisations will begin to comprehend that the perceived image of the organisation by its customers is one of the most important filters in the communications process.

Trends

Before we discuss the filtering process affecting marketing communications, let us explore some of the significant trends impacting the ability of organisations to communicate to their key audiences effectively and efficiently.

First, the most important trend is that the entire developed world, and a great part of the developing world, is rapidly moving from a need for content to a desire for context. While futurologists continue to write about the coming Information Age, I suggest that much of the world has already entered this era. Today's problem is that there is too much raw information and data available. The problem will get worse with the proliferation of the Internet and the wide availability of CD-ROMs packing an amount of information that previously required encyclopedias or mainframe computers to store. The need of the immediate future is to package and deliver this content in a meaningful and timely manner.

In business, we have already seen the types of information systems go from transaction processing systems to knowledge work systems (eg computer aided design) and office automation systems (eg the early word processing units). In other words, technology was used first for operational

Corporate Image Management

activities and then for knowledge and information gathering. Today, management information systems support (and sometimes lead) decision making while providing executive information systems that put the core data into an understandable context. But I am not just talking about the need for 'knowledge workers' in tomorrow's growth industries either. Customers are going through the same information transition. Very few organisations deal with uninformed customers these days (though your front-line and customer service people may not agree with this statement!). The market today comprises intelligent, demanding customers who have the mobility and the freedom of movement to go elsewhere if their rational and emotional needs are not met. At the same time, all of us are bombarded with tens of thousands of marketing messages *every day*. These messages are contributing to a feeling of information overload, resulting in many marketing communications messages going undigested or barely noticed.

What does this have to do with the communication process? Everything the organisation does, and does not do, communicates a message about it (and thus has a direct impact on its perceived corporate image). Organisations are going to have to do a much better job of communicating to their target audiences *the context* of their messages and *why their messages are relevant and important to the recipient*. Those who do not will find their customer bases dwindling and their efforts at relationship development fraught with disappointments. Informed customers no longer need more information and raw data, they need information put into a tangible, pertinent and usable format.

The second trend impacting the communications process is that a huge disintegration gap has developed between the marketing communications messages being sent by organisations and the receipt and comprehension of these messages by the marketplace. Five reasons for this communication gap are:

- the massive proliferation of products, services and brand options available,
- the focus of too many marketing communications messages on brand and product names. These hope to generate name recognition and recall at the point of sale, instead of developing and communicating unique brand characteristics,
- a near-universal acceptance that many product categories are now

commodities in terms of product features, promotional activities, pricing and distribution,
- higher levels of mistrust by the general public of both advertising and product claims, and
- informed and demanding customers replacing the uninformed.

The fourth factor, consumer mistrust in advertising and brand claims, may be the most worrisome for marketeers. When surveys such as one conducted by Video Storyboard Tests reveal that as many as 75% of respondents think all or some television advertising is unbelievable, marketeers must stop and re-evaluate how and why they are still engaging in one-way, unconvincing forms of communication.

A third trend, greatly enhanced by modern technology, is that the *individual has become the mass*. This trend is just starting to evolve and develop, and we are certainly a long way from seeing it applied from pole to pole across all industries. Customisation and personalisation have always been key differentiating factors in defining levels of customer service. Now, however, the trend toward customisation of both product offer and service delivery is already having an impact in some manufacturing sectors. Levi Strauss already offers customised jeans to be ordered, so customers no longer have to fit into jeans made to standardised sizes. Dell Computer and Gateway 2000 revolutionised the personal computer industry, by allowing customers to order PCs to individual specifications and needs. If you want an off-the-shelf computer product, visit a retail outlet. If you want to have your own modified version with more memory, a different processing chip, or more bay slots, give a call to either of these organisations and your new, *personalised computer* (a major step up from it just being a personal computer) will be shipped in a few days or sooner.

The last significant trend to mention is again one that is evolving slowly and is weaving its way into the annals of marketing literature and practices. This is the move from integrated marketing communications to integrated marketing. As explained in their book *Driving Brand Value*, Tom Duncan and Sandra Moriarty describe the primary differences between their version of integrated marketing and traditional marketing concepts as:

- shifting the emphasis from acquiring customers to retaining and growing them,

Corporate Image Management

- communicating *with* rather than just *to* customers and other stakeholders, and
- expanding the 'marketing' responsibility beyond the marketing department, making marketing less a function and more a philosophy of doing business.

On these we agree. These authors place the integrated marketing concept squarely at both the product brand and corporate brand levels. This is used to drive relationships with customers and other stakeholders through marketing and communications efforts. By comparison, we advocate using the corporate image management process as a philosophy of doing business in order to develop relationships at the organisational level that are delivered through consistent experiences and interactions. The differences between the two approaches are not great. Theirs is a more outward looking perspective with integrated marketing strategies aimed at customers and other stakeholders. Ours is an outward and inward approach, which takes into greater consideration the need for an organisation to develop a unifying corporate culture and an agreed upon set of corporate behaviour patterns that allow for the seamless execution of the desired corporate image. With the corporate image management process, employees, business partners and suppliers become equally important target audiences as customers, shareholders and other 'outside' audiences.

Another thing we agree on is that the integration of marketing communications tools and efforts will be to no avail if the organisation is projecting more powerful and contradictory messages through its actions. In our opinion, such contrary messages not only make integrated marketing communications efforts fruitless, but they result in negative consequences for the organisation as it gains a reputation for being (at best) inconsistent or (at worst) dishonest.

Filters to Relationship Building

Relationships are made and broken on three things: communications, experiential involvement, and perceptions. When relationships break down, it is just as likely to be from miscommunication as from actual bad experience (witness the number of troubled marriages in which the partners either 'don't communicate any more' or constantly miscommunicate with one another). The same holds true for commercial relationships.

The Importance of the Corporate Image on your Communications and Audiences

All messages go through a filtering process before reaching the cognitive stage within the receiver. On an individual basis, many of these filters are cultural: ethnocentrism, stereotypes, status and power, language, political, etiquette and non-verbal behaviour. An example of the last is the circular linking of the index finger and thumb: in America it means 'OK' but is interpreted as an obscene gesture in Brazil, Greece and Turkey. Other filters include the time and place of message receipt, the topic and subject matter, things falsely attributed to the subject matter, the medium used as the message channel, and any noise or distractions in the message channel that may interfere with message delivery and content. Filters impact both the message being sent (the sender attaches filter elements with the message) and the way the message is received (filters block, impede or add to all or part of what is captured).

There is a more important filter that takes priority before the recipient has the opportunity to consciously or unconsciously put other filters to use. I call this the source credibility filter. When the message is sent by an individual, the recipient first judges whether the sender is a trustworthy source for the type of message being sent. In the world of commercial and organisational messages, the source credibility filter is known as the corporate image.

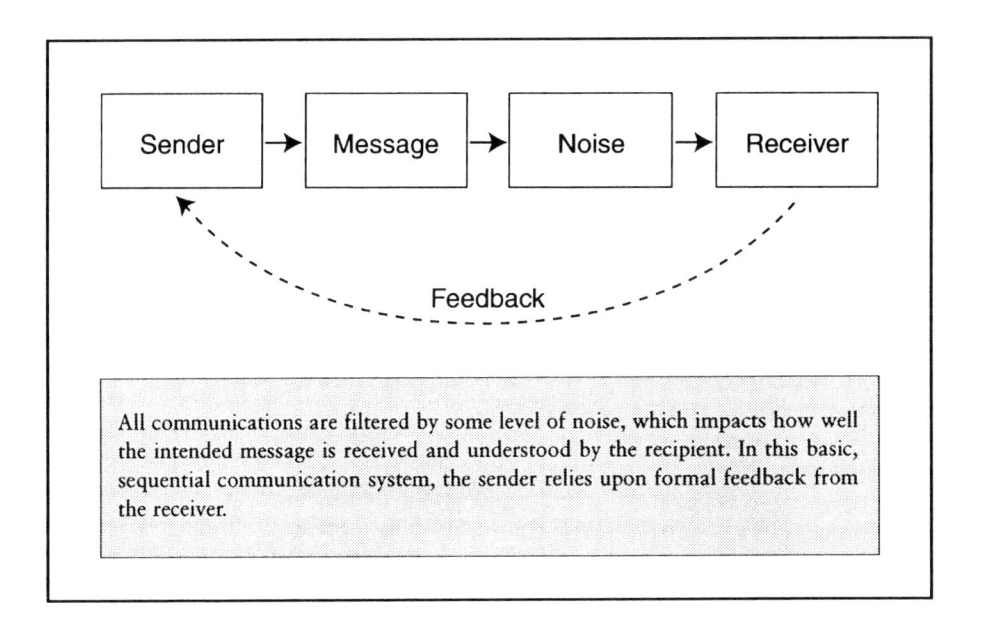

Sender → Message → Noise → Receiver

Feedback

All communications are filtered by some level of noise, which impacts how well the intended message is received and understood by the recipient. In this basic, sequential communication system, the sender relies upon formal feedback from the receiver.

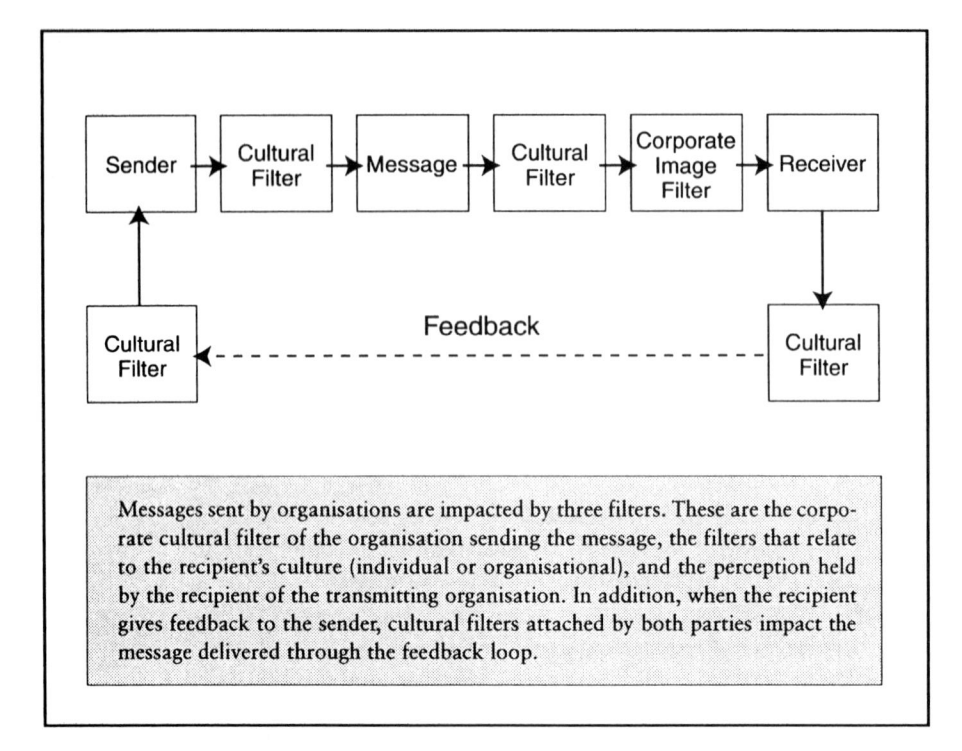

```
Sender → Cultural Filter → Message → Cultural Filter → Corporate Image Filter → Receiver
                                                                                    ↓
Cultural Filter ← - - - - - - - - - - Feedback - - - - - - - - - - - Cultural Filter
      ↑
(loops back to Sender)
```

> Messages sent by organisations are impacted by three filters. These are the corporate cultural filter of the organisation sending the message, the filters that relate to the recipient's culture (individual or organisational), and the perception held by the recipient of the transmitting organisation. In addition, when the recipient gives feedback to the sender, cultural filters attached by both parties impact the message delivered through the feedback loop.

You'll notice the distinct one-way, circular flow of the communications sequence in the above diagram. The sequential nature of this process results in the sender waiting for the receiver to formulate and return a response message, labelled as feedback in the diagram. This convoluted process is too time-consuming for today's fast-paced business world.

A new communications process is required if organisations are going to be more adept at forming long-term customer and partnership relations. The process in the diagram opposite places the obligation on the sender to observe how its message is being received and to make any necessary adjustments and re-send the message without waiting for the formalised feedback process to take place.

Relationships are built during the sending, analysing and re-sending steps. This communication process is a series of circular flows that resembles a person-to-person conversation. Of course, this is not a coincidence since one of the criteria for relationship excellence is engagement in personal dialogues with important audiences (a form of the individual becoming the mass).

The Importance of the Corporate Image on your Communications and Audiences

By analysing *how* its messages are being received by its audiences, the organisation is effectively saying 'We care about your perceptions and want to work with you in helping you understand our message'. This is a much better approach than the current methodology, which implies 'Here's our message, we hope you understand. If you don't, please let us know through your feedback. If you do, please buy our products and services'.

This new methodology not only impresses the receiver, the process is perceived as credible and trustworthy by the recipients. In other words, by exhibiting an open, honest and engaging demeanour in its communications, an organisation can effectively raise its own profile in the corporate image filters used by its audiences. To paraphrase McLuhan, 'The message is the process'.

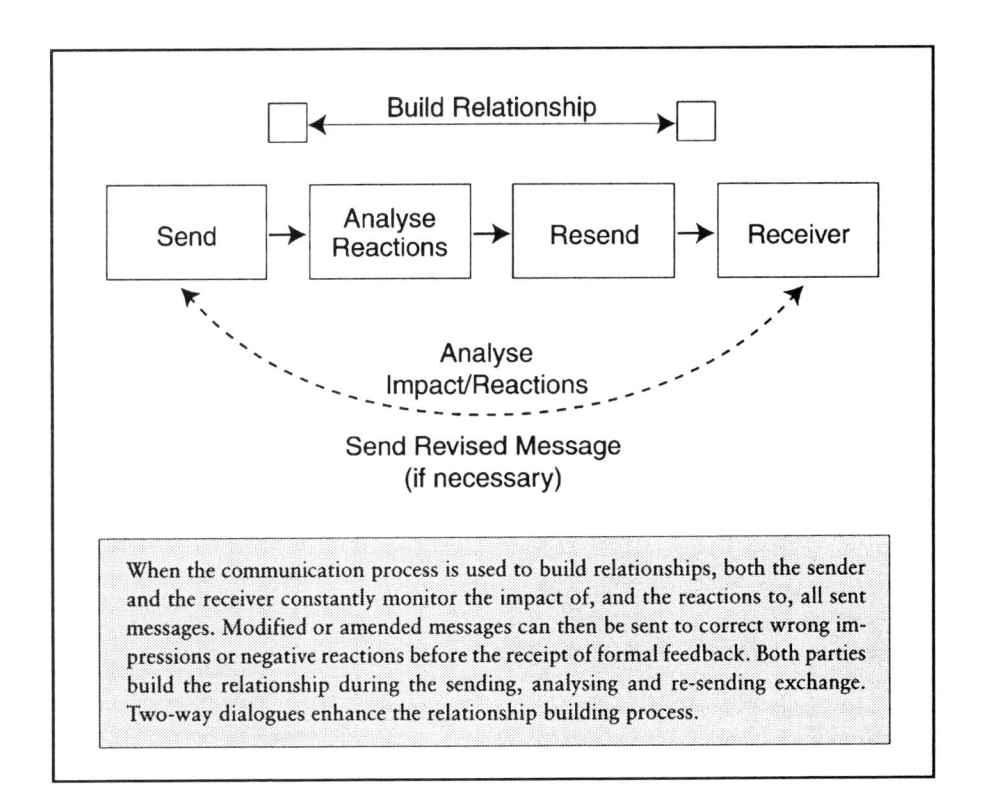

```
        ☐ ←——— Build Relationship ———→ ☐

  ┌──────┐   ┌──────────┐   ┌────────┐   ┌──────────┐
  │ Send │ → │ Analyse  │ → │ Resend │ → │ Receiver │
  │      │   │ Reactions│   │        │   │          │
  └──────┘   └──────────┘   └────────┘   └──────────┘

              Analyse
              Impact/Reactions

           Send Revised Message
              (if necessary)
```

> When the communication process is used to build relationships, both the sender and the receiver constantly monitor the impact of, and the reactions to, all sent messages. Modified or amended messages can then be sent to correct wrong impressions or negative reactions before the receipt of formal feedback. Both parties build the relationship during the sending, analysing and re-sending exchange. Two-way dialogues enhance the relationship building process.

Corporate Image Management

Interlocking Circles

There are three keys to communicating the corporate image:

- the strategy and the structure of the organisation,
- the people within the organisation, and
- the corporate culture.

As shown below, the corporate culture is found where the interlocking circles of the strategy and structure and the people overlap.

These are the three elements that must be communicated through the corporate image management process, not the visualisation of the image. If the organisation focuses too much on projecting an image through its communications activities, then it risks sending contradictory messages through its actions and corporate behaviour patterns. Projecting a good corporate image, without changing and managing the actual experiences provided by the organisation, is analogous to people who go to church on Sundays but act amorally during the week. Who do such people really think they're fooling? And for how long? It is the reality behind the corporate image that counts the most, and that will be found out over time through experiences and interactions with your organisation. In today's age of modern communications and a glut of competitive offerings, no

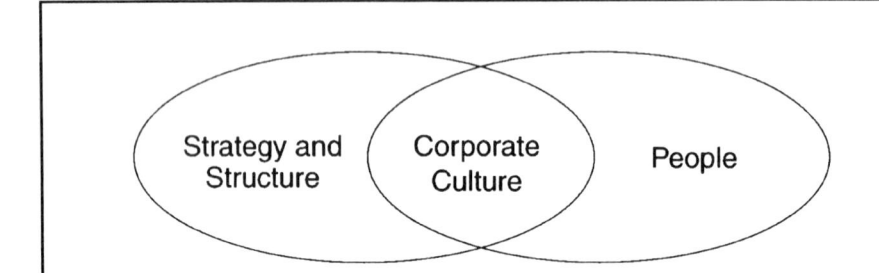

The corporate culture is found where the interlocking circles comprising the organisation's strategy and structure overlap with its people. Too many organisational leaders view the corporate culture as an outgrowth of corporate strategy or structure. This belief impairs their understanding that the collective culture and beliefs of their fellow employees have a direct and important impact on the organisation's culture and corporate behaviour patterns.

172 Chapter 13

organisation can afford to base its future existence on 'fooling enough of the people enough of the time'.

In addition, by putting the organisation's greatest emphasis on managing the actual reality behind the corporate image, you minimise the risk of being perceived as inconsistent, dishonest, or both. Instead, the organisation is better positioned to become known, and respected, for its true core values.

Speaking of values, many organisations struggle with how to communicate corporate values and beliefs to key audiences. It isn't easy, because any marketing communications efforts, particularly advertising, used to communicate core values are most likely to be perceived as self-serving and less than fully believable. I recall seeing a full-page colour advertisement in early 1996 for a multinational conglomerate that had been formed by the acquisition and merger of various business entities around the globe. The firm's new logo had the obligatory swirl in it to illustrate that this is a dynamic, growing, future looking organisation. Also, corporate colours of green and blue were used to assure us that this industrial concern is environmentally friendly. Beyond that, the copy text informed the reader that the new (name of company) stood for:

- technological leadership—most of the group's companies are leaders in their fields whose goal it is to offer their customers top value for money;
- globalisation—the group is actively engaged in 50 countries around the globe with 150 operational companies employing 18,000 people;
- customer focus—its employees focus on the specific needs of their customers, offering them individual solutions to increase their efficiency, and
- flexibility—the company combines the strength of a large industrial group with the flexibility of decentralised companies in close touch with their markets throughout the world.

These are all grand and good corporate values. But would reading about them in an advertisement in the *Asian Wall Street Journal* convince any potential customer, future business partner, or investment analyst that these values are sincerely executed throughout 150 separate, decentralised companies employing over 18,000 people? The point is not whether

Corporate Image Management

or not this is a good piece of corporate advertising; it is that corporate values need to be experienced to be believed. And if the corporate values cannot be personally experienced, then the marketing communications materials need to show these values in action, not simply list them as bullet points in a self-serving, one-way piece of communication.

It is far more important for the organisation to constantly communicate its core values and beliefs to its internal audiences than to spend massive amounts of corporate funds on so-called image building advertising campaigns. I particularly like the booklet produced by Dow in the mid 1990s for its employees. In the words of then CEO Frank Popoff, the document was intended to '...blend the best of Dow's tradition with our ongoing need for strategic direction'. In his president's message, Popoff writes to the company's senior managers 'I urge you to read the Strategy carefully, understand it, commit yourself to make it happen and use all of it as a guide. Above all, you must communicate the Strategy, explain it, and secure the commitment of all your people to its success'. The booklet, produced in 1994, then goes on to cover the five integral elements of the Dow strategy: technology, business, geography, organisation and people. It also has a page devoted to a listing of the critical issues facing Dow and another outlining the company's financial goals for 1995 and the year 2000.

As a potential investor in Dow, I would be far more impressed by its determined efforts to cultivate a unifying corporate commitment to its five-point strategy, as exhibited through this internal document and the cascading process outlined by CEO Popoff, than if the company had told me about their efforts in a slick advertisement placed into an expensive business magazine. This is a company that plans to 'walk the talk'. If Dow's senior executives build acceptance and commitment for this strategy throughout the organisation, then they have a damn good chance of achieving their financial goals before the dawning of the new millennium. More importantly though, from a long-term customer and business partner relationship building perspective, the inculcation of Dow's vision and mission throughout the organisation will result in a consistent delivery of its products and services.

By managing the circles of strategy and structure on the one hand, and people on the other, Dow is furthering the development and reliability of the overlapping corporate culture in the middle of the two interlocking circles. The resultant corporate image will be based on how these three components deliver the customer experience, not on how the Dow name and corporate symbol are projected through marketing communications.

Projecting the Corporate Image Through Action

While the example of Dow may seem a straightforward, back-to-basics approach, it may very well be the exception rather than the rule. An American Management Association (AMA) survey in 1996 of more than 10,000 US manufacturing and service companies found that 'most executives expressed middling confidence, at best, in the ability of key internal and external groups when it came to their understanding of, and ability to articulate, some of the basics, including their company's mission, vision and values, financial and marketing objectives, or what distinguishes them from competitors'.

From my own experience in working on corporate image management problems in half a dozen countries in Asia, the same is true in this region as well. While many senior managers profess that employee communications are a top priority in their organisations, the focus is too often on the speed of communication (installing electronic mail) than on ensuring that strategic messages are clearly understood.

Other findings in the AMA survey follow.

- The company mission, vision and values were better understood by stockholders than by its own employees, competitors, customers, suppliers, the business press or local communities.
- A majority of managers and supervisors in the finance, human resources, and marketing areas lacked a high level of understanding of their firms' mission, vision and values.
- Senior management expressed relatively low confidence in how well leaders of these function areas could articulate the fundamental business drivers.
- Less than half of the survey respondents believed that managers and supervisors working in most of their company's key functions thoroughly understood its financial and market objectives.
- Customers had only a slightly better understanding of what distinguished their organisation from competitors than either employees or stockholders, while suppliers had even less understanding, ranking a distant fourth.

Corporate Image Management

The highlight of this survey, though, was that *'less than a third* of the executives surveyed said their firms regularly sought feedback to make sure their messages were received as intended' (italics added). Not only is the credibility gap growing between organisations and their audiences because of the five disintegration factors discussed earlier, it would appear that senior managers are not even bothering to measure the ever dwindling acceptance of their key strategic corporate messages.

The 1990s have focused too intently on the bottom line, quarterly results and corporate share prices. Management is starting to forget that customers and employees matter, not as a means to a quarterly result that surpasses Wall Street projections, but as the core elements required to ensure the organisation's success in the future. The five factors of disintegration are not only going to lead to disenchanted customers, but to the eventual demise of numerous organisations if they do not refocus on customer needs and consistent corporate behaviour patterns.

The good news from all this is that the current vacuum in corporate message credibility and understanding can easily be overcome by any organisation that can fill the void through action. This must take the form of corporate behaviour patterns, and include new methods of authentic, two-way communications with key constituents, not more glossy, well-produced and well-written corporate advertising campaigns. The former will have long-term results; the latter, short-term results, if any, and it risks creating negative images for the organisation if its actions contradict the messages conveyed in the paid communication.

The Importance of the Corporate Image

The bottom line is that it takes informed, motivated and committed employees to achieve and maintain customer and business partner relationships. From a communications standpoint, the more well-informed the organisation and the customer become about each other, the greater is the chance of a mutually beneficial relationship being developed and sustained. The more your audiences know about your organisation, the more they understand its core values and appreciate its endeavours, the greater is the chance that they will identify with the organisation. This is one of the most elevated forms of bonding and attachment available for sustaining a desirable relationship with either customers or business partners.

The Importance of the Corporate Image on your Communications and Audiences

A planned and well-managed corporate image is the most promising marketing prescription for conquering the current attitudes audiences have towards today's marketing communications efforts. There is no other marketing panacea as powerful as an organisation that understands itself, knows where it is headed, has dedicated, committed and enthusiastic employees, and that relishes two-way communications with its key audiences.

Everything your organisation is currently doing is already communicating to each of your intended and unintended audiences. To ensure that the right messages are being communicated *and* received, the organisation must put into place the most powerful marketing discipline available—the corporate image management process.

Chapter Fourteen

Making the Corporate Image Management Program Succeed (Worth Repeating)

We broached the topic of how to make your corporate image management program succeed in general terms in Chapter Five. Having taken the reader through a more detailed explanation of the corporate image management process, and its tremendous benefits, we should now look at the 'how to succeed' topic in greater detail.

The three basic premises to the corporate image management process are:

- *everything an organisation does, and does not do, has a direct impact on its corporate image,*
- *everything an organisation does, and does not do, communicates a message about it, and*
- *the projection of a corporate identity through marketing communications is a futile effort in relationship building if the organisation projects more powerful and contradictory messages through its actions.*

To implement a corporate image management program successfully in your organisation, you, your senior managers, and perhaps the entire staff, need to deeply believe all three of these principles. Secondly, you and your senior executives must build your future growth strategies around all three principles.

The corporate image management process goes beyond corporate pride and is more like sharing a common value system. You can think of this in terms of family values. What ground rules do you set for your children's behaviour? Are these usually defined by what is acceptable to the family's values and the desired perception of the family by neighbours, relatives, friends and others? That's basically what corporate image management is all about, establishing the ground rules for corporate behaviour patterns that enable the organisation to live up to the desired image of the organisation as perceived by customers, business partners, employees, government entities, the media and the general public.

Making the Corporate Image Management Program Succeed (Worth Repeating)

Organisations, unlike families, also need to have their products, services and brands marketed in a competitive environment. For that reason, the corporate identity system is added to the corporate image management equation. However, in the corporate image management process, the corporate identity system becomes subordinate to establishing the corporate image through shared values and consistent corporate behaviour. This differs from the strategic design approach, where the corporate identity system is created as a strategy of competitive recognition and positioning based on a graphical system.

The second thing to remember about the corporate image management process is that *it is a sequential process*. You cannot jump over any phase, or skip any part of a phase, in your hurry to 'get the project done'. Like all strategic initiatives, the corporate image management process requires extreme executive patience because every program is different and every project has its own in-built schedule. There are no benefits to be garnered from trying to speed the process along. And there are no advantages to be gained from skipping a phase. You cannot go from the Phase I Research to Phase III Creative Exploration without doing the Phase II strategising. Skipping Phase I altogether (the 'we already know where we stand' argument) is a foolish path to take. Twice I have seen this attempted and twice I have witnessed a great deal of wasted money, time and other resources. As a result, I would not personally become involved in any corporate image project with an organisation that tries to save money by eliminating or minimising the Phase I research.

The corporate image management process has three over-riding objectives:

- to carve out a corporate philosophy, personality and image based on inherent and substantiated corporate characteristics,

Corporate Image Management

- to ensure that the organisation practises corporate image management as an on-going marketing discipline, and
- to establish corporate behaviour patterns that will be meaningful and relevant to key audiences outside the organisation by encouraging them to enter long-term relationships with the organisation.

Checklist for Success

Let us now summarise the key factors discussed elsewhere in this manuscript that comprise the critical checklist for successfully attaining the above three objectives.

Management commitment

Senior management should commit to the corporate image management program as an on-going process and provide the necessary capital, human resources and executive time as required to keep the process moving forward at all times. A commitment to the final image and corporate identity system is also required, even if the final selection somehow happens not to be the manager's favoured choice.

Holistic approach

The program must cover all aspects of the organisation, not simply the design and implementation of an identity system comprising name, logo and other visual elements. You need to understand, going into the corporate image project, that the end result will probably impact just about every aspect of your business: hiring practices; internal communications flows; policies, procedures and guidelines; physical working environments; customer interaction environments; supplier relationships; business partner relationships; performance measurement yardsticks; customer communications procedures, methods and tonality; customer relationships; community relationships; media relationships; management information system requirements; future technology investments; marketing strategies; new product development strategies; customer service standards; and others.

This holistic approach is a way of re-energising (one is tempted to say 're-engineering' but that word now has such negative connotations) the organisation towards a common goal using a common compass and roadmap.

Determine corporate vision, mission, philosophy and values

These will be partly uncovered during the Phase I research and fully determined during the Phase II strategy development sessions. They cannot be mere words on a page with the hallowed tone a national anthem. Once agreed upon, they will serve as a countercheck for all future organisational behaviour.

One of the biggest complaints about the Royal Family during the week between Princess Diana's death and her funeral was that the 'stiff upper lip' and empty emotional conduct of the House of Windsor was in stark contrast to the openly public outpouring of emotions by the British public. The standard of conduct being set by the Royal Family, and the corporate values that this conduct reflected, was completely out of sync with that of the British people (and much of the rest of the world as well). Coming soon after all the monarchy's other problems during recent years, this public outcry against the behaviour patterns of the Queen and her family was another major blow to the corporate image of the House of Windsor (which, funnily enough, refers to its rule of the British domain as 'the Family Business'). As the Royal Family undoubtedly wishes to maintain and further its relationship with its subjects (ie its customers, from a corporate image perspective), then one suspects that it will have to alter some of its corporate values and many of its corporate behaviour patterns in the future. Otherwise, the Windsors as head of the monarchy, or the British monarchy itself, may not be around for the dawning of the 22nd Century. (As preposterous as this may seem, history provides plenty of examples where monarchies have been replaced or eliminated, such as in France, Germany and Italy.)

The corporate vision, mission, philosophy and values should also be used as a counterpoint for short-term and strategic decisions. Should the organisation enter into a partnership arrangement with another that does not share a similar set of values? Should this short-term investment be pursued, even though it's not within the strategy? A well-developed set of corporate beliefs would ensure that an organisation is not tempted to behave outside its corporate character, even if this means missing some perceived short-term financial opportunities. It's interesting, but so many times short-term deviations and detours that are out of character for an organisation end up costing the firm, either financially or in terms of diminished image equity.

Corporate Image Management

Planned image

The corporate image that ensues from the corporate image management process must be planned. It must also be based on a clearly defined corporate image strategy and a set of objectives created to cover every key constituency of importance to the organisation. Management must also remember that the planned image is *the goal*, and that this goal may take several months, even years, to achieve. The planned image is not something that can be created by 'running a couple of ads and telling everyone about our new image', as one former client seriously suggested. The planned image is going to be achieved through the combination of corporate interaction and two-way marketing communications with the organisation's key audiences.

The importance of planning the image is exemplified by another scene (remember the red roses?) from *Alice in Wonderland*. Alice is walking through the gardens, very lost, when she comes upon the Cheshire cat. Innocently, she asks the cat for directions on which way to proceed. The wise old Cheshire cat answers in response, 'Where do you want to go?'. Alice replies that she really has no idea, to which the cat shrewdly retorts, 'Then it doesn't matter which path you take'. The moral of this story should be presented to every organisation contemplating a corporate image program.

The crux of a successful program is that organisations must choose where and what they want their respective images to be. The Phase I research stage helps to identify the existing image (as perceived by both internal and external audiences), the greatest equities embedded in the image, and how it compares with those being projected by identified competitors. The Phase II strategy sessions complete the matrix by identifying where the desired corporate image should be. Phases III–V are the creative and managerial means of getting from the Phase I existing position to the Phase II desired position. Without the goals established in Phase II, it really doesn't matter, to paraphrase Alice's Cheshire cat, which corporate image or corporate identity route you take.

Communicate internally first

All changes to the corporate image position platform or to the corporate identity system need to be communicated internally at first, before any public exposure or announcement of the planned changes. When the process results in significant changes to the corporate structure or the procedures of business, then open channels of feedback must allow any misgivings about these changes to be communicated freely.

Achieve internal acceptance
In addition to uncovering potential obstacles and hazards to the implementation phase, the internal communications process must be given sufficient time to achieve full acceptance by all members of the organisation. A single-shot communications approach to the staff a week before the new corporate identity program is publicly unveiled is not sufficient time for employees to internalise changes and to dedicate unchallenged commitment to the new systems and image. Recall the process used by Dow to cascade its new five-point strategy throughout this enormous organisation. This process takes time, but if it is short-circuited so will be the end results.

Monitor, monitor, monitor
There's no such thing as a hands-off approach after the new corporate image system is inaugurated. Like the three keys to real estate investment (location, location, location), the three most important factors are to constantly monitor, monitor, monitor. This process uses feedback systems that are both formal (quantitative and qualitative research) and informal (customer and employee feedback, media reports, etc). The key point to remember is that the corporate image is a strategic weapon, and thus it should not be changed or altered for tactical reasons. The monitoring process is not designed to determine how to tweak the image, but rather to monitor the perceptions of the image in the minds of the key audiences and how these perceptions are being impacted by corporate behaviour and corporate communications.

Gatekeeper
A senior executive with wide connections and respect throughout the organisation needs to be assigned as the corporate image gatekeeper. This person should serve as the focal point for all feedback received through the monitoring activities. The gatekeeper is responsible for ensuring strict adherence to the corporate image guidelines and the corporate identity standards, and for recommending changes to policies and procedures that support or enhance the organisation's ability to deliver upon the corporate image through its activities and actions.

Leadership

Change requires leadership, none more so than the changes created through a corporate image management process. It is best that the employees perceive a collective leadership for these changes, rather than leadership from a single person. If the latter, the corporate image management process becomes too strongly identified with one individual (often the CEO) and it becomes hard to separate resistance to the change from resistance to the person. This is so particularly if the CEO is relatively new to the organisation, and cites 'fixing the corporate image' as one of their top priorities in the new job. A collective leadership approach, which includes participants from across the various functions and units of the organisation, helps to achieve quicker acceptance of the changes and the change process. This leadership of change issue is so important that the entire next chapter is devoted to it.

Outside resources

A successful corporate image program will require the assistance of outside resources. These may be limited to the research aspects of Phase I, to the creative exploration and execution of Phases III and IV, or to the brainstorming and strategy sessions of Phase II. Most likely, however, the organisation will require the external consultants to lead the project from the time of designing its scope through to implementation, internal communications, acceptance, and public exposure. After the initial public launch, the outside resources should be kept on tap for the first six to twelve month monitoring period, the length of which is determined by the calibre and experience of the gatekeeper.

Checklist for Failure

Including the above factors in your corporate image management program will help to ensure its success. It is equally important that you avoid the mistakes commonly made by those less dedicated to executing the process in its entirety.

Trying to fool people

This will always work a while, usually a very short while. Creating a corporate image platform and identity structure on false pretences or superficial corporate values may seem like an acceptable route to take. But in the long run the organisation's weaknesses will be exposed and the positive equities of the corporate image, once lost, are extremely difficult or impossible to regain.

Relying on identity positioning strategies

What works well in the battle for mind share is unlikely to work as well in the battle for heart share (relationships). The world is moving, albeit slowly, to one in which relationship excellence will separate the organisations best equipped to be competitive from those likely to be relegated to the second tier. While it is hard to consider changing when one's positioning strategies are working so well, this kind of thinking is required to win tomorrow's battles. No one wants to end up like the manufacturer of slide rules because they were too busy counting today's profits to realise that the future holds no place for them or their products and services. Industries experiencing rapid change today are banking and financial services, airlines, media, government owned and operated businesses, telecommunications, specialty chemicals, and tourism. Organisations in these industries, as well as many others, should no longer be contemplating positioning excellence strategies. All, or at least those who wish to be survivors and leaders in the next century, need to start thinking right now about how to define and achieve relationship excellence with the customers who will be critical to their success.

Expecting the logo to communicate who and what the organisation really is

The corporate symbol is a great mnemonic device for assisting customer recall at the various points of interaction. It is not, however, helpful for understanding or appreciating the corporate entity. Logos, symbols and other visual elements of the corporate identity system are great for reminding people that your organisation is different to others. They can go only so far in actually communicating how the organisation differs, which is best explained through corporate behaviour and the use of integrated marketing communications strategies. And, just as a woman's perfume doesn't really change her character or her values, the symbol selected and used by organisations will have little or no impact on the corporate character and the core values of the corporation. Perfume tells us no more about the innate characteristics, qualities and personality of a woman than a corporate symbol explains the who, what, and why of the corporate persona.

Using the corporate image for short term solutions

This is one sure way of splintering the organisation's personality. Just as the organisation cannot be all things to all people, it cannot be constantly repositioned in order to gain short-term market advantages. One cannot

Corporate Image Management

be 'everyday low prices' one year and then 'unsurpassed customer service' the next. Customer memories are not that short, even in today's world of information overload. Gradual change on a strategic basis is both understandable and acceptable. A one-off major change in the corporate persona is often necessary for strategic marketing reasons (the change from Kentucky Fried Chicken to KFC because of the perceived health concerns of fried cooking is one noteworthy example). But constant tinkering and changing of the corporate image provides little gain and many problems.

When it comes to customer service, it is good to have the philosophy that 'the customer is always right'. Actually, of course, the customer is not always right as they do make mistakes. In the area of corporate image, however, there is no debating that the *customer's perception of the organisation's corporate image is always right*. Whether you like it or not, that is the perception held by the customer. That perception is going to form the basis for the corporate image filter used by the customer on each and every message sent by the organisation. To make your corporate image program succeed, you have to monitor the perceptions of your customers, match them against your desired image, and then make changes to your corporate actions or to the way your corporate communications activities project your corporate behaviour patterns.

When all else fails, go back to the Phase I start of the corporate image management process. It's an on-going, never-ending process. But then again, so is your organisation. Or at least you hope it is.

Chapter Fifteen

Can You Manage Change?

Can you manage change? If you cannot, it will manage you. And none of us would want that inscription on our corporate tombstone.

In truth, you cannot *manage* change. Change management is a misnomer. Change has to be *led*. Trying to manage change means reacting. Leading change requires pro-active mental and physical states, combined with a sense of purpose, a spirit of optimism, and an ability to communicate plans and goals. To properly lead change, however, one must have more than the gift of the gab and the power of inspiration. One needs a set of powerful change tools, and the best implements to include in this corporate change tool set are the:

- vision statement—the ideal future state of the organisation and the place it would like to find itself (and its customers) at some destined point in time. Note that neither of these may ever be achieved, but that is not a problem. Sometimes the vision will change over time; in other cases it may be a never-ending goal, like a person's desire to be 'the best parent possible'.
- mission statement—a stated and measurable set of desired outcomes that should be achievable, understandable, believable, specific, time-bound and relevant to customers as well as staff. At the same time, the goals should stretch the organisation to accomplish and perform consistently at levels that surpass current performance; exceed customer satisfaction criteria and employee satisfaction levels; and that build, maintain and enhance customer and business partner relationships.

Corporate Image Management

- corporate culture—one that fosters individual and organisational growth in line with the vision and mission statements. The corporate culture will help to ensure that individual and collective patterns of behaviour consistently enhance relationships with customers, prospects, business partners and other key influential audiences.
- marketing strategy—one that is customer focused and that drives the organisation to identify and monitor changing customer needs, to create and deliver value-added solutions to these needs, to understand the relationship requirements of customers and business partners, and establish a basis and framework for relationship development and perpetuation. The marketing strategy should be the underlying business driver for organisations, not the quarterly or yearly financial goals.
- market perception—a clearly definable understanding by key target audiences of who and what the organisation is, where it is heading and why it is relevant. This perception must be projected through both the organisation's communications and its corporate behaviour patterns. These need to reinforce one another, resulting in unified and solidified messages that are clearly perceived by those who interact with the organisation.

The tool that unifies these elements into a holistic corporate change mechanism is the corporate image. Manage and lead the corporate image, and the organisation is more likely to accomplish the tasks and goals desired of it by its leaders and stakeholders.

In recent years, management practices related to change have covered the entire spectrum from 'If it ain't broke, don't fix it' to 'Change everything from top to bottom'. The re-engineering processes of the 1990s ran the gamut from changing internal processes and procedures to 're-inventing the organisation' by throwing away practically everything (and often almost everyone) including the proverbial kitchen sink.

Unfortunately, such practices approach the corporate entity as an inanimate object and the relationships with customers as inorganic inclinations. In doing so, many corporate change agents attempt to fix organisations the same way one would fix a problem with a car or a house. If the bath leaks, call a plumber. If the brakes on the car are causing problems, change the lining and the pads. Each individual problem is viewed in isolation with no connection to the rest of the object. Rarely is it considered that the leaky bath may indicate rusting pipes or that the problem with the brakes may relate to the gearbox malfunctioning while the car is reducing speed.

But the organisation is not an inanimate object and its valued relationships with customers, partners and others need not be temporary tendencies subject to changing whims and passing penchants. In fact, the corporate body should be thought of as an individual's body. One can rarely fix the health problems associated with being overweight merely by going on a diet. Rather, all the tools available to the individual need to be used: dieting, changing activity levels, exercise, modifying eating habits and the types of foods eaten, removing or managing causes of stress, etc. The same applies to corporations and organisations. Those who wish to lead change should use all of the elements in the corporate change tool box, not merely one or two of the most obvious gadgets. The blueprint for how to effectively use these tools, of course, lies within the corporate image management process.

Global Forces at Work

In Chapter Two, we highlighted some of the changes that are having an impact on tomorrow's business-customer relationships. Some of these are becoming widespread forces that will form the foundation for all relationships in the near future. They include:

Marketing
- Powerful regional trading blocks (EEC, AFTA, NAFTA) resulting in new trading rules within regions and between organisations.
- Faster rates of industrialisation in newly developed markets (Indonesia, Thailand, Poland, Mexico, etc) and an increase in the number of newly industrialised nations. The combination of these two factors is causing changes in the availability and supply of raw materials, in the product development and distribution patterns for manufacturers, and in the type and location of competitors everywhere.
- Increased strategic alliances being developed to share resources, markets, technologies and even customers. These strategic alliances are going beyond the code-sharing practices of airlines to encompass industry-rattling announcements like the Apple Computer/Microsoft linkage.
- Emerging markets (India, China, Eastern Europe, and Africa) with blossoming upper and middle classes whose purchasing power is on a

par with those in any developed country. India alone has over 250 million people (approximately the size of the entire United States population) with the purchasing power capability to afford almost any product or service in the world. In Indonesia, the purchasing power in Jakarta alone is estimated to be at least twice that of neighbouring Singapore.

Once the trade barriers and high rates of import duties are eliminated through the treaties enacted and enforced by the regional trading blocks, the marketing opportunities and competitive threats found in these emerging and newly developed markets will escalate for all to see.

Technology

- Instant communication of voice, data, text and images is changing the pace of business and relationships. Information is power, and needs to be accessed rapidly. Fast-paced customers will want relationships with organisations that serve them with both quality and speed. If I cannot get the information from you *when* I need to make a purchase decision, then I'll go to a source that can.
- Flexible manufacturing and distribution in order to meet changing and customised customer requirements.
- The use of outsourcing, for both technological and non-technological solutions, in order for the organisation to become (and remain) fluid, flexible and responsive.
- Reduced product development and delivery times. Customers are not going to wait for your organisation to get its act together.

If your bookstore doesn't have the title I want, why should I wait two weeks for your shipment to arrive when I can order through Amazon.com and have the book delivered to my doorstep within days?

Competition

- Your competitors no longer live down the street or across town. They're just as likely to be found halfway across the globe. Even if the competitor is not fighting you for the same clients (eg customers of a local bank are not likely to be pursued by a multinational bank eight time zones away), it may very well be fighting you for the same capital and human resources, the same raw materials, or the same distribution channels.

- Additionally, if the product or service can be sourced from remote suppliers and delivered by a third party, the Internet removes all barriers and borders to where your competitors can be found. Already today, I can live in one country and have my banking facilities, book store, music store, news and information sources, software suppliers and much more all located outside my home country. This is just the start.

Managers spend an awful amount of time monitoring and worrying about the competitors they know. Leaders understand that tomorrow's competition may just as likely come from someone or something that they don't know today.

Customers

- There is an increased demand across all industries and markets for higher quality, greater service and better value for money regardless of (but sometimes actually because of) the name of the manufacturer or service deliverer.
- Global trade, more streamlined distribution methods, and an increased ability to travel means that customers have the ability to access a wider range of products and services than ever before. Remember the cheap shopping paradises of Hong Kong and Singapore? Both are mere reflections of their former selves. The range of items in major commercial centres such as Kuala Lumpur and Jakarta now nearly equals that to be found in either Singapore or Hong Kong, and usually at fairly comparable prices.
- With all the time constraints they face in their daily lives, customers need to find organisations that understand their needs, with whom they can identify, and upon whom they can depend for consistency and customisation.

Customers today are armed and dangerous—armed with information, and dangerous to your future growth if your organisation believes it can continue to transact business in the same manner year in and year out.

Government

- Governments will remain the biggest players in the commercial arena, even in spite of the continued privatisation of government companies and organisations throughout the world.

Corporate Image Management

❑ Governments will also continue to set technical standards, policies that impact on market regulation or deregulation and, of course, taxation policies.

Additionally, governments will continue to compete with the private sector for raw materials, technology, capital, facilities, human resources and information.

Being able to lead your organisation through change requires a knowledge of the change agents in the marketing environment as they occur, combined with the right analytical techniques to fully understand their *future* impact on your organisation. Like the analogies above about fixing only one part of the problem, organisations cannot afford to focus on only one or two of the global trends impacting their future business-customer relationships. Not only are all of these trends constantly in play, they all are interwoven and interconnected, since each affects how your customers view their purchasing options.

There is no need to be reactionary when it comes to these global forces, particularly when it comes to the organisation's corporate image. How well your organisation meets or leverages the effects of these global forces will greatly depend on how well your organisation executes the corporate image management process. This is your only tool for weaving the corporate vision, mission, and culture together with the corporate strategic marketing plan and the organisation's public perception. The corporate image management process is a leadership tool for helping the organisation stay ahead of environmental change and on top of changing customer requirements.

Sadly, even some of the best-known and respected corporations react badly to the global forces of change. The reason is that they often apply tactical marketing techniques to situations requiring strategic corporate image management processes. In one of the most public examples of 1997, McDonald's Corporation in the USA reacted poorly when trying to deal with the above change trends.

McDonald's sales and earnings have achieved record levels *every year* since the company was founded in 1965. In 1996, the McDonald's brand name even surpassed the legendary Coca-Cola to become the 'most powerful brand in the world', according to an annual survey by Interbrand Group. Most of this sales and brand image growth, however, was international, not within the company's US domestic market. In the US, sales at stores open for at least 12 months see-sawed up and down during the first half of 1997.

So what did this highly successful and strongly perceived company do? It launched a huge promotional campaign across the country that discounted its famed hamburgers to 55 cents. The goal: lift store traffic and sales. The result: confused customers who now wonder why they ever paid full price for a McDonald's burger. After six weeks, the nationwide promotion was halted and the company admitted that the campaign had cost its franchisees (those often overlooked business partners!) dearly and had done little to increase either lunch or dinner traffic in its outlets.

Once again, the obvious occurs. Customers are not going to be wooed by price discounts if the organisation isn't meeting the other criteria in purchase and relationship decision making. There are simply too many choices available, and the 'armed and dangerous' customers of today and in the future are unlikely to be persuaded or fooled by short-term price and promotional gimmicks.

When an organisation reacts to changing environments, as McDonald's did in the US, the chance of using the wrong tactic or designing the wrong solution is extremely high. For one thing, change is not static. By the time you implement your solution to one part of the problem, the situation is likely to be different. As the wise philosopher once said, 'You can never stand in the same river twice'. Like the current moving the waters of the river along, change constantly sweeps the marketing environment along to a new predicament with new conditions. Reacting to 'what is' results in solutions to what no longer is or what will not be true for long. Change leadership, through the corporate image management process, means aligning yourself and your organisation to what *will be* in the future.

Apple Computer and IBM are two firms that know the importance of being aligned properly in order to achieve optimum returns from the future. When Apple Computer introduced one of the earliest personal computers in 1976, there were many other PC makers around. But it was the Apple

Corporate Image Management

II that really launched the PC revolution. This was followed by the Apple Macintosh, which popularised the hand-held mouse and the graphical user interface. Within five years of its birth, Apple Computer had sales high enough to place it onto the Fortune 500 list.

Of course, after IBM entered the PC market and allowed IBM compatibles to offer higher performance at lower prices, Apple lost market share and the firm, long known for its innovation, fell behind in the race to improve and to innovate. It also misunderstood the need for partnership development at the software level (Apple Computer's key partners have mostly been chip makers such as Motorola), whereas IBM early recognised the importance of forming a relationship with Bill Gates and Microsoft.

Even IBM, however, has misjudged change patterns. The company that had dominated the mainframe computer business misread the PC revolution. It not only allowed the makers of compatibles to steal away its market share, it also lost sight of the fact that the new, more powerful PCs were having a direct impact on IBM's mainframe and minicomputer business lines. IBM went from being the third most profitable US company in 1984 (net earnings of US$7 billion) to a firm that reported an US$8 billion loss in 1993. During this period, the company was forced to reduce its staff by almost 200,000.

Now, IBM once again has leaders who understand changing market environments and the importance of leading, rather than reacting to, change. In 1996, the company reported a profit of US$5.4 billion, still short of what was achieved a dozen years ago, but a huge turnaround from three years earlier. And, of course, today it is Apple Computer that is struggling for corporate survival. In both cases, these organisations have learned (we hope) that it takes fresh ideas to stay ahead of changing trends. Leadership is for tomorrow, management is for today. The corporate image management process requires leadership, not managers.

Even worse than reacting to global change factors, of course, is not reacting at all to the fact that markets and the environments for products are constantly changing such as the example of the slide rule manufacturer cited earlier. In the early 1980s, portable electronic typewriters were all the rage. Only a few years later, they were made obsolete by notebook computers and portable printers. The corporate tombstones for both should read: we failed to understand what was happening around us.

Leading Change

Leading change requires a matrix approach that is fundamental to the Phase I of the corporate image management process. In this matrix, one takes the five key global forces (marketing, technology, competition, customers, government) plus human resources and applies a series of analytical questions to each one:

- What are the biggest problems facing the organisation from these global forces?
- What are the biggest known opportunities the organisation could turn into measurable advantages?
- What might be the biggest unknown or unexpected opportunities? What would have to happen to turn these into known or identifiable opportunities?
- What are the organisation's growth needs, in terms of geographical or product expansion plans, franchising, downsizing, cost reduction, customer bases, and image perceptions, and over what time frame are these being planned?
- What are the organisation's marketing and sales goals? How are these numerated and measured? How are they monitored, tracked and reported?
- What are the key financial issues facing the organisation?
- What are the organisation's assets and strengths? Its liabilities and weaknesses?
- What is the current state of relationships with key audiences? How do you know? How would you improve these states if you could? Why?
- What is the organisation's technical prowess or weakness?
- What ranks first on the organisation's future agenda?
- What were the last new ideas, creativity, and new directions undertaken by the organisation? Were they successful? Why or why not? How was success defined and measured?
- How will your customers in the future be different from those the organisation serves today?
- How will your distribution channels in the future be different from those used to market the organisation's products and services today?
- Which of today's competitors will still be the organisation's competitors in the future? Which ones will go away? Why?
- What type of competitor is the organisation likely to face in the future?

Corporate Image Management

- What are the key components of your value chain today? How will these differ in the future?
- How will your profit margins, and the source for these margins, differ in the future?
- What skills or core competencies will it take to make the organisation unique in the future? How can these be achieved?

Again, each of these questions needs to be asked against all five global change factors, as well as against the organisation's current and planned human resource activities. Asking and evaluating the responses to this set of questions will help to determine whether the organisation collectively understands what is happening around it. Then one can determine whether to start preparing the organisation's tombstone and epitaph, or whether to embark on the change leadership path.

These questions will also propel the corporate image management executor into a deeper understanding of how the organisation perceives the outside world, the first step in comprehending how the organisation engages in relationship building and relationship maintenance practices. One goal of the corporate image management process is to enable the organisation to develop sustainable relationship advantages with its key audiences. This is markedly different from corporate identity practices and re-engineering processes that aim to develop sustainable competitive positioning advantages. In the corporate image management process, the focus remains clearly on the customer and other key audiences critical to the future success of the organisation—not on attempts to derive temporary competitive marketplace advantages.

Sustainable relationship advantages come from leading change and understanding where the needs of customers, and indeed even the customers themselves, will be in the future. Sustainable competitive positioning advantages, on the other hand, are reactionary to current market conditions and are sustainable only until the marketing environment changes. Thus, the corporate image management process is a leadership process and should not be used only as a reaction to current market conditions or to current competitive situations.

The corporate image management process is an instrument of change that may alter, modify or even completely change the assumptions and premises that determine or support current business decisions and activities. Not only will new core competencies and skill sets be identified in this process, new methods of organisational decision-making and improved patterns of corporate behaviour are also likely to result. When taken to this extreme, as in the case of CISCO discussed in Chapter Three, the organisation will undergo an important transformation (sometimes even without a new name or significantly changed corporate logo).

Changing relationships
Whether it was labelled the 'me decade' or the 'greed decade', the 1980s seemed to be a time when materialism and cut-throat competition ruled. The top selling business books at the time had titles like *Swim With The Sharks Without Being Eaten Alive*, *What They Don't Teach You at Harvard Business School*, *Search for Excellence*, Sun Tzu's *The Art of War*, *Marketing Warfare* and various 'live action' reports from the trenches by corporate leaders such as Lee Iacocca. The marketplace was considered a battlefield. One of the corporate image books I recall from that era was *Image Wars: Protecting Your Company When There's No Place to Hide*.

Then in the early 1990s, managerial emphasis shifted to re-engineering, transformation and taking a scythe to corporate costs and head counts. CEO bookshelves became populated with titles like *Transforming the Organization*, *Reengineering the Corporation: A Manifesto for Business Revolution* and *Business Without Bosses*. In line with the thinking that corporations needed to be redesigned, along came *Image By Design: From Corporate Vision to Business Reality* and *Marketing Corporate Image: The Company As Your Number One Product*. The latter basically advocated using corporate advertising to support brand sales and build the organisation's perceived value in the minds of investors, employees and other key groups.

Today, the world continues to change and evolve. As the Baby Boom generation passes through the throes of middle age and struggles with the concept of old age and the reality of death, at the end of the century the world is searching for...something. Corporate leaders, consumers and others have become keenly interested in seeking deeper meanings, values and relationships in both their professional and personal lives. A review of the best sellers in the late 1990s shows titles like *The Celestine Prophecy*, a whole range of *Chicken Soup for the Soul* books, *The Seven Spiritual Laws of Success* and Pat Riley's *The Winner Within*.

Corporate Image Management

The evidence is all around us. The books being read, the focus on healthier and less self-indulgent lifestyles, the rise in religious service attendance and the creation of major public events such as the Million Man March and the Promise Keepers gatherings are all manifestations and demonstrations of pent-up desires. As we gradually close the 20th century, our customers, global business partners, employees, and neighbours are all seeking ways of satisfying something more than their material needs. Customers want something more than products and services in their personal lives. Employees crave something more than a monthly pay cheque in exchange for the time spent in their business lives. Business partners desire something more than new assets or another joint venture to manage. The 'something' they each seek is relationship satisfaction.

Relationships that are successfully developed, maintained and satisfied in the future will be multifaceted, multidimensional and will provide mutually beneficial rewards and experiences at multiple layers along the numerous points of the interaction chain. This will require a significant change in the ways that organisations interact with customers, prospects, business partners, employees and other important constituents. The one-dimensional, unidirectional relationship between the organisation and its audiences, as so adroitly depicted in the *Dilbert* series of cartoons and books by Scott Adams, will no longer suffice or satisfy. Companies that treat their employees, customers or partners in a 'Dilbertised' fashion are headed in one direction: towards the trash bin of corporate and business history.

Relationship satisfaction will come when the products, services *and* organisations with which customers deal add value, enjoyment and fulfilment to their personal lives. Organisations will need to deliver these added-value elements through emotionally bonding experiences that reward both the individual customer and the organisation. Organisational leaders should not think of this in terms of spirituality, for the fervour for your products and services need not take on religious overtones. Rather, the relationship enhancing experiences need to create bonds of affinity *between* the organisation and the critical constituent (as opposed to *with* the targeted audience, an attitude that treats customers as collective groups and not as individuals with customised needs, concerns and desires).

Your customers, partners, employees and other audiences want relationships that help them meet their self-knowledge and self-determined definitions of success, satisfaction and fulfilment. To deliver this, the organisation will need to be flexible and adaptable, as these definitions will change from customer to customer, partner to partner and employee to employee. Your products and services, and the perception of your organisation, will need to match these definitions and will need to reflect the values, ethics and other intangible attributes of the individuals with which the organisation desires a relationship.

The competition for relationships with customers, business partners and employees will be contested and determined at individual levels using the emotional and intangible criteria discussed above. However, this does not mean that the tussle for customers, partners and staff will *shift* from the mind to the heart. Competition on the commercial playing field also will not go to wide-eye marketing zealots who attempt to create a religious-style acclaim or linkage for their products and services. Rather, the relationship winners of tomorrow—and by definition it will be the relationship winners who become the marketplace leaders—will be those who can capture the minds, hearts *and* emotional souls of their intended audiences.

Using Corporate Image to Lead Change

Leadership during times of change is mandatory. The change in marketing excellence to the new era of relationship excellence is exactly the kind of change that will require astute organisational leadership. The leadership of change, however, cannot exist solely at the top of the organisational pyramid structure. Change leadership, particularly in terms of corporate image management and relationship excellence, must exist throughout the organisation at all levels.

When planned, change can be good—for the organisation as a whole, for its individual employee members, and for its relationships with key constituencies in the market place. Using the corporate image management process during times of change provides the organisation with the strongest set of tools for executives to use in leading and implementing change. It provides an understanding of how the organisation perceives its marketing environment, how the market place perceives the organisation, and what criteria key audiences will use in their decision-making processes about relationships.

Corporate Image Management

Corporate image management always focuses on the process. This enables management to lead the overall direction of the organisation, providing in-built flexibility for manoeuvring through changing conditions, rather than emphasising specific targets or goals. By keeping the corporate image management goal visionary, the on-going corporate image management process provides corporate leaders with a tool for dealing with the unpredictable future.

Given that change is inevitable, continuous, unstoppable, and occurring at a faster pace than ever before, the key issue for organisational leaders is whether they want to react to change in a crisis mode or in a prepared and planned manner. The change agenda can be set by the global forces of the market environment, by your better prepared and equipped competitors, or through your own organisation's readiness and willingness to take the lead. When you embark upon the latter course, the corporate image management process enables you to identify and exploit the experiences, foresight, creativity, customer knowledge and enthusiasm that exists throughout your organisation.

In short, corporate image management is a wonderful tool for executive leadership, particularly suited to today's changing times.

Chapter Sixteen

The Value of Outside Resources

The development of relationship excellence in all organisations requires perpetual innovation and improvement. As such, the never-ending corporate image management cycle, with its emphasis on the Phase V monitoring and managing stage, becomes the mandatory marketing discipline for building relationships. The most effective way to introduce the corporate image management process to an organisation is usually through the experience and expertise of outside resources.

In today's highly competitive business environment, the standard operating procedure for most executives is to get so caught up in the affairs and problems of the day-to-day business grind that the larger picture of what the organisation is, what it stands for and where it is headed often is shunted aside. In the era of relationship marketing, this treatment of the corporate image must change; the success of organisations, their products and their services will depend on how they are perceived. Many organisations use outside image consultants to help them initiate programs to ensure that the corporate image management process is dispersed and fully embedded.

Successful marketing has always been about correctly identifying or anticipating customer needs and fulfilling those needs. This will not change in the immediate future. However, the change in priorities will come from a world in which the deeper, emotional needs of relationship fulfilment

Corporate Image Management

become the predominant factor, by an overwhelming margin, in the customer purchase decision-making process. Hence, organisations that are to be the success stories of the future will be those whose management of the corporate image sustains and enhances all other relationship building efforts by the organisation. Of course, the public must see, understand and appreciate these relationship efforts—another reason why the corporate image management process emphasises monitoring and managing the public perception of the organisation.

Humans generally resist and resent change. This is unfortunate because the corporate image management process, by its very nature, dictates change. Sometimes this change is evolutionary, sometimes revolutionary. Either way, it is merely a precursor to the future organisational state, in which change will be a constant as the organisation flexibly adapts itself and its processes, procedures and protocol to cater to the changing and evolving desires of its audiences. Perhaps, when change becomes more prevalent, and adaptability becomes the norm in organisational relationships, today's natural discomfort with change will cease or subside.

What is Required

The role of the outside image consultant is to help the organisation pass through the various stages of change resistance, acceptance and implementation. Before this can be tackled, however, the leadership of the organisation, at all levels, must give its full commitment to the corporate image management process.

Naturally, anything as strategic in nature as the corporate image management process does not come cheaply. Management must be willing to pay the price for future success by investing the necessary financial and human resources, a commitment that often requires explicit approval and direction from the board of directors and, if applicable, significant shareholders.

Additionally, as the combination of professional skills, specialised knowledge, image management experience, and impartiality necessary for the initiation and execution of a corporate image management program are unlikely to be found in-house, the organisation is best advised to secure these services from the most suitable sources available.

Most importantly, the organisation's collective leadership *must believe* in the applicability of the corporate image management process as part and parcel of its future success. The process will stretch, test, validate or repudiate every aspect of the organisation; how it conducts its business dealings with clients, customers, suppliers, employees and others; how it collectively views its role in this world and its future existence; and how the vast majority of individuals and organisations with which it deals and transacts view its *raison d'être* and viability as an on-going concern. Additionally, the corporate image management process will stretch, test, authenticate or negate the skills, experiences, personal beliefs, management practices and marketing theories held by the organisation's leadership, management and staff.

In many ways, undertaking the corporate image management process is like having an annual physical examination. The process is going to poke, prod, bleed, examine, analyse, test and question almost every nuance, belief, practice and behaviour of the organisation. As one image management consultant I used to work with was fond of saying about the corporate image management process, 'It isn't a blind leap of faith, but it may very well be the closest thing to a religious experience that the organisation will ever encounter in its corporate life'.

Why an Outside Resource?

The most important value of an outside resource, particularly in the early stages of the corporate image management process, is the advantage gained from an independent diagnosis of the organisation's current market and image situation and its future potential in both these areas. Additionally, the early stages of the process require an enormous time commitment by a range of specialists and marketing practitioners, time that is unlikely to be available by appropriate people within the organisation unless they are completely relieved of all other commitments, duties and responsibilities.

The image consultants will need to be empowered by management to conduct a thorough review and analysis of the organisation, not simply a review of its corporate identity practices and procedures. The wider the latitude given to the consultants, and the greater their access to information and key people (both internally and externally), the better will be the recommendations and strategies. Empowerment, however, does not mean

The Value of Outside Resources

Corporate Image Management

abandonment. Both the consultants and the client should view corporate image management as an 'arm-in-arm' process in which the client remains actively engaged at all stages. The only area of the process to exclude the client is research, in order to maintain the strictest levels of confidentiality and openness during the qualitative interviews. Remember, the process itself is an important feature of the corporate image management cycle and the use of outside resources does not absolve the organisation from active participation in all phases. Also, since the implementation and post-implementation monitoring and managing phases are most likely to be handled exclusively (or at least mostly) by the client, it is imperative that senior members of the client organisation have a full understanding and hands-on experience in each step of the corporate image management process.

The second greatest benefit comes from the impartial and confidential role of the consultant. Impartiality allows objective appraisal and analysis of the information uncovered during the research stage. Confidentiality allows a wide range of unknown issues, beliefs, feelings and concerns to be raised safely by the interviewees. In my experience, such issues have run the gamut from inconsistent and confusing instructions from senior management to previously unspoken complaints about the quality of the food in the company canteen.

Other benefits of using an outside resource are:

- ❏ to provide purpose, and to harness across-the-board commitment to the project. Engaging an external consultant is often a key signal to the organisation that the project is serious and that management is willing to admit that it does not have all the answers. Also, external resources can often keep a project moving along, without it becoming delayed or bogged down by new priorities and day-to-day concerns.
- ❏ to facilitate communication throughout the organisation. Making information available to all is an important aspect of the consultant's role, particularly in organisations where information tends to trickle rather than cascade. A good image management consultant always has an eye out for stagnant communications processes and should be a strong and vociferous advocate for ensuring that a consistent message about the project is conveyed to all relevant parties.
- ❏ to create attention and spread the gospel for both the project and the process. Without the proper attention throughout the ranks, the

implementation stage will be mired in the same webs of disbelief, disenchantment and deep-seated resentment as any other poorly planned change process program. Experience has shown that the consultant is usually aware of these problems as they develop and has greater experience in anticipating and heading off such pitfalls.
- to form a shared understanding of the organisation's future and create a common language that expresses that future. By removing language barriers, particularly those that reside between layers of the hierarchy, the capacity to act in unison becomes a new element of the corporate culture. The shared language may also improve the organisation's operating efficiencies through better interdepartmental communication, improved work flows, greater coordination and integration of dispersed activities, and shared purpose, objectives and measurements.
- to distinguish between process information and results information. If process information is overlooked (eg how *deeply held* are the beliefs expressed during the interviews), then solutions will be missed. Too often I have witnessed management teams dissecting the verbatim responses delivered in the Phase I management report in an attempt to rationalise or justify what has been revealed. It is the role of the consultant to both protect the sources of the testimony and to present the information in the proper context so the best possible solutions and recommendations can be tabled.

Strategic Transformations

There will be times when the corporate image management process will lead to a major, strategic transformation of the organisation. This occurs when the process results in redefined business objectives, the creation of new businesses or strategies, the evolution or redefinition of core competencies, a change in marketing focus from product and service excellence to relationship excellence, or other wholesale changes.

All strategic transformations face a unique set of challenges, but there is one thing that all have in common: the need to convince staff, partners, suppliers and sometimes even customers that change has become a prerequisite for future success. Most organisations are not fully equipped to contemplate massive change and it becomes the chief role of the consultant to guide them through the strategic transformation minefield.

Corporate Image Management

True strategic transformations really do not take place unless corporate behaviour changes. The corporate image management process enables such behavioural changes, either before or after a new corporate identity is developed. The strategic design process, on the other hand, only transforms the projected image of the organisation and does not attempt the depth and breadth of the corporate image management process. To achieve a pandemic transformation within the organisation, the outside resource will need to challenge (and eventually help to alter and modify) the underlying assumptions on which the organisation's business decisions and behavioural patterns are based. This challenge to the status quo and existing protocol is best left to the external resource, otherwise every challenge and new methodology will be tainted by political hues or personal agendas of the internal advocate.

Much of the transformation process of recent years has usually been measured in terms of financial results and impact. While such measurements are certainly included in the monitoring phase of the corporate image management process, a better yardstick for evaluating the true effects is how entrenched the new corporate culture is in all units of the organisation. Admittedly, this is often a difficult criterion to quantify, but like many other subjective aspects of management (eg what makes a good advertisement? how well written is a subordinate's report? do the front-line staff care for and empathise with customers?) it is something that can be both felt and sensed.

Working with an Image Consultant

The first step in working successfully with an outside consultant is that the organisation has an understanding of what it wants to accomplish in terms of corporate image management. As simple as that may sound, my personal experience is that this is not the case in over half of the initial client meetings. As a result, the client wastes too much time in talking to the wrong type of consultants, or in trying to weigh and evaluate the different methodologies, goals and costs of the strategic design approach on the one hand against the corporate image management process on the other. This is like evaluating whether you should order a pizza to be delivered or go to a nice Italian restaurant for a complete meal: you really cannot compare one with the other.

To help you avoid the normal errors associated with engaging an image consultant, the following sections provide an overview of what the client should include in the initial briefing session and a range of criteria that have proven useful in choosing the most appropriate consultant for your situation. In the project brief, the client should be able to:

- provide a list of your needs, as seen from the perspective of the organisation, including a short background description on why each need is relevant and important. They should be expressed as problems requiring solutions, not as an end objective or outcome. If you brief the prospective consultants that 'We believe we have an incoherent image with our key audiences', that tells them they need to verify your belief and then develop a solution. If you state, 'We need to be projected as a high-tech company', then that's exactly what you will get, whether it's the right or wrong image for you.
- identify any special considerations or unusual circumstances that may appear during the length of the project, such as planned management changes, revamped organisational structures, new business ventures or new product launches.
- clearly identify key stakeholders, their roles in the organisation (or their relationship to the organisation if external). The stakeholder list should include any individual or group that has a large interest in the outcome of the project and could include unions, government officials or statutory bodies, media, community leaders or groups, marketing intermediaries, and financial providers.
- define deadline expectations, the reasoning behind the timetable, and advise on whether the expected delivery date has been fixed arbitrarily or is cast in stone.
- identify the steering committee members who are most likely to play an active role in the project (even if only tentatively). If possible, identify the key liaison person and detail their professional background.

Once a consulting team has been chosen, fully communicate additional information, particularly internal political issues. At this point, the consultant becomes one of your most trusted partners and advisers and it would be unwise to keep professional secrets from each other.

Agree on the evaluation criteria for selecting the consultant *before* the start of the presentation cycle. This enables each member of the evaluation panel to focus on the key criteria during each presentation, or to

Corporate Image Management

have the opportunity to raise important issues during the presentations. I have assisted clients to select external consultants and have been on the pitching side of this business. There are few things more frustrating than having three to four teams of professional consultants make their pitches, and then have the evaluation panel spend precious time afterwards trying to determine which criteria to use in comparing very different methodologies. In the end, someone always suggests an arbitrary scorecard, a vote is taken and the results are fairly split across all the candidates with no clear winner. The rankings are then rationalised, a group consensus forms, and the selection is usually the team that exhibited the closest chemistry to the evaluation panel.

This is not to suggest that chemistry is not important, because it is. But it should not be the ultimate and final criterion unless it is used simply to break two closely ranked bids.

The selection criteria should include:

- relevant experience—not necessarily within your industry, but in successfully handling projects of similar size and nature.
- understanding needs—how well did the consultants understand your initial brief? Did they take your brief and respond to it, or did they also investigate your situation and add valuable points for you to consider? Are they likely to react only to your stated concerns, or will they help you by expanding your horizon and thought processes, challenging you to think outside your existing belief boxes?
- integrity—a critical factor. Your image consultants are going to be exposed to vast amounts of company data and will be privy to your growth plans, business strategies, hiring practices and other corporate secrets. They will also come to learn about most, if not all, of the organisation's 'dirty laundry' and internal political issues. If the consultants are too willing to share secrets or exchange rumours with you about the organisations with which they have worked in the past, that is often a good sign that your own stories and gossip will be spread after the conclusion of the assignment.
- consulting team—the composition of the consulting team to be assigned to the project is the most critical factor to be evaluated. The experiences of the consulting team members should be probed fully and the client should not be satisfied with pat phrases like 'Bill worked on the XYZ project'. Ask for details on exactly what Bill did on that project.

Did he merely attend a few client meetings and presentations? Did he conduct any of the interviews? How many and what was the percentage split between the internal and the external interviews? Did he facilitate any of the cross-department or executive team meetings? Also ask how many times has this team worked together and on what business and types of projects. The last thing you need as a client is to find out mid-way through your project that the consulting team has developed its own internal political problems because this is the first time they have worked closely together on an assignment.

- size of the firm—I place less emphasis on this category than on the size and make-up of the consulting team to be assigned to the project. Unlike many other consulting assignments, the corporate image management process does not require large support teams in the consultant's head office. Additionally, the image management consultants do not necessarily need to have their own in-house design teams. The creative development and execution of the corporate identity system can be managed by the image consultants using third-party resources or through one of the client's advertising or graphic design suppliers.
- communication skills—evaluate both the written and oral communication skills of the consulting team to be assigned to the project. I always advise clients to insist that all key members of the consulting team attend the pitch presentation. If any are not actively participating in the presentation, then questions should be directed to them in order to ascertain how well they communicate to your group. The successful implementation of your corporate image management system relies heavily on how well the image consultants can communicate with all levels of your organisation, as well as with many of your external constituents. Additionally, if the short-listed consultants are likely to be interfacing with any of your existing communications consultants (advertising agencies, public relations firms, design studios, etc.), then they should be asked to meet with each of these firms. Again, it is important to ensure that you will not have poor chemistry or communications problems when it comes time to implement and execute your new corporate image program.
- methodology—one of the keys to success is the actual process used in developing the corporate image management program. The evaluation panel should therefore require explicit details on the methodology proposed by each competing consultant. If it appears that any steps are missing, or if the project scope stops short of fulfilling the entire assignment, the evaluation panel must ask why. As I have

Corporate Image Management

emphasised throughout this book, experience has taught that *the process drives results* and the process must be followed in sequence to avoid failure or suboptimal results.

- availability—all consulting team members need to be immediately available for your assignment. Unfortunately, this is rarely the case as they will undoubtedly be involved in other projects at the time of their pitch. Thus, the evaluation panel must ascertain how quickly the consulting team can be brought together, what other assignments each member is currently engaged in, and how much time each has available for your project.
- diversity—depending upon your organisational composition and the region of the world in which you operate, the diversity of the consulting team may or may not be important. Where feasible, the make-up of the consulting team should reflect that of the client organisation, in terms of gender, ethnicity, market experience and cultural roots. Such diversity will help to break down barriers and resistance to change and, at the same time, often help to speed and enhance the communications process.
- skills gap—however, there is one key area where the consulting team *should not* mirror the client, and that is in the specialised skill base that the consultants bring to the project. If the client team is weak in the areas of marketing or strategic planning, then the consultant team must be strong in this area. However, if the client team is strong in a particular area, such as in having its own design studio, then the consultants should seek to leverage these strengths and not insist on using their own resources on the assignment.
- style and fit—lastly, the consultants should have some natural fit with the organisation and its corporate culture. This should be with the bulk of the organisation, and not only with the 'suits' located on the executive floors. This is another reason for advising that the consulting team should mirror, as much as possible, the entire client organisation in terms of diversity and composition. While some aspects of style and fit relate directly to chemistry, other details include communications style, documentation, dress, vocabulary, jargon, social interests, and demeanour.

When it comes time to compare the various consultants and their proposals, the client evaluation panel should score each consultant on all of these criteria, plus any others that have been agreed to in advance. It should discuss and list the strengths and weaknesses of each consultant proposal, along with any concerns that any of the evaluation panel members have. Lastly, a list of 'bonus point' items should be developed that identifies any extra comments or positive surprises that were revealed during the proposal presentations.

The final selection decision should be as unanimous as possible. If a split decision is taken, the chances of the project progressing smoothly is hindered right from the start, particularly if any of the evaluation panel members in disagreement with the selection decision are to be participants in the project steering committee. If a near unanimous decision cannot be made by the evaluation panel, then this is probably a sign that the panel's members are not clear about the objectives of the project or that the organisation is not truly ready to undertake and proceed with a corporate image management program.

Project Pitfalls

Any project as lengthy and complicated as a corporate image management program is likely to be beset with turmoil and pitfalls during the course of execution. Many of these problems, however, can easily be avoided through proper planning and acute observations. Here are some of them.

- ❑ Using the wrong approach—a design approach will not identify nor fix underlying problems affecting the way the organisation is perceived in the market. The strategic design approach is a very valid method for organisations needing to derive competitive advantages through positioning projection and for those organisations that are happy and contented with their current public perceptions. The corporate image management process is more suitable for organisations moving into the realm of relationship excellence and for those whose public perceptions are not consistent with corporate strategy.
- ❑ Unwilling to accept advice—there is little point in engaging outside expertise if the organisation's management is not going to heed the advice received. It is rather like going to a doctor and then ignoring the advice received. If the organisation has neither the intention nor the internal resources to proceed with the recommendations from the consultant, then it is a pure waste of corporate resources to engage the consultant in the first place.

Corporate Image Management

- Wrong selection process—time and again I have seen organisations use one team to make the corporate image or corporate identity resource selection, only to have another task force comprising different individuals be assigned to work with the selected consultants. That's like having management ordering the food and assigning another team to do the cooking: it's doubtful that management will get the meal they had in mind. Without making the evaluation team too large, it should always include some key players who will also be assigned to the project steering committee or corporate image management task force.
- Getting charmed—by the slick, professional presentation given by the most senior executive from one firm when in fact their methodology or understanding of your needs is not the best option available to you. One also needs to be careful that the charming presenter will actually be assigned to work on the project. Sometimes these 'rainmakers' are merely the consulting firm's best sales representatives, who are often too busy doing new business presentations to actually work on any individual client projects. If you are excessively impressed by Mr or Ms Smoothie, be sure to clarify how active they be in your project. You don't want them only showing up when the major presentations are planned.
- Dictating the solution—if you state your desired results in the brief and use this in the judging process of the prospective consultants, you are almost sure to get what you ordered, even if it is not the solution to the right problem. Remember, one of the most valuable roles of the consultant is to help identify your *true* problems, not merely to confirm those already on your own list. The real goal of the project should be to identify all the important and tangential problems, and then to develop solutions to each.
- Making the scope too narrow—limit the project to a focus on the creative identity solution and you will not get the most value from your investment in the external consultants. A good image management consultant will bring you experiences and professional skills that transcend and integrate the disciplines of marketing, management, human resources, recruiting, marketing communications, training, strategic planning, leadership, motivation, interpersonal relationships, team building, and forward thinking.
- Refusing to work as a team—the corporate image management process calls for close teamwork by members from both the consulting and the client teams. At the end of a well-executed project, it is often hard to

determine which side and which individuals were responsible for many of the specific solutions. This is not a project where individuals should be seeking to create personal glories. The satisfaction comes from creating winning solutions for the entire organisation, not from trying to make a hero of the person or persons who scored the winning points.
- ❏ Abdicating—while control and management of the process ideally resides with the consultants, key decisions and approvals must remain with the client. Management cannot relinquish its need to be represented in the process and its responsibilities for ensuring that decisions are taken in a timely fashion. The consultants should be tasked with creating and recommending solutions to your problems, inclusive of the responsibility for giving their judgements on the probable results (good and bad) for each recommendation if accepted and implemented. Push your consultants to make strong recommendations to you, but do not allow them to make your final decisions. Strange as this may seem, some clients get so afraid of evaluating recommendations and making a decision that they simply accept any and all suggestions, disavowing final ownership.
- ❏ Accept reluctantly—if you feel that you are being forced into accepting a less-than-suitable solution, particularly during the corporate identity design development stage, then something has gone wrong during the process. Chances are that either the designers do not understand the results and conclusions of the research and analysis stages, or that the client remains entrenched with an unwillingness to change or with a preconceived creative solution. Neither the client nor the designers should be bullied into accepting a creative design solution simply because 'the project has progressed so far' or 'we've invested so much time and money and still don't have a solution'. If the project becomes bogged down at the creative development stage, it would be better to change either the design team or the client decision-making team (or both) than to proceed with an unsuitable design solution.
- ❏ Being creatively swayed—allowing the consultant to convince you that their most beautifully designed new corporate logo for you is an artistic masterpiece that will be revered and adored by all who come into contact with it. Designers are rightfully proud of their creative executions and will go to great lengths to persuade you that they have created the single best possible design for you. Take that claim with the proverbial grain of salt and then subject it to the same hard-nosed evaluation criteria you would use for any other subjective issue, like the architectural design of a new office building.

Corporate Image Management

I have had the luxury of working on corporate image management projects where almost everything has gone smoothly, right through to execution and post-launch monitoring, and the misfortune to be in projects that never got past the initial creative design stage. Those that went smoothly still had the odd hurdle to overcome and the occasional misstep. Those that were disasters usually got off on the wrong foot and either the consultants, the clients, or both decided to ignore the early warning signs.

Management Is the Message

When it comes to managing external consultants, in particular image management consultants, your management process becomes one of the key messages to your internal audiences. Like the corporate image, everything managers say and do (and do not say and do) delivers a message to the staff and to the consultants.

As a result, your communications and actions with the image management consultants need to be consistent, clear and concise. You will need to allocate massive amounts of senior executive time to the consultants, partly to help them understand the organisation and the way it conducts business and partly to understand the cultural and professional beliefs of the organisation. Additionally, you must live up to your commitments to the consultants, both in terms of making resources available and in making decisions on a timely basis so that the project continues to move forward.

At the same time, your communications with your staff also need to be consistent, clear and concise. They may also need to be repeated frequently, as it will take time for the entire organisation to fully hear, understand, accept and believe the messages about change. It is important to remember that organisations can only truly connect with their employees through values, beliefs, and feelings. This cannot occur only through one-way communications: it must be reinforced by consistent corporate behaviour patterns, particularly at the executive, senior management and middle management ranks. Spouting that the organisation believes in honesty and ethics, while allowing the troops to know that an overseas contract was secured through the use of 'facilitation money' sends out contradictory signals. When two divergent messages are received, the one reinforced through action and deed is almost always believed over the one communicated only through words.

Additionally, the trust of your employees during a time of change is founded on two parameters: predictability and capability. In any organisation, people need to know what to expect and that these expectations are predictable. During any period of change, their concern about the predictability of their expectations continuing to be met is at the source of much change resistance. Both the employees and the management must determine that each is now capable of performing whatever new roles result from the change process.

The Value of Outside Resources

One of the key roles of the image management consultants is to facilitate the change process so that predictability is preserved and capabilities are easily recognised and reinforced. At the same time, management actions must also reinforce both the credibility of the consultants to the staff and its own solid belief in the changes being implemented. As part of this communication by action, any change management task forces or transformation management teams should be staffed by executives, managers and staff who are well respected throughout the organisation and who are recognised as key players for the future. These teams are not the place for creating a new layer of bureaucracy within the organisation, nor for placing executives and managers who are on the downward slope in their careers. If these teams are seen as the kind of 'temporary assignments' given to executives just prior to their removal from the organisation, then the resistance to change will escalate through the informal communications channels that tunnel through each and every organisation worldwide.

Managing the Process

Management of the corporate image management process is both complicated and easy. The complications come from the holistic approach of the process, which is designed to sweep through the entire organisation, from top to bottom and from outside to inside. The ease comes from following the process, step by step, in sequential order.

The corporate image management process is a major undertaking, one that requires the full commitment of the organisation and the allocation of appropriate financial and human resources. For most organisations, the scope of a corporate image management project is too large and the range of skills required is too vast for it to be handled internally. In such situations, the value of outside resources, such as corporate image consultants and design consultants, and the benefits of the resultant long-term strategic solutions generated by these external resources, far outweigh the costs.

Epilogue

There is no single marketing or management panacea. The marketing arena is too dynamic and diffuse for a single methodology to be applied to each and every situation.

Although numerous recent attempts have been made to proclaim a single solution, none have proven universally sufficient. We have gone through service quality, total quality management, quality is free, re-engineering, down-sizing, building conglomerates, spinning off unrelated businesses to focus on 'core competencies', globalisation, 'think global, act local', and other permutations. In a similar vein, the impression one would get from browsing through the management shelves at the local bookstore is that we have been: searching for excellence, driving brand value, playing territorial games, operating under fatal illusions, planning strategically, and trying to drive our competitors crazy while, at the same time, re-engineering the corporation and transforming the organisation.

Phew! That's a lot of activity.

But activity does not equate to action. One of the problems, of course, is that most of these attempted activities tend to look at only one aspect of the organisation: production, finance, marketing, leadership, organisational structure and behaviour, etc. Even re-engineering (some might say *especially* re-engineering) was not a balanced approach between the organisation's internal and external worlds. Perhaps unintentionally, many also became one-off approaches, the kinds of activities that management could check off on their management scorecards during shareholder reporting seasons.

The corporate image management process can help you overcome these problems. Corporate image management is a holistic, never-ending approach to creating the leadership, direction and corporate behaviour patterns that will enable your organisation to develop strong relationships with all of its key constituents (internal as well as external). When implemented properly, corporate image management is a greater precursor of marketplace success than is any other core competency defined for the organisation: product innovation, price leadership, distribution prowess, clever advertising campaigns, excellent service quality, superior manufacturing capabilities, efficient process management, visionary leadership, skills in change management, or financial strength.

At the same time, corporate image management is not a cure-all for every organisation. Organisations go through various stages of corporate development, face different marketing challenges, and have varied human and financial resources to put to use. For those not already engaged in the process, the implementation of an integrated corporate image management process into the organisation may be too costly, too time consuming, and take too much senior management attention away from the realities and priorities of the day. In effect, the cost of the medicine and the time for implementing the cure may outweigh the current costs and troubles caused from having a sick or ill-defined corporate image.

On the other hand, every organisation has both internal and external customers and other constituents with which it needs to partner and form relationships. Thus, at some time in the organisation's existence (and for most, the sooner the better), every organisation will need to assess, define, and pro-actively manage the projection of its corporate image through its corporate behaviour patterns.

As we have stated before, the battlefield for marketing success is shifting from the minds of the consumers (where perceptions are formed from projected corporate imagery) to the emotions, hearts and souls of consumers (where relationships are formed and maintained from both projected corporate imagery and experienced corporate behaviour patterns).

There is no greater marketing issue facing senior managers in today's increasingly competitive markets than the issue of corporate image management.

Lastly, the impact from properly managing the corporate image will become greater and more pronounced as organisations move up the marketing excellence ladder into the realms of relationship excellence and partnership excellence. This is what makes corporate image management a strategic marketing weapon at the cutting edge of marketing and management technology.

Corporate image management is *the* marketing discipline for the 21st Century.

Glossary

Bromides
A precise reproduction of the corporate and SBU signatures, cast onto a special bromide-coated (slick) paper from the Master Artwork. Also known as a 'stat' in North America.

Corporate Colours
A specially formulated combination of colours identified for use in a Corporate Identity System. For most systems, a set of recommended colour variations should be included. Also, the designers should recommend a set of secondary colours, to be used as support colours in marketing communications materials.

Corporate Identity Manual
See Corporate Identity System Graphics Standards Manual below.

Corporate Identity System
The elements and graphic style that visually represent the organisation. It includes a nomenclature structure, Corporate Signature system, Corporate Colours and a Corporate Logo or Mark. The system should be used consistently, as prescribed in the Corporate Identity System Graphics Standards Manual.

Corporate Identity System Graphics Standards Manual
Written and illustrated instructions and guidelines on how to consistently use the Corporate Identity System. The information is usually compiled into a binder and disseminated widely within the organisation and to outside suppliers. Also known as the Corporate Identity Manual.

Corporate Signature
The combination of the Corporate Symbol and Logotype. The Corporate Signature should only be produced from Master Artwork and should never be reconstructed or produced by any other means. The Corporate Signature nomenclature system needs to be designed for the parent company and any subsidiary companies in the group.

Final Artwork
The 'mechanical' or 'camera ready' artwork made ready for use in printing. Final Artwork should be made of 'bromide' pieces, as per the standards in the Corporate Identity System Graphics Standards Manual. Laser prints from computer workstations do not constitute Final Artwork.

Graphic Standards
The detailed instructions for usage, reproduction and protection of an organisation's Corporate Identity System. See Corporate Identity System Graphics Standards Manual (above) for more details.

Legal Signature
The Corporate Signature with the full legal name of the organisation. This may be required in certain cases, particularly for legal purposes. It should not be used for marketing purposes.

Logo/Symbol
A graphic representation or icon used as a fundamental aspect of a Corporate Identity System. Also known as the Corporate Mark. Should appear with the Logotype to form the Corporate Signature. It is up to the designers of the system whether the Logo can be used on its own, such as on products, packaging, signage, etc.

Logotype
The typeface and letters that form the name of the organisation when used in conjunction with the Corporate Symbol. This is usually a special typeface designated for use only for the Corporate Signature and SBU Signatures. The typeface selected for signatures would not normally be used in supporting text.

Mark
See Logo/Symbol. Also known as the Corporate Mark.

Master Artwork
The original version of the Corporate and SBU Signatures. This is often hand-cut and produced by the designer.

SBU Signatures
The combination of the Logo and Logotype used to depict SBUs or other operating entities in the organisation (other than subsidiary companies).

Glossary

Signature

An identifying name or group of words used consistently in a particular typographic style, or in combination with a Logotype and a Logo. Used to identify organisations, SBUs, legal entities, subsidiary companies and other business units.

Support Typography

Any additional typography, such as address and legal information, that appears with the Corporate Signature.

Index

A
Adams, Scott, 198
Adidas, 80
Agassi, Andre, 121
Air Canada, 112
Alice in Wonderland, 44, 182
Allegis, 100
Amazon.com, 53–55, 61
American Express, 93, 118
American Management Association (AMA), 174
Apple Computer, 36, 63, 105, 193–194
Asian Wall Street Journal, 41, 117, 173
AT&T, 81, 118
Audi, 35
Australian Financial Review, 69
Avis, 60–61

B
Bacardi, 30
Balmain, Pierre, 89
Batey Advertising, 88
BHP, 81
Bigio, Jenny, 140
Boston Consulting Group, 36
branding strategies, 86–87
Britain's Royal Family *(see* House of Windsor*)*
British Airways, 88
BSN, 33
BMW, 35, 85

C
Cadillac, 35
California Bankcard Association, 119
Carlson, William, 22
Cassin, James, 96
Cathay Pacific, 59
Chan Boon Kiong, 21–23, 25
Charles, *Prince of Wales*, 116
Chemical Bank, 32

Chicken Soup for the Soul, 197
Cirrus, 33, 93, 94, 95
Citibank, 49, 154
Clinton, Bill, 105
Cobb, Charles, 31–32
Coca-Cola (product), 33, 86, 87, 98, 100, 122, 193
Coca-Cola Company, 29, 30
Colgate, 87
Commercial and Industrial Security Corporation (CISCO), 20–27, 197
Compaq, 36, 75, 80, 81
corporate culture, 10–11, 83, 84
corporate personality, 75–77, 83, 85
Costner, Kevin, 29

D
Dai Nippon Printing, 96
Dallas Cowboys, 114–115
Danone Group, 33, 87
Darcy Massius Benton and Bowles, 121
Dell Computers, 81, 167
Diana, *Princess of Wales*, 116, 149, 181
Digital Equipment Corporation, 36
Dilbert, 198
Disneyland, 43, 145
Dom Perignon, 58
Dow, 174–175, 183
Dow Jones, 41–42
Driving Brand Value, 167
Duncan, Tom, 167

E
EuroCard, 33
European Wall Street Journal, 41
Exxon, 29, 70, 81
Exxon *Valdez*, 29

F
Falwell, Jerry, 98
Financial Times, 69

Index

Fonda, Bridget, 94
Ford Motors, 81
Fortune 500, 81
Fortune magazine, 10, 69
Fraser & Neave, 87
Frito-Lay, 148
Fuji, 86

G

Gates, Bill, 148–149, 194
Gateway 2000, 81, 88, 167
Gemplus, 96
General Motors, 35–36, 81, 100
Geo Prizm, 35
Gerstner, Lou, 31
Grant, Hugh, 30
GTE, 97

H

Hertz, 100
Hewlett-Packard, 63
Hilton, 100–101
Hitachi, 96
H.J. Heinz, 33, 87
Hoechst Chemicals, 75
HongkongBank, 91
 Care for Nature MasterCard, *see* MasterCard (product)
House of Windsor, 116, 124, 149, 181

I

Iacocca, Lee, 197
IBM, 31, 36, 63, 73, 74, 86, 97, 193–194
Image By Design, 197
Image Wars: Protecting Your Company When There's No Place to Hide, 197
International Herald-Tribune, 41–42
It Could Happen to You, 94
ITT, 100

J

Jackson, Michael, 30, 64, 86
Jaguar, 35
Jobs, Steve, 63
Johnson & Johnson, 29, 44
Jordan, Michael, 121
Jurong Town Corporation, 22

K

Kenzu, 80
Keppel, 22
Keycorp, 96
KFC, 148, 186
Kia Motors, 81
Kleenex, 86
KLM, 63
Kodak, 80, 86
Kotter, John, 84

L

Landor, Walter, 28
Lasorda, Tommy, 73
Lee Kuan Yew, 111
Leo Burnett Advertising, 88
Levi Strauss, 167
Lewis, Carl, 121
Lexus, 35
Lincoln-Mercury, 35
Lippincott, George, 140–141
Lippincott & Margulies, Inc., 140
Lufthansa, 112
Luvs, 8, 12

M

Madame Tussaud's Wax Museum, 111
Madonna, 30, 64, 86
Maestro, 33, 93, 94, 95
Magnovox, 74
Major, John, 105
Major League Baseball, 120
Malaysia Airlines, 58, 59
Malaysian-Singapore Airlines, 88
MAOSCO, 96
Maradona, Diego, 121
Margaux, Chateau, 80
Marketing Corporate Image, 197
Marketing Warfare, 197
Marlboro Friday, 8
Marlboro Man, 88
Martini & Rossi, 32
Maslow, Abraham, 99
MasterCard (product), 33, 56, 93, 94, 95, 119–120
 American Airlines MasterCard, 55
 General Motors MasterCard, 55
 Gold MasterCard, 55
 HongkongBank Care for Nature MasterCard, 55, 90–91
 Shell MasterCard, 55

Index

MasterCard International, 33, 63, 92–97, 119–120
MasterCharge, 119
McDonald's Championship, 121
McDonald's Corporation, 122, 192–193
McGraw-Hill, 28, 97
McVities, 33
Mercedes-Benz, 34, 35
Microsoft, 63, 97, 148–149, 194
Mondex International, 96–97
Moriarty, Sandra, 167
Motorola, 80, 97, 194
Mount Blanc, 34
MULTOS, 97

N

NASA, 69, 105
National Basketball Association (NBA), 120–122
Nesbitt, John 55
Nestlé, 87
Netscape, 97
New Rules, 84
Newsweek International, 69
New United Motor Manufacturing (NUMI), 35
New York Times, 69
New York Times Company, 42
Nike, 80, 122
Nokia, 80
Northwest Airlines, 63, 98

O

Oldsmobile, 100

P

Pampers, 8, 12
Pan Am World Airways, 31–32
Parker Pen Holdings, 32
partnership marketing, 63–64, 101
Passages, 112
Pelé, 121
Penfolds Grange, 80
Pepsi (product), 86
Pepsi-Cola Company (PepsiCo), 64, 87, 148
perception, 85
perception (5th 'P' of marketing), 80, 101, 165
Perrier, 8, 29, 30, 34, 44, 81, 86
Pertamina, 74

Philip Morris, 8, 88
Philips, 63
Pixar, 80
Pizza Hut, 148
Popoff, Frank, 174
Port of Singapore Authority, 22
PrimeEast Capital Group, 157
Proctor & Gamble (P&G), 8, 12, 87
Prudential Insurance, 118

Q

Qantas Airways, 52

R

relationship building, 97–101, 196–199
relationship marketing, 55–57, 59, 73, 81, 83, 99, 101
Riley, Pat, 197
RJR Nabisco, 32
Rodman, Dennis, 121
Royal Dutch Shell, 118

S

7-Eleven, 8
SAS, 112
Schechter, Alvin, 117–118
Schechter Group, 117
Search for Excellence, 197
Sears, Roebuck & Co, 114–115
secondary identifiers, 88–90
Secure Electronic Transaction (SET), 97
Sembawang, 22
Shell Eastern Petroleum, 23
Sheraton, 100
Siemens, 97
Silk Air, 59
Sim Cheok Lim, 23–25
Singapore Airlines, 22, 52, 57–59, 62, 73–74, 88–89, 104, 106, 111–112, 118
Singapore Girl, 58, 88–89, 111–112
Singapore Telecoms, 22
Sony, 52, 63, 86
Spielberg, Steven, 29
Stern, David, 120
Sun Tzu, 197
Swatch, 34, 35
Swim With the Sharks Without Being Eaten Alive, 197

223

Index

T
Taco Bell, 148
Texaco, 70, 81
Thai Airways, 112
The Age, 69
The Art of War, 197
The Body Shop, 90
The Celestine Prophecy, 197
The Economist, 11, 69
The Seven Spiritual Laws of Success, 197
The Winner Within, 197
Tide, 12
Time Warner, 81
Tokyo Disneyland, 43
Toyota Corolla, 35
Toyota Motor Company, 35–36
Transforming the Organization, Reengineering the Corporation, 197
Turner Broadcasting, 32
Tyson, Mike, 30, 64, 86

U
UAL, 100, 112
Unilever, 87
United Airlines, 100
USA Today, 42

V
ValuJet, 64
VeriFone, 32
Visa, 63, 93
Volvo, 35, 85

W
Wall Street Journal, 41
Wal-Mart, 115
Walt Disney Company, 81, 145–146
Walt Disney World, 43
Washington Post, 69
Washington Post Company, 42
Waterworld, 29
Western States BankCard Association, 119
Westin Hotels, 100
What They Don't Teach You at Harvard Business School, 197
Write-Angles, 140

X
Xerox, 86